# Home Is Where the Suitcases Are

Marilyn Beckwith

abbott press®

A DIVISION OF WRITER'S DIGEST

# Home Is Where the Suitcases Are

Abbott Press books may be ordered through booksellers or by contacting:
Abbott Press
1663 Liberty Drive
Bloomington, IN 47403
www.abbottpress.com
Phone: 1-866-697-5310

ISBN: 978-1-4582-0160-7 (sc)
ISBN: 978-1-4582-0159-1 (e)

Library of Congress Control Number: 2011962684

Printed in the United States of America
Abbott Press rev. date: 12/29/2011

For the people and places I've known in the third world,
and to family and friends who are my first world—
with grateful thanks for the times these two worlds coincided

# Foreword

Marilyn Beckwith knew how to dream big dreams. I knew this as soon as her daughter Karen introduced us, when I learned she was writing a memoir chronicling her family's adventures in Africa in the early 1970s. That experience was in itself the realization of another of Marilyn's dreams. As a girl growing up in Medford, Oregon, she'd dreamed of traveling the world. Married to Jim, she did just that— many times over.

When I met Marilyn, she and Jim were retired, which allowed her time to pursue her book-writing dream. In fact, she envisioned *Home is Where the Suitcases Are* as the first of several books about her family's many years abroad. Marilyn was an experienced communicator: a lifelong letter-writer and editor to her husband's technical missives, she was also writer and editor for the National Iranian Television Network. She was, in fact, heading for a position as an anchor before politics forced her family's evacuation of Tehran.

I, meanwhile, was a fledgling freelance writer who taught memoir writing at the local community college. We each had something the other needed: another writer's keen eye to hone our work in an iron-sharpens-iron way.

Over the next decade, Marilyn continued to revise her manuscript until at last it was completed. She then cast her eye on the next big dream: to see it published. Sadly, this didn't happen. In early 2011, Marilyn suffered a brain hemorrhage from which she never recovered. On February 15, 2011, she died at the age of 78.

Her husband, Jim, however, wasn't about to let her dream go, and the book you hold is the result of his determination to see it through. You'll be so glad he did. *Home is Where the Suitcases Are* is brimming with Marilyn's warmth and wisdom and wit. You'll feel she's speaking directly to you in all of her candor and humor. You'll see that her stories were written for the adventurer-at-heart—people like her, who dared to dream big.

And if you're one of those folks whose dream still beckons you—if Marilyn's stories inspire you to take that next step toward whatever adventure calls your name—well. That was one of Marilyn's big dreams too.

Katherine Jones
November 11, 2011

# Moving

◩ ◧ ◩

We arrived for my husband's job in Africa via airplane and one year of unemployment. Our hopes were high, our finances low, our family moderately large with four children.

We began the 1970s in Seattle with the big Boeing layoff. The airplane manufacturing company dismissed some sixty thousand of its employees. The government said, "Recession." We more intimately involved in losing livelihoods said, "Depression." We said some other things too.

There is no denying that, as one of life's low spots, that year of unemployment was a trudge along the bottom of the Grand Canyon—or, from a later African view, maybe the Great Rift Valley. It was a very bad year, with jumping and shooting records set. But the first was off bridges and the shooting wasn't sport. Suicide never is.

And yet, the time also produced humor. I liked the reaction to adversity of those persons who somehow kept their sense of humor and enough money to erect that famous billboard, "Will the last person leaving Seattle please turn out the lights."

Some medical observations suggest that having a sense of humor is good for a person, that laughter may even lengthen one's life. Or as a new twist of an old proverb puts it, he or she who laughs, lasts. So, a sense of humor can be a natural sturdy strand of one's lifeline. Africa would stretch mine.

My husband and I and children had already moved a number of times in the course of his aviation career. This to the point where a friend burst

1

out with, "That does it. You are ruining the entire B section of my address book. From now on, I'm penciling you in!"

My mother, in Medford, Oregon, was used to our moving and living at least several hundred miles from her. But in that year of unemployment, my letters to Mother tried to ease her to the realization that my husband's next job would probably take us even farther away. This because her son-in-law was willing to move anywhere there was a halfway-decent job. I supported him in this thinking.

When Jim, my husband, returned from Nairobi, Kenya, after a successful job interview with East African Airways, I telephoned my mother to share the good news. Whether from heightened awareness or long-suffering resignation, Mother sighed and asked, "Well, where is it this time? Timbuktu?"

"You're close," I said and sent up a silent prayer. I hoped the prayer would rise faster than Mother's blood pressure. When the shock wore off, she appreciated the humor, at least a little bit.

Actually, Timbuktu in Mali, and Nairobi in Kenya, are about three thousand miles apart. But both are in Africa, and I was talking about moving halfway around the world. "Close" was a relative term.

Moving to Africa! What an adventure! My husband and I were eager for it and hoped the children would be infected with our positive enthusiasm. Their questions were vociferous and varied, taxing our patience and knowledge. The encyclopedia and atlas became invaluable, as did the brochures Jim brought back from Nairobi.

A weight limit made answering some questions easy…

"Yes, you may take your teddy bear."

"No, you may not take your rock collection."

I knew those rocks had long since ceased to be a vital interest. Had it been otherwise, that collection might have had to accompany us at the expense of something else, or several something elses.

An imminent move points up the value of possessions. It's often difficult to decide what must be discarded or left behind. Monetary value doesn't necessarily enter in. A seemingly worthless object becomes priceless in its invisible wrapping of emotion and memories. So, despite a certain requisite ruthlessness, we've moved our share of questionable-priority possessions for our children and odd mini-mementos for ourselves.

We were familiar with the mechanics of moving. Memories of past mistakes served to prevent their repetition. Articles to be given away were not even temporarily stored next to things we were keeping. I had no wish to inadvertently donate another card table to charity, nor end up with a box of outgrown ice skates in our shipment. That particular box lives in memory as the first one I opened in tropical Puerto Rico after an earlier move.

Every cupboard and drawer would be emptied. I knew I'd check their reassuring lack of contents many times because I'd skipped one of each in past moves. My "when in doubt throw it out" act would take place with no audience participation to delay the performance. If something hadn't been used for a year or two, it was a candidate for casting out. Actually, I often checked the importance of something with a family member. But one son has yet to forgive me for encouraging him to give away his boxes of baseball cards. Can't say I blame him. I too now wonder how valuable those cards would be today. And was there really a Mickey Mantle one?

Our suitcase supply was ample, and there would be no cases of mistaken identity enroute. We learned that lesson years before on our honeymoon. That was when Jim grabbed my suitcase's twin from the pile of limousine luggage and checked it to our destination. That flight ended in our first argument. "Damn it, I don't care if the numbers on the baggage claim-check do match. I'm telling you, that is not my suitcase!"

On our move to Nairobi, East African Airways was picking up the tab for our travel and transport of a limited amount of household goods. Some other expenses would come out of our own pocket. The state of our finances dictated that packing not be among them. Our confidence in our ability to do it ourselves was not misplaced. That shipment arrived halfway around the world with less damage than most of our professionally managed moves before or since. Let me hasten to add that, unless necessity dictates, I still prefer to give the nod to the professional movers. Not because they'll do it better. After lo these many moves, I bow to no one on packing ability. However, it is a tremendous job. The British aptly describe it as "moving house."

The logistics of a long-distance move can be mindboggling. To prevent my mind from screaming, "TILT," I made lists of things to do. These little pieces of paper marked the path to moving day. They helped in getting things, and me, organized. This despite the fact that it may have been

Friday when I finally crossed off the last item on last Tuesday's list. To one particularly daunting and lengthy list for the move to Africa, I facetiously added, "Find time to have a nervous breakdown."

My husband and I learned a great deal about official paper work on that move to Kenya. It was our first overseas move to a truly independent, foreign country. There seemed to be innumerable forms to fill out, most in at least triplicate and of course multiplied by six. Moving internationally requires passports and visas, which in turn require birth certificates. In applying for copies of those, it came as something of a shock to learn that Washington state credited us with only three children. Bureaucracy's computer evidently burped at our last baby's registration of birth.

It struck me as ironic that Karen was the supposed non-person. She seemed sure of her identity at an early age. She was three that year in New York when we gathered the kids for a short story about the first Thanksgiving and a parental plug for homely virtues such as thankfulness. I suggested they each voice a thankful thought and led off with our oldest child Roxanne, then age ten. Whether she was practicing diplomacy, truly meant it, or was maybe trying to butter up the bosses, she said she was thankful for good parents. Jimmy was thankful to have two extra days off from school. Mike was bored by the whole business, but he expressed appreciation for the turkey in the oven. Karen melted my heart when she spoke in her wee and wispy three-year-old voice. Softly but positively she stated, "I'm thankful for being me, Karen Beckwith." I liked that sure sense of self and felt that we must be doing something right.

Five years later we were thankful to have readily at hand the hospital certificate indicating the date I'd given birth to Karen. We also had her baptismal record. These convinced the State of Washington to promptly, if belatedly, record Karen on their rolls and issue a Delayed Registration of Birth.

The practicalities and myriad details involved in moving a family of six halfway around the world loomed large. To meet the reporting date in Nairobi, Kenya, in less than a month, added a sense of urgency to our organizing. Even with all the pressure, though, it sure beat the heck out of unemployment—and Jim and I felt ready to tackle anything. This supreme supply of overconfidence dwindled of course, but I suspect without it we might never have made it.

Each day became a unit of controlled chaos. Lists, passports, forms, lists, shots, and lists begat lists. Sometimes problems, and also blessings, multiplied by a factor of four. Our children are named Roxanne, James Jr., Michael, and Karen. At the time of our move to Africa, they ranged in age from sixteen to eight.

The boys suggested they could be of immense help if allowed to drop out of school immediately instead of the day before departure as planned. This was vetoed, with the acknowledgment that it was a nice try. Our family never operated as a true democracy. I felt that my husband and I jointly headed a benevolent dictatorship, with our children occasionally questioning the benevolent adjective.

The thought of living in Africa was exciting, and the children couldn't help being infected with our positive enthusiasm. They also couldn't help greeting the whole idea with decidedly mixed emotions. It was a difficult time for them.

As for myself, I was buoyed by the fact that my husband had another good job, never mind that the pay was low. I concentrated on making everything work. It was certainly great to have Jim enthusiastic again. The unemployment year had been difficult. There had been a number of potential-job disappointments. I remember that I stopped chirping, "Cheer up, things could be worse."

I stopped on the day Jim growled in reply, "You're absolutely right. I cheered up the other day and, sure enough, things got worse!"

But his job interview in Nairobi had gone well. All management-level jobs for East African Airways were interviewed there at the home office. The airline had invited me to accompany Jim to Nairobi for the interview, but I'd regretfully declined. Very regretfully, because I had more than a touch of wanderlust in me. My favorite songs in my teen years were "Red Sails in the Sunset" and something about being called by "Far Away Places With Strange Sounding Names."

Never did I imagine, as a small-town teenager, that I'd someday live in and be familiar with a whole list of places with strange-sounding names: San Juan, Nairobi, Kinshasa, Teheran, Addis Ababa, London. I would even eventually learn to sail and have more than a musical acquaintance with red sails in the sunset. Ah, but living on a sailboat half of each year is another story.

In our moving-to-Africa year, my wanderlust streak was overlaid with practicality. I was thrilled to be invited to accompany Jim to the Nairobi job interview. I desperately hoped that my declining would not adversely affect his chances for getting the job. But we had four children, and no one to leave in charge of them. Also, halfway through that unemployment year I'd gotten a job—low paying, but at that time it was, financially, the difference between our making it or not making it. I felt I had to subscribe to the theory that a bird in hand was worth two in the bush—even the African bush.

Jim's unemployment compensation from the government was soon due to stop. In those days it wasn't that much money anyway, though we were grateful for it. We'd already sold our car and used most of our savings. In fact—and I cringed at the thought— we were about six weeks shy of applying for food stamps and welfare. Somehow we were managing to keep up with the mortgage payment on our house, which we'd bought two months before Jim was laid off from Boeing. My minimum-wage job was important. It was helping to keep the proverbial wolf from our door. Though in the still reaches of some nights, that wolf seemed to howl ever closer…or maybe that was just the anguish of my heart heard in my head.

So I was delighted that Jim got the job, and I would get to see Kenya too. My enthusiasm faltered only briefly when he told me he'd narrowly missed being involved in a coup that began at Entebbe Airport in Uganda. The East African Airways plane Jim was on had Ugandan registry. He later learned that this fact caused Idi Amin's contingent to delay their coup a few minutes. They didn't want bullet holes in their own plane, so they delayed shooting until Jim's plane was safely airborne. Whatever their reasoning, I was certainly glad not to have bullet holes in my husband. And I let him reassure me. It was most unlikely that anything unusual would be going on again at Entebbe when our East African Airways plane stopped there enroute to Nairobi with all of us aboard. He was right. Our stop at Entebbe was uneventful, though sometime later that airport was the scene of a dramatic rescue of hijacked hostages.

# School

❑ ❑ ❑

*ambo!* The Swahili word of greeting seems to encompass so much more than our simple hello. The English word can seem more dismissal than salutation in its curtness, sometimes more wary than welcoming. But *jambo* seemed to greet, to welcome, to offer an invitation to friendship and understanding. We were immeasurably enriched by our exchange of *jambos* in Kenya that year.

The plastic prestige of a high-rise hotel was not for us this trip. We were kind of glad that East African Airways put us up at Nairobi's Mayfair, an older, British-style hotel. We were anxious to quickly fit into our new life.

We were missing a family member. Roxanne would join us later. She had stayed in Seattle with friends in order to finish her junior year of high school. What persuaded us on this was the unusual fact that her high school was permanently closing at the end of that school year. She desperately wanted to remain behind for the grand finale.

Our other children were tasting and testing their new environment. This included the Mayfair Hotel's dining room. Knowing that restaurants in the United States serve meals at all hours, it came as a shock to our children that there was any other way. Kenya was less than ten years into independence then. It had been colonized by the British. Wherever they were, the British seemed slow to give up the notion that it somehow served the discipline of the soul if one's stomach was served only at strictly prescribed times. In the British way of thinking, lunch began not a moment before noon. Nor was it served past two o'clock, or perhaps half-past two in some cases.

Tea, a lovely tradition, was served promptly at four at the Mayfair. Fortunately, "tea" also included food. This was usually substantial enough to prevent hunger pangs from growling too loudly before dinner at seven. We tried to set our stomachs on local time.

Our children found it fun to change their table manners. These were not bad, just American. If a time and motion study were done on the use of knife and fork when cutting one's portion of meat, I think the European manner would win hands down, or up as the case may be. In this method of eating, hands are rested at the ready each side of the plate, with knife and fork held poised to pounce. People schooled and skilled in this manner of eating even manage to make it look graceful. Effort and motion are kept to a minimum by keeping the fork in one's left hand, and thus, with that fork, raising to one's mouth each bite as it's cut. The knife remains at the ready in the right hand. Our American family's switching back and forth of knife and fork brought people clear across the hotel dining room to ask what part of the United States we were from.

My own table manners were sorely tried in another way. The first time the waiter addressed my husband as *Bwana*, I spluttered my soup. There are times when a sense of humor can be a mixed blessing. *Bwana!* The word triggered childhood tales of Tarzan on my mental movie screen, and my husband really didn't fit any image there.

Hearing myself addressed as *Memsahib* also took a little getting used to. As for the children, Karen learned to respond to "Missy" and the boys to "Young Sir." As he came to know us better, our friendly hotel waiter called our children by their first names.

Jim plunged into his job right away. My first priority was getting the kids squared away in schools. In our straitened circumstances, that might prove difficult. My husband was on a pay scale geared to the British who got some form of help on school fees. We did too, but not enough from East African Airways for four children who wanted to continue American-style education.

In Africa then, we were what I call freelance-type Americans. That is, we had no connection with a parent organization anywhere else. My husband was under direct contract to one particular African airline. This in contrast to being loaned or seconded from some other company, or employed by a large American firm on a technical-assistance contract.

Consequently, school-fee assistance was minimal or nonexistent. And we lived off the local economy. There was no question that the whole situation beat unemployment back in the United States, and we were delighted to be there. The real question was how, under the circumstances, to best educate our four children. I did not feel competent to homeschool them.

Looking for schools in Kenya reminded me of a few years earlier, when we moved to Puerto Rico. There we had to find schools with an English-speaking curriculum rather than Spanish. At that time the difficulty was more lack of space in the Puerto Rican schools than our lack of ability to pay. But four was a problem then too. We tried to get them into Catholic schools in largely Catholic Puerto Rico. I got used to the following scenario there.

"Oh, I'm sure something can be arranged, Mrs. Beckwith. We like to think there is always room for one more. How many children do you have?"

"Four, Sister."

That always brought a flustered gasp. And then, if not outright and immediate rejection, I sometimes got a, "Perhaps if you had just one or two."

I was sorely tempted to ask the good nuns if they were advocating birth control, but I could never quite muster the nerve.

Schools were crowded when we arrived in Kenya too. The American, or International School, was the least so, but this didn't seem to help us. It also had the highest tuition rate, perhaps the one fact accounting for the other.

Roxanne obviously had to have our priority on American schooling. She was a senior in high school. We couldn't fight it, there was no way she could switch educational systems at that point. It was bad enough that she had to change schools, though that was eased slightly by her knowing that the permanent closure of her stateside school would have caused her to transfer anyway for her senior year. However, a transfer halfway around the world was admittedly different than one halfway across town.

I wasn't totally happy with our decision allowing Roxanne to remain behind in Seattle those few months. It wasn't a bad decision, but with the wisdom of hindsight, I feel a better one would have been for her to accompany us. Had she spent those three months in her Nairobi school, she would have made new friends with whom to share the summer and a sense of belonging. Without friends her own age, that summer in a new place, though interesting, was lonely for her when it needn't have been. I also suspect her extra, unfilled time made the normal dread of fitting into a new school grow to more traumatic proportions than necessary.

After an explanation of our finances, Nairobi International School allotted Roxanne a half-price hardship scholarship. It was aptly named. We found even the cut-rate price a hardship.

Had our finances permitted, we might have contemplated boarding school for our children. This would have provided the continuity of schooling, and perhaps a certain stability that they missed with all our moving around.

Boarding school was a way of life that seemed to work well for the overseas British. Though even with them, confusion could result. I knew one little British girl, on Home Leave from Kenya with her family, who was quite surprised to find England peopled with persons of all ages. Prior to that visit, she had thought England the exclusive preserve of school boarders, grandparents, and Her Majesty, the Queen.

We found space and acceptance at good local schools for Jimmy, Mike, and Karen. There was no free schooling of any kind in Kenya. We were able to afford the tuition rates, though just barely. Our budget worked perfectly. That is, our budget worked providing everything of monetary cost in our lives held to a perfect plan. More than once I pondered the possibility that a calendar should contain more Februarys. Too often the money, the milk, and the butter ran out before the month did.

Michael and Karen attended Westlands Primary School in Nairobi. Neither had ever been a discipline problem in school, but even so, they seemed to worry a little over the ever-present threat of "six of the best."

Corporal punishment persisted in schools in the British Isles until an Act of Parliament abolished it in 1986. It may still be common in parts of the Commonwealth. The punishment takes various forms, often six good swats ("six of the best") with a paddle to the child's posterior. At Westlands this punishment was administered by the headmaster for serious infractions of the rules.

Anxious not to incur anyone's wrath, Karen curbed her tongue. This was an accomplishment that would have surprised some of her former, and future, teachers. The more diplomatic of these wrote on Karen's report cards something such as, "Karen always has something to contribute to class discussion." Or, "I can always count on Karen for comments." The less diplomatic would bluntly state, "Karen talks too much in class!"

In Kenya, she talked less and in a British-cum-Kenyan accent. Karen was one of those people who picked up accents unconsciously and then found them difficult to lose. Small wonder she was thought to be a non-American at her next school. Her math teacher at the American School of Kinshasa, in Zaire, was most understanding of her low scores.

"It's not unusual, Mrs. Beckwith, for non-American children to have difficulty with the chapter we're on now. All the problems are concerned with American money, and for the children not familiar with it, it is difficult sometimes."

I clarified Karen's nationality at that point, and the teacher and I agreed that lack of familiarity with American money did not necessarily equate with lack of American citizenship. But there did seem to be, at least in our children's cases, a relationship between math and moving. In our travels there came to be a stock question, to which I gave a stock answer.

"How does all this moving around and changing schools affect the children?"

"Well, their math studies suffer, but they're great at geography!" This flippant answer proved all too true later when low math scores kept Mike out of West Point.

Meanwhile, Mike seemed to be settling in well at Westlands Primary in Nairobi. He was never one to rant and rave in rebellion, but he'd been known to be a quiet nonconformist when it suited him. Consequently, I tried to impress upon him the importance of keeping up with his daily school work and accepting whatever new requirements might arise. I had no doubt that Mike could do the requisite school work, but I couldn't help thinking back a few years.

I remembered how eager Mike had been in New York to start first grade. He reminded us the night before his first school day to be sure to call him, along with his older brother and sister. The next morning, it was obvious he'd decided not to completely trust my memory. I stumbled over him as he lay curled up on the hall floor, sound asleep, leaning against his big sister's bedroom door.

Knowing his quick mind and keen interest, it therefore came as a distinct shock three weeks later when Mike's teacher spoke to me about him. She told me that he showed no interest in reading and the concept of numbers seemed totally beyond him. She suggested he might not be up to doing first grade work and showed me his blank arithmetic papers. I saw but I did not believe. Somehow there had to be more than mere numbers that weren't adding up.

I thought the simplest solution probably was to ask Mike, "Why?"

"They're blank because I don't want to draw those stupid balloons!" he burst out.

"Balloons?"

"Yes. The teacher wants us to draw a balloon, put a plus sign, draw another balloon, put an equal sign, and then draw two more of those idiot balloons! I thought you got to do real arithmetic in school. Why can't I put one plus one equals two?"

A simple solution. "And the reading?" I asked. "Let me guess. You didn't like the 'stupid' book. Right?"

"Right! It's got baby words, and I like the one with hard words that some of the other kids get to read." The rest of his first-grade year went well. Both Mike and the young first-time teacher learned a lot.

But perhaps I'd forgotten a lot when Mike came home one day from Westlands Primary. He had a question.

"Mom, I got it wrong on a test today. What's the capital city of the United States?"

I worried that growing up overseas would somehow alienate our children from their own country. This question from Mike really blew my mind. Talk about ranting and raving—I verbally tore him in two, ending with "Michael John, Washington, D.C., is the capital city of the United States. Not only should you most certainly know that because you are an American, but for heaven's sake you've lived there. Don't you remember our year in Silver Spring, Maryland? It's a suburb of our nation's capital."

"Yeah, well, that's what I thought. And I put Washington, D.C. But the teacher said the capital of the United States is New York. I tried to tell her but..." His shrug finished the sentence.

"Oh." And *oh-oh*. "Yes. Well, you're right. She's mistaken. And I'm sorry I blew up at you."

"Yeah, but will you tell her she's wrong?"

"Well, I guess I will because as a teacher she particularly needs to be accurate about such things. But it's not exactly an easy situation, Michael. I need to think about it, about how to tell her. But I promise I'll take care of it."

"Tomorrow?"

"Not tomorrow," and I shook my head in emphasis, but also partly in bewilderment at the whole problem.

"The day after?"

"Yes, probably."

I felt the situation was a delicate one. I had met Mike's teacher, a native-Kenyan woman, and I'd been favorably impressed. I'd also met the British headmaster and detected more than a tinge of his feeling decidedly superior to women in general, and local women in particular—and maybe local men, for that matter. Anyway, I felt that Kenya needed to develop and encourage native teachers. Granted, not at the expense of my child. However, the teacher seemed fairly well educated. I was already learning that the United States is not the center of everyone's universe, but even so, this mix-up of Washington, D.C., and New York didn't compute. I couldn't let the mix-up continue of course, but I wanted to be careful that I didn't undermine the woman's confidence in herself as a teacher. Plus, I certainly didn't want to get her into trouble with the headmaster. I didn't want *anyone* in trouble, including my visible, vulnerable American children. I didn't have a clue as to what to do, but a policy of *when in doubt, don't* seemed in order—at least for a day.

It worked. I didn't need to do anything. Michael came home all smiles the next day. The teacher had made everything right first thing, in front of the whole class. She also sent me, via Michael, a very gracious note of explanation-cum-apology. In it, the teacher applauded Michael's attempt at respectful persistence the day before. This prompted her to check the reference books after class. There, she saw again the statement that had led her memory astray: "New York is the financial capital of the United States."

For Jimmy, perhaps too much was new and overwhelming. He'd left eighth grade and an uncertain educational approach in the United States. That seemed a time in his school when a policy of *learning should be fun* was too often misinterpreted by the children as *don't strain the brain.*

13

In Nairobi, Jimmy entered a boys' school in Form 1A where thirteen solid subjects, including four languages (English, Swahili, French, and German) and at least two science courses (physics and chemistry) were the norm. An indifferent student under any system, young Jim seemed unable to buckle down to the work required in his new school.

His new school was in session six days a week. At least five of those days were made very long by the mandatory sports program. Now this was something Jimmy could relate to. Always athletically inclined, young Jim switched from baseball to cricket, and American football to rugby, with a certain amount of enthusiasm. He happily sacrificed a tooth to the latter sport and knowledgeably spoke of wickets and scrums. Unhappily, the enthusiasm Jimmy displayed on the playing field was not transferred to scholastic endeavors.

I think too that he had trouble fitting into his new peer group. His situation was unlike Mike and Karen's, the only Americans in their school. Though not in the same standard (grade), they could at least compare notes on mores and manners. They lent a certain amount of moral support to each other, but Jimmy was on his own. With no compatriot to interpret or provide guidance, he proved easy prey for his peers. Too gullible by half, he believed his best friend, for instance, when he told him the next day was a school holiday. And none of us knew any better either. There was no school calendar handed out. One was expected to know the routine—at least somewhat.

That incident was just a small contribution to his end-of-term report card, which could hardly have been worse. We took Jimmy and our persistent plea of poverty to the Nairobi International School. They accepted both.

As time went on, our children agreed it was easier to assimilate into international and American schools overseas than into neighborhood schools there and stateside. In the former, they didn't have to fight new-kid-on-the-block syndrome because many of the students were new to the school—to the country. They could all relate to moving. It made for quick common ground.

# Things are Different

Jimmy's quick temper caused us concern. More than one expatriate family has been invited (ordered) to leave a developing country because one of its children hit someone at school—"someone" usually turning out to be the relation of an important someone else in local government. It was an uncomfortable thought, the idea that a career and livelihood could depend on one's children's abilities to exercise restraint and self-discipline.

The idea that freedom of speech could be considered a mere indulgence, often not to be tolerated, rather than a basic right as in the United States, was a concept foreign to our family. We discussed this among ourselves before ever leaving America.

We also briefly discussed the issue of color and quickly decided it simply wasn't an issue. It would be a different experience for us being a part of the white minority in a black-majority country, but not a problem. Skin color may give a hint of heritage, but I don't think it defines or measures a human being—or a nation. Martin Luther King Jr.'s hope that someday people would be judged by the content of their character and not by the color of their skin rings true with me.

I was anxious for the new nations of Africa to show the world that they could govern themselves. I hoped they'd do an even better job of it than their colonial rulers. I was somewhat young, naive, and idealistic. I even expected altruism in the new leaders of Africa. Of course I would learn, if I didn't know it already, that good, bad, and greed come in all colors. Color us all human.

Jim and I felt we could handle the fact that our American rights stopped at America's shores. We knew we'd be subject to our host country's laws. We would have no diplomatic immunity. We were not official Americans officially representing our country.

This wouldn't prevent us from trying to be diplomatic, however. Diplomacy would prove especially helpful in one or two parts of the world, especially when faced with the question, "And what do you think of our country?"

"Oh, I find it very interesting," can be a true statement. It can also be true diplomatese for an opinion that, in some countries, can't be more accurately—or safely—expressed by a good and prudent guest.

And this was the theme I hammered into our children. "Be polite. We are guests in this country. It is bad manners to blatantly criticize one's host or hostess. If you can't say something nice, then don't say anything. But look for the good things."

"There are too some!" I insisted. We all had our down days.

I suppose I harped about good manners and being a good guest in a foreign country because I saw this as a natural, positive, and probably safe approach to getting along and surviving there. Besides, to me basic good manners aren't artificial but flow from a respect for one's fellow beings. And didn't someone once describe good manners as being the oil for the wheels of civilization? To avoid squeaks, it behooves one to be knowledgeable, and aware, and willing to learn. What is polite, or at least acceptable, in one part of the world may not be in another. For instance, to an American, a thumbs-up might mean *okay, right on*, or that someone wants a ride. It's an obscene gesture in the Middle East and some parts of Africa.

So much was new to our kids—to all of us when we went to Africa. I didn't want different-from-America to be a burden for our children, but rather an opportunity for learning and broadening their outlook and understanding. It seemed a chance for an expanded education, one not easily graded with the usual A, B or C.

After our year of unemployment, lack of money sometimes constrained our being able to take advantage of as many trips and opportunities in Kenya as we would have liked. We certainly didn't consider ourselves "rich" Americans, and my husband commented as much in conversation at work one day in Kenya. His secretary overheard and paused in her typing. Jim heard her quietly comment to her typewriter, "All Americans are rich." And then she added, "Some of them just don't know it."

We all tried hard to adapt to and learn about our new environment. Sometimes we seemed to trip over little things. A coin got young Jim thrown off a Nairobi bus. To him a shilling was a shilling, but he learned that a Tanzanian shilling wouldn't buy him a ride on a Kenyan bus. It might have done so not long before, but the East African Community formed by Kenya, Tanzania, and Uganda was already cracking, and they were no longer accepting each other's money.

Another time, at work at Embakasi, Nairobi's international airport, Big Jim obliged a Kenyan coworker with the loan of a shilling. He casually flipped the coin across the room to the young man, who missed catching it and picked the coin off the floor. Jim found the next couple of days mystifying. He became aware of a strained office atmosphere. He didn't know the cause, except that he might be it. Where before the office personnel were polite and friendly to him, now they were only polite. Jim knew he must have inadvertently offended in some way. He enlisted the aid of a British manager who discreetly investigated and reported back. By flipping that coin, Jim had insulted President Jomo Kenyatta. The Kenyan shilling had Kenyatta's image on it, and the Kenyans thought Jim had treated that image with a distinct lack of respect. He successfully apologized.

Our children were shocked one day to see what they thought was a lack of respect by Kenyans for the Kenyan flag. They had been taught to respect their own and other countries' flags. Reared in the American tradition that allowing our flag to touch the ground was disrespectful, our children were startled to see stacks of Kenyan flags tossed down to the street from a lorry (truck) distributing flags to be hoisted for a holiday.

I was more appalled at what was tossed into, rather than out of, a truck in Nairobi in preparation for festival days there. Cleaning up the streets meant a sweep of the beggars. They were tossed, none too gently and yet not really harshly the time I witnessed it, into the back of a lorry. The beggars were then driven miles out of town. It would take them awhile to make their own way back, by which time the festival would be over and complaints about the beggars' presence would have subsided. It was one way of solving the perceived problem, at least temporarily.

There were more men than women begging in Nairobi. However, one of the women was systematically working a car park near the market on a day when I waited alone in a car there for a friend. Usually the police kept the beggars from plying their trade in the market parking lot. Evidently this woman escaped their scrutiny. I watched people give her a few coins when she approached them, and I knew I was not going to do so. This because I saw her periodically, surreptitiously dump her booty into a strong leather pouch. The pouch hung from a thong around her neck and then hid itself in her voluminous attire. Once, I saw her briefly remove from the pouch a large roll of paper money in order to better dump in the coins. I figured her cash flow was better than mine at the moment.

I tried to make it a policy to give only to organized, reputable charity efforts. Though this beggar woman's efforts were organized, she looked far from reputable. Dirty and disheveled, she had a wild look about her that should have warned me. She accosted me at my car window, which was down a few inches. I indicated refusal to her request for money, and the beggar woman went into a rage. Her hand shot through the narrow opening of the car window straight at my face. Her hand was a claw, whose talons might have dripped with my blood had I not quickly dodged. My quick reflexes saved my face, and hers her hand as I got that window closed. I momentarily feared I would roll the car window the wrong way, opening rather than closing it. That woman had the longest, dirtiest fingernails. Had they connected with their target, my face, I would have had blood poisoning for sure. Even with the window closed, the witch wasn't through with me. I began to realize that all the people I'd seen give this woman money had probably done so to contribute to their own safety rather than her welfare. Her fingernails flailed a frenzy on my car window as she spewed verbal venom at me. I was determined to maintain a calm demeanor despite being scared. Suddenly the woman stepped back a pace, going from hissing hysteria to icy calm. In what I presumed to be the best voodoo manner, her palms down and fingers spread, she extended her hands at arm's length toward me. Her curses before were oaths—this one looked to be the real thing. The woman's gaze bored into mine as she began her malevolent mumbo jumbo. I deliberately broke eye contact. I was afraid, and not totally sure of what. She finished with a high-pitched cackle and loped off to more lucrative liaisons.

I didn't really believe in curses, at least I didn't think I did. However,

I usually cut my own hair and I was surprised to find, from then on in Africa, a slight change in my behavior. Some little primeval part of me prompted a more careful disposal of hair clippings. I guess images of voodoo dolls danced in my head. Into my mind popped a mean little realization too—that I'd like to nominate that particular beggar for the next festival truck-toss tour.

It never occurred to me that a curse could be a labor problem until my husband came home and told me how his day had gone. "You're not going to believe this, but we have a typist who can't type."

"How did she get hired as a typist?"

"Oh, she could type when she was hired, but now she can't because she's cursed."

"You're kidding!"

"No, really. She thinks her fingers are cursed and she really can't type."

"Are you sure she's not putting you all on?" It sounded like an inspired excuse for incompetence to me. But no, my husband assured me it was all for real, very real in the typist's mind—and consequently her fingers.

Nairobi's Mayfair Hotel did a good job of easing us into life in Kenya, but with three children, hotel living palled quickly. I was delighted to hear that we could move into our new home. It was a maisonette, one of a row of houses connected by common side walls—a town house. It was located a long walk from Adam's Arcade, a small shopping center. There, among other small shops and a post office, was a bakery that produced salivating smells and great loaves of bread, usually sold unwrapped and each an armful in itself.

The post office, however, was the object of my first visit to Adam's Arcade. Few, if any, countries in Africa have door-to-door mail delivery. I wanted to get a post office box, not realizing they were in short supply and we could simply continue to receive all our mail through Jim's work place. That was, in fact, quite a normal way to get one's mail.

Maybe my being new and naive appealed to the nice young man at the little post office. For some reason it was a case of ask and you shall receive. Only later did I learn, to my astonishment, that there was a long waiting list for postal boxes, and that people who knew we'd gotten one so quickly assumed one of two things—either we were of some special importance or we paid a bribe. Neither assumption was true.

I suspect the nice post office people tried to do me another favor later that year. Surface mail from the United States was taking six weeks to three months or more to reach us. Too often people in the United States assumed that all mail traveled by air regardless of destination and postage paid. But usually a surface price meant a surface route for overseas mail. I sometimes thought the proverbial slow boat to China might be a mandatory part of the routing. Therefore, when Christmas cards went on sale in September in Nairobi, I took the hint. With our budget I didn't want to pay airmail postage for our Christmas cards, so I sent them surface, mailing them with what I thought to be good timing in late October.

Well, Happy Halloween! I took a lot of ribbing from the recipients of my Christmas cards, which reached everyone by October 31st that year. If it was a postal favor, it certainly backfired on me. Ever after overseas, I paid the price and purchased airmail stamps for Christmas cards—which I mailed in December.

# Meet Okech

🖾 🖾 🖾

Our maisonette had been vacant for three or four months, which accounted for the thick layer of red dust over everything. I never knew why the house wasn't available to us sooner. Though I came to realize that seldom do events or people move quickly in the developing world.

As I set to work cleaning our new home, so we could move from the hotel, I thought longingly of my trusty vacuum cleaner in the United States. But there had been no point in bringing it; Kenya, along with most of the world, operates on 220-240 volt 50-60 cycle electricity for everything. That is, it does when and where electricity is available. North American 110-volt appliances would burn out, cause damage, or be damaged if plugged into a higher volt system such as Kenya's. American 110-volt appliances could be used there only if plugged into an often expensive—and usually heavy—transformer box, which in turn plugs into the 220-volt system. A transformer is not necessarily the same as an adaptor. An adaptor can be just a plug that does not in any way change the flow of electricity. Sometimes it simply enables the plug on the cord of an appliance to have access to the local electricity.

There are a number of different types of plugs and outlet boxes around the world. Sometimes, in England for example, appliances were sold without any plug at cord's end. This way one could choose and attach a plug compatible for use, wherever. More than once I was expected to simply plug bare wires into the electricity supply in the third world. No, I didn't do it. Anyway, in contrast to some adaptors, a transformer actually transforms the current of electricity, stepping it up or down as the case may be. I tended to find transformers a nuisance for those appliances in frequent use. I worried that I'd forget and plug the appliance directly into the wall outlet instead of the transformer, thus blowing everything. I preferred my iron, mixer, electric kettle—and vacuum cleaner, if I had one—to be directly compatible with the local electricity supply.

But at that point in Nairobi, I was on my own with the cleaning up. I couldn't afford a vacuum cleaner and had the naive notion that I didn't need a servant. After all, I was an efficient American housewife and our budget was tight. The realization soon dawned that a servant could be a necessity rather than a luxury.

I found that the laundry was done daily, in the bathtub, by hand. This was a time-consuming chore for a family our size, made more so by the red Nairobi dirt—or mud, as the case might be. No child of any age or nationality could avoid getting this on his clothes, and it always meant extra scrubbing to get it out.

Until I lived in Africa, I associated hand-washing of laundry with the word delicate, as in "fine or soft in touch or skill." Delicate fabric, delicately laundered. That idea changed when I saw the vigorous sloshing and scrubbing applied to dirty clothes by household staff in Africa. Seemingly, their hands knew no delicate cycle.

Then came the ironing, and not just for appearance's sake. The heat of the iron killed any eggs the mango fly might have laid in the damp clothes on the clothesline. There was no temptation to allow skipping or skimping on the ironing after I read the following: "If not killed, the larvae will burrow under the skin to produce a most unattractive slug which must be squeezed out."

However, I did hope my husband wouldn't come to consider ironed underwear the norm and expect it other times and other places. We'd have a rough time back in the United States if he ever expected me to add ironing underwear to my job description of housewife.

When it came to hiring servants, I had been saying, "No," to hotel personnel. They all approached me with suggestions that I hire their brother, sister, cousin, or friend. Maybe I needed to rethink my refusals.

I pondered the problem while cleaning our empty maisonette's downstairs toilet. Thus preoccupied, I jumped when the first flush produced a baby lizard swimming for its life. My startled reflexes were too slow to save it. Down on my hands and knees scrubbing, I kept a wary eye out for momma and poppa lizard. I wondered if they'd pop out from some nook or cranny to condemn my failure as a lifeguard.

Servants was not a subject I'd ever dwelt upon. The very word evoked, in my mind, images of lady-of-the-manor or plantation living. Certainly that lifestyle was as foreign to me as anything I expected to encounter in Africa. At the thought of servants, my mind conjured visions of spotless, white-coated retainers gliding noiselessly as they went efficiently about their household duties. The reality of Okech was, in every sense of the term, something else.

In the midst of my cleaning, his unheralded arrival was announced with a timid knock at the kitchen door. He looked to be about forty years old and was dressed in a sport shirt and walking shorts. Both must have seen a lot of walking because, though clean, they were stained and patched and gave real meaning to the word "threadbare." Poverty punctuated our conversation with each nervous shuffle of his ragged sneakers, sans laces or socks. Okech's English was considerably better than my few words of Swahili, but I still understood little of what he said beyond "houseboy." His need of a job was obvious, his eagerness to work apparent. Still, his written references were dated three years before and earlier. Surely if he were any good he'd have a job or more recent references. I mulled the possibilities. Maybe he'd been ill. He was surely thin. I didn't want to chance exposing our four children to anything serious. Common sense dictated a polite brush-off to be rid of him.

The next knock came at the front door only minutes later. Finding Okech again, I wondered if my brush-off had been too polite. Then I noticed that he'd brought an advocate, my next-door neighbor. She introduced herself and launched into an explanation of Okech.

Her half-hearted assurance that I was in no way obliged to hire him was followed by the expressed hope that I might see my way clear to do so. It seemed he'd worked for the previous tenant of my new home. He'd stayed on in the maisonettes' communal servant quarters in hopes of working for the next occupant of the house. Jobs were scarce and it was good planning. He had no way of knowing that several months would elapse between tenants. Odd jobs and a little charity from the neighbors had kept him going.

This is another reason why it is usually good to employ household help in developing countries. Jobs are hard to come by. Unemployment, almost inevitably, is far greater than any percentage one can envision in the rest of the world. Becoming an employer adds to the health of the local economy. Your own life is made easier. Not only is someone physically doing some of the work you would otherwise have to do, but also you experience a better acceptance locally because you've conformed to tradition and contributed to the economy. Foreigners who don't hire someone to help in the house when it is local custom are apt to be thought of as stingy, unfeeling, and undesirable. They are sometimes treated accordingly.

My neighbor continued her entreaty. Long before mention of two wives and umpteen dozen children, I knew I'd inherited a houseboy. Okech knew it too. As my neighbor continued to plead his case, I watched Okech's hopeful smile turn to a grin that showed a sunny disposition and several missing teeth.

Okech

I couldn't help liking him and felt my family would too. He seemed a willing worker and there was an air of honesty and cheer about him. This, I hoped, would compensate for what I suspected would be a certain lack of competence in household skills. It did, but sometimes just barely. This was indicated soon after in a letter to my mother.

> *Everything I think of doing this morning seems impossible for one reason or another. For instance, I can't finish unpacking the suitcases because I have to go buy hangers. I can't go buy hangers because I haven't got the car. Jim has it at work. I can't unpack the rest of the dishes and get them washed and put away because the drains in the house are all plugged up. All the drains run together at one point, and of course that is where they are plugged.*
>
> *Have I mentioned that I have a house servant? Right this minute I consider that fact a mixed blessing! Guess how the drains got plugged? Okech was fixing Mike some toast on the grill of the stove. While the bread was toasting, Okech went to empty the kitchen trash. While doing so, he discovered I'd thrown out a cup which had its pedestal base broken in moving. Well, this was quite a find. Okech was so pleased and excited when I said he could have it that he forgot about the toast. The next thing we knew, smoke was pouring from the stove's broiler and filling the kitchen. Now Okech wasn't about to waste the toast so he scraped it off (it was very thick bread) into the kitchen sink, ran the water to wash the mess down the drain, and I've already mentioned the result. And no, there is no garbage disposal to turn on.*

Our group of ten maisonettes constituted a miniature United Nations. The British had a slight edge in numbers, Kenya then being less than ten years into independence after British rule. Fortunately for our lone and linguistically-lacking American family, everyone there spoke English, if not as their first language, then as their second or third. True, there were some slight disparities, mostly amusing, that arose due to differences in British and American English. However, our children and the neighbors' played Monopoly with equal facility, whether it was Park Lane with pounds or Park Place with dollars. The interchange of cricket with baseball was less easily accomplished.

Variety spiced our group with various occupations and interests as well as nationalities. It was tremendously interesting to get together and compare notes, to listen and learn. Would that the whole world could go and do likewise.

A week or so after my arrival, the neighbor ladies welcomed me officially with a gathering for morning coffee. It was there that I received a compliment of sorts that I still cherish because it was so spontaneously well meant. I'd sensed some minutes into the coffee hour that I'd passed muster. Confirmation of that came with a delightfully impulsive outburst from my normally reserved British hostess.

"Oh, Marilyn, I'm so glad you've joined us. You fit in so well. You're not at all like an Ameri . . . Oh dear, oh my, oh goodness. This isn't coming out at all right, and I meant it so well!"

I interrupted her rather pink confusion to assure her that I quite understood. I too had met the brash and brassy American. I was glad of the chance abroad to prove that we weren't all stamped from that mold. Not that boorishness was ever strictly confined to any one nationality. It has been my experience that brash bigots and careless clods can be found in any culture. It wasn't long after that, in a larger mixed gathering, that I leaned toward my new British friend and said, "One of yours, I trust," in regard to a self-important young man making a fool of himself. She nodded and returned my wry smile.

The neighbors' knowledge and advice was invaluable. Not that I slavishly followed it. A commonsense sifting of what I gleaned was necessary to find what was comfortable and applicable for our family.

There was no way I could ever bring myself to lock up all, or any, of the food in the house to prevent servants stealing it. Only one neighbor advised this, but it was a common enough practice throughout Africa. My own approach was to try to establish a degree of mutual trust and liking. That, I hoped, would work in lieu of locks. This didn't mean that I left money and valuables carelessly lying around to provide temptation.

I gave the servants free rein on certain food items during their working hours. I made it clear that they could eat on the job, but they were not to take food home with them without permission. In Kenya, the items available to the servants were tea with milk and sugar, and bread, sometimes with butter or jam if our supply was ample. Later in Zaire, it was again tea with milk and sugar, but rice in lieu of bread, which was often in short supply. Anything else they wanted, I expected them to ask. Generally speaking, it was me they were to ask. My husband did not want to be bothered with what he considered the trivial details that were part of my job of running our household.

As for our children, we instructed them from the first that they had no authority over the servants. Our children were to give neither orders nor permission to the staff. I suspect this parental edict quashed some secret dreams along the lines of, "Peel me a grape, Alphonse."

Though I'd like to think my allowing the servants to eat on the job stemmed first from the higher motive of feeding the hungry, there is no denying its practical justification. Adequate nutrition makes anyone healthier, happier, and able to work better.

I think establishing good rapport with the servants, a mutual feeling of trust and respect, is important. Situations can arise in Africa, and I suppose elsewhere, in which you find yourself entrusting the care of your children, your worldly goods, perhaps your very life to them. It behooves one to be a good judge of character so as to choose wisely in the first place, and then to proceed in the relationship with cautious assurance.

The preceding sounds almost a prescription for marriage. I recall a day in Zaire when my husband and our head houseman happened to arrive at our house simultaneously after lengthy, separate absences. Truth to tell, I wasn't at all sure which of the two men I was happier to see at that moment. As welcome as my husband was, I knew it was our employee, Victor, who would solve some pressing problems, the biggest of which was our not having any water. Only Victor could succeed in finding and bribing the man with the tanker truck to fill our empty underground cistern. Victor would take care of the balky cook stove, comfort the clamoring chimpanzee, and probably cook a special treat of delicious French fries for my soon-to-be clamoring children. For that one problem-filled moment, I might have been happier to see my houseman than my husband.

# Do It My Way

⬚ ⬚ ⬚

But before Zaire came Okech and Kenya. My feelings for Kenya were straightforward enough, love almost at first sight. Okech, however, evoked a wider range of emotion—from amazement, amusement, and appreciation, to a zeal to reform.

Maybe this last is best exemplified in my quelling of Okech's delight in using the potato peeler. A simple gadget, it was the first of its kind he had seen. He wielded it with a joyous abandon that daily created a floor-to-ceiling montage of peelings in the kitchen. This being completely contrary to my neat and tidy way of doing things, I tried to rein in Okech's happy enthusiasm.

To a certain extent I succeeded, except then I found that I missed something. Gone was Okech's cheerful exuberance. I decided to rethink the situation. What difference did it make if he turned the kitchen into a disaster area? He always cleaned it up. Sure, Okech was making more work for himself, but he didn't mind that. And maybe it wasn't really more work. In his hands, that handy-dandy gadget made potato peeling a pleasure for him. That is, it did until I, Memsahib, took all the fun out of it.

None of this was really articulated between us, but Memsahib got the message. The mess and wasted effort would not bother me if I didn't see it. Therefore, I made a point of staying out of the kitchen when Okech created his daily mosaic of potato peelings and carrot curls. We were both happier at my absence. I returned to do most of the actual cooking.

There were so many differences in our household in Africa compared to how we had lived in the United States. Though embassy Americans and similar official-types in Africa usually had washers and dryers and servants trained in their use, we left the washing machine, clothes dryer, vacuum cleaner, et cetera behind. In Kenya, Okech served in lieu of these appliances and consequently supported his family. He supported our family too in a different way. We would have been hard pressed to manage without him. Perhaps he lacked the efficiency of a well-oiled machine, but, as a machine never could, Okech added a totally interesting dimension to our life in Kenya. It was a dimension most often measured in smiles.

How impossible to stay somber when coming upon Okech literally kicking up his bare heels to one of our records. Herb Alpert and the Tiajuana Brass could be counted on to set Okech's toes tapping and his broom dancing across the living room.

We all liked Okech's naturally sunny disposition. He and the children got along well, though there were times when he'd get annoyed with them. These times were easy to tell. Normally he called the children by their first names. However, if he was annoyed with them, the girls became "Missy Roxanne" or "Missy Karen," the boys "that Jeem" or "that Mike."

When the children and Okech were enjoying good rapport, which was most of the time, friendly warnings sometimes passed between them. One of these went to Jimmy one evening. I stepped out of the kitchen for a moment, and young Jim took the opportunity to grab a spoon and sample something I had cooking. Okech smiled, wagged a finger at him and said, "Ahhh, Jeem. Memsahib weel keel you!"

I heard and hoped his choice of words was due to a limited English vocabulary rather than to any thought that I was actually that bloodthirsty a disciplinarian. In retrospect, I wonder if it might have been a bit of wishful thinking on Okech's part.

I've just recently learned, during some family reminiscing, that a favorite trick of young Jim and his best friend was to sneak my cigarettes. Though I would give up smoking a few years later, in Kenya I was a pack-a-day smoker, give or take a few, and my cigarettes were always lying around. It was easy for the boys to snitch some without my becoming aware of it. It seems that Jimmy and his friend gave these cigarettes to the servants, but you can forget any motive of generosity on the boys' part. They often doctored my cigarettes by inserting tiny firecrackers, creating a smaller version of a comedian's exploding cigar. They then gave these altered cigarettes to the unsuspecting servants. Had I known at the time of my son's misguided sense of humor, I probably would have at least half-keeled "that Jeem."

The children really cared about Okech though, and I once overheard them trying to protect him. "Okech, *please* don't laugh about it. Memsahib is really angry with you this time!" I suspect that my overhearing this defused the situation. I don't even remember why I was mad.

The warnings continued to flow both ways and often worked to my benefit. "Jeem, Mike, Karen. No bother Memsahib now. Memsahib really sick. She drink tea."

Okech's quick understanding that I then rarely drank tea except when ill was in marked contrast to his noncomprehension of my coffee habit. Early on, Okech and I had to come to an understanding about my coffee cup and the coffee therein. He was to consider both nearly sacrosanct. I insisted that neither the coffee nor the cup was to disappear just because my back was turned or I happened to be temporarily elsewhere. In this one case, it was possible for Okech to be too efficient. I liked cold coffee. To be precise, I liked cold coffee to which I added hot coffee to make warm coffee. This I could then drink immediately. My first cup of coffee of the day sometimes got cooled quickly with half an ice cube, a whole cube in and spooned out when it was half melted. From then on, through a good part of the day, I drank my particular blend of old (cold) and new (hot) coffee. It took some doing to convince Okech to allow me this idiosyncrasy, but we slowly progressed.

At first, Okech zapped that cup under the tap and into the cupboard the moment I or my attention wandered. Next, he took to washing my coffee cup sparkling clean and returning it, empty, to the exact spot in which I had left it. Then came the phase where he seemed to fear it was some kind of fetish. He was afraid to touch the cup, even to move it out of his way. Okech would circle my coffee cup warily, and make little darting jabs toward it with the dust cloth. He never understood, but he finally relaxed and did it my way. He realized that at some point during the day he would find Memsahib's coffee cup in the kitchen sink. This became the signal that he might, with a clear conscience, wash that cup. Otherwise and other places, it was hands off.

While the timing of the washing of my coffee cup was a personal preference thing, with some chores it really did matter as to the order in which they were done. This message was sometimes difficult to put across. One such chore was the division of laundry. Not the sorting and separate washing of white clothes and dark clothes, but rather "our" clothes and "your" clothes. There was no color issue involved, just health and odor.

I always hoped, in vain, that the subject wouldn't come up, but it did, usually because I raised it. However, the odor theme was an onerous one for me. Perhaps I'd seen too many bad-breath and body-odor commercials in the United States. I think I somehow identified with the lady in television's early years who looked askance at the man with body odor and murmured, "Oh, I could never tell him."

Yet there were sound health reasons as to why the servants' clothes and ours should not be mixed together. The servants' exposure to disease was greater than ours due to a number of reasons—crowded living conditions and an inadequate water supply, to name but two. They tended to wear their clothes for longer periods of time without laundering than we did. Consequently, there was a definite odor-transference problem if all our clothes were soaked together. Even so, I all but became tongue tied trying to explain that our clothes should be washed in the water first before theirs. I didn't want to insult anyone, so my tongue tiptoed and tripped around the whole topic. Therefore, the message the servants got was weak and ineffective. The servants misinterpreted and thought I really didn't care strongly one way or another. For a while the laundry would be done my way and I'd relax my vigilance until one or another of us found cause to complain.

"Mom, these clothes stink!"

By the third time I had to speak on this subject, I was so annoyed because my orders hadn't been followed. The servants then received my message loud and clear. Perhaps not as bluntly as my children put it to me, but the servants were left with no doubt as to how and in what order the clothes were to be washed. Even if they didn't quite understand why I was finally so vehement in laying down the law about the laundry, it got done my way from then on.

Okech's handwashing of our laundry took its toll, particularly of the bedsheets. I wasn't able to afford a new supply, so some of them were wearing thin. Okech would bring them to me to mend. I'd always hated sewing and never learned to use a sewing machine. In fact, I felt intimidated early in life by the one or two I'd tentatively tried. Consequently, all my mending was done by hand, though I hadn't bothered mending bedsheets before Kenya. But I sewed them there, as well as mending the rips and tears in the clothes of our family of six. Dogged determination made me almost adept at removing the hip pockets on the boys' jeans and sewing them back on as knee patches, the iron-on kind being unavailable.

Okech was impressed with my ability to mend things so well that they could survive his laundering. I don't think he realized I disliked plying that needle and thread. He saw only how happy I was when any sewing job was finished. Understandable, then, that he thought it the sewing itself that made me cheerful. Perhaps he thought he was doing me a favor when one day he came with a special request. Memsahib's mending was so good, would Memsahib please mend this for him?

"Now wait just a doggone minute," I exploded. "This isn't how the rules work. I'm not supposed to be mending my servant's clothes. You work for me, not vice versa."

"Sorry, Memsahib, sorry." Okech backed away with a scared look on his face. And of course, then I was sorry. He looked so crushed. He probably didn't understood half of what I said, but I wished I'd been more diplomatic anyway.

"It's all right, Okech. It's okay." I gestured a calming hand and smiled rather ruefully. I knew that, to make amends for my rudeness, I was going to do Okech's mending this one time. But I made clear to him this was going to be the *only* time.

All jobs have their fringe benefits. Their clothes washed and ironed at their employer's expense is one of the valued perks for household help in Africa. In their villages, sometimes even in servants' quarters, they are lucky if there is so much as a communal faucet tapping a piped-in water supply. As often as not their water supply, which may be the nearest river or stream, is a difficult distance away. As for electricity, even the single-bare-bulb variety is still a luxury in much of Africa, particularly for the not-so-well-off lower strata of society.

Sometimes I'd see Okech ironing something for his young number-two wife with whom he was absolutely besotted, or for one of their children. This was a violation of unspoken rules, as custom allowed for the washing and ironing of the servants' own clothes but not those of their family. Though Okech and I both knew I was aware, I pretended not to notice the occasional extra ironing. He didn't do it often, and I figured it was probably done for some special event. His number-one wife and their children usually remained in their home village a couple of hundred miles from Nairobi.

There was plenty of ironing for just our family alone, and Okech tried to do a good job of it. Despite having clean, freshly ironed clothes to wear each day, our younger son, Michael, started looking rather rumpled as he left in the mornings for school. I figured, since Mike seemed to be ready for school in plenty of time, that he was probably playing, turning somersaults on his bed or something while waiting to leave. I wasn't that bothered about Michael's morning appearance, but Okech was upset because he felt it reflected poorly on himself when Michael walked a little wrinkled out the door. I was unaware of Okech's sentiments, but he grumbled to young Jim, who promptly reported to me.

"Mom, you know how lately Mike's all ready for school so early? Well, Okech is mad because he's sleeping in his clothes."

"Who's what?"

"Michael. He's sleeping in his school clothes."

"He sleeps in pajamas," I said in bewilderment.

"Yeah, but underneath he's got on his clean school clothes, and Okech is mad because they're getting all wrinkled."

Sure enough. Michael had thought about his problem of getting ready on time for school and solved it by dressing himself the night before. I directed him to rethink the problem…and the solution.

But there was no solution to the telephone problem. Telephones in Nairobi were in even shorter supply than postal boxes. Ordinary people simply didn't get one no matter how nicely they asked. It was an inconvenience we adjusted to without much difficulty, actually. One simply went in person to accomplish things one would have used the telephone for at home, or sent and received messages and notes via someone else. All this was time consuming, but it worked.

I learned not to underestimate the local grapevine. It was sometimes surprisingly efficient. One day our family went downtown, there splitting up to accomplish errands in various directions. We agreed to meet later. My husband's tasks didn't take him as long as expected, so he headed for the

Nairobi Market in hopes of catching up with me. Misjudging my agenda and shopping speed, Jim went first to the greengrocer section to wander about looking for me. He'd been there only a time or two before, yet he was soon stopped by the people at one stall.

"Bwana, are you looking for your wife?"

"Yes, I am."

"She is not here yet, but you wait. She will be here soon. She is still buying meat." Jim and I both were amazed at their awareness of us. The meat section was totally separate, unable to be seen by the people in produce.

Another instance of the grapevine at work was when my sister telephoned one Saturday from the United States. She could not conceive of us living in a city and not having a telephone in our home. Therefore, when our aunt became seriously ill, my sister undertook to reach me via telephone. That she did so, despite my not having a telephone, was a tribute to her persistence and the Nairobi grapevine. When I arrived at the church rectory for choir practice that Saturday, I was told that someone in the United States was trying to reach me, that I should call a certain operator number. The church people apologized for not getting the message to me sooner. They explained that no car had been available, but they'd known I was due there soon.

My sister had not been aware of my schedule, nor exactly which church we attended. I believe someone in the Nairobi telephone company happened to know of us and put that knowledge to helpful use.

What wasn't helpful to me was finding that my sister expected me to drop everything and return to the United States to care for our aunt, who was expected to live only a few more weeks. I felt torn and my heart went out to all concerned, but I simply couldn't comply with my sister's wishes. She had it all figured out…I could get reasonably cheap transportation because my husband worked for an airline, and there would be no problem with leaving my family because I had a housekeeper to do everything anyway. My sister had the first part right. I probably could have gotten reduced-rate airline tickets, though it would take awhile and I would have to apply for an exit visa to leave Kenya. But "a housekeeper to do everything anyway"? Okech?

This pointed up the difficulty in describing differences in living conditions and lifestyles. People in the United States seemed to picture us living as they did, with most of life's conveniences—only better because we had fulltime household help. Their idea of a servant was as naive as mine had been before I became better informed through the actuality of Africa. To family and friends back home, a servant was a luxury. To me a servant was a necessity, and God bless Okech. Luxury would have been screened windows and doors, television, perhaps even a preciously saved egg carton or plastic grocery bag.

It was hard to not be able to respond more to the needs of family back in the United States. However, since we were still new to living halfway around the world, I felt that my priority had to be my husband and four children—helping them, and me, with the ABCs of our new life : to Adjust, to Belong, to Cope.

# Yes, Memsahib

◫ ◫ ◫

Glad as I was to employ Okech, having a servant was not an unmixed blessing. Morning coffee klatches in Kenya abounded with amusing, and sometimes not so amusing, tales of what one or another of the servants had done. At such times that impish little corner of my mind, the one that punctures pretension and prods perspective, would start to work. Invariably my irrepressible inner voice would soundlessly whisper to me, *Hah! La-de-da. Listen to you, discussing The Servant Problem, no less.*

It was at one of these coffee gatherings of ladies that a neighbor shared a tidbit from a recently received letter. The missive was from the former memsahib of my maisonette. The lady sharing her news made certain that none of the servants were within earshot. She then told us the story that became known among us as "Okech's Revenge."

That he and the departed memsahib didn't think much of one another was no secret. After all, she hadn't given Okech a reference, not even one condemning with faint praise. No reference at all could have made him virtually unemployable if my neighbor hadn't vouched for him. Most of the neighbors liked the lady, but not her attitude toward servants in general, and Okech in particular. His opinion of her I'd gleaned as much from what he didn't say as what he did say. However, at that coffee klatch with the reading of the letter from England, it became clear that Okech had finally expressed his true opinion of and to her.

On arrival in England, the memsahib unpacked her favorite outfit which had been washed, ironed, and carefully folded by Okech. You just bet it had. There, on the posterior of her pants suit, Okech's former employer discovered a gaping hole the size and shape of an iron. We ladies gasped but agreed—most of us anyway— that Okech administered a cleverly executed kick in the assuredly appropriate spot.

Small wonder then that I suspected Okech might be trying to tell me something when I found he'd melted the collar of my favorite blouse. However, I decided later it was carelessness rather than comment.

Early problems with Okech's ironing were mostly my fault. When I bought an iron in Nairobi, I bought the kind I would like to use. An excellent steam iron, it also sprayed, sprinkled, or squirted on demand. It caressed the clothes with the aid of a fine-tuning dial clearly labeled with multiple settings.

All this was wasted on Okech who couldn't read in any language. He never had the opportunity to go to school. In the course of our year together I realized that fact continued to rankle. His family could afford to educate only one child. His elder brother was the chosen one; his sister of course had not been even considered. I also got the impression that, perhaps, elder brother did not properly appreciate, nor make the most of, his education.

Okech was not in the least stupid, nor were any of the servants. He was usually very quick to catch on to things, particularly provided he had some degree of familiarity with the subject beforehand. Problems arose with the language barrier or the fact that he couldn't read instructions.

I erred in my explanation of the steam iron to Okech, assuming him to have some prior knowledge of it, which in fact he lacked. My instructions were therefore perfunctory. Plus, I too lacked knowledge. I'd not yet learned there was significance in the inflection that Okech gave the word yes.

"Do you understand?"

"Yes, Memsahib."

A few days passed before the new steam iron shorted out, ample testimony to excellent engineering in view of the fact that Okech had consistently poured water into the wrong part of the iron. Also, he had seldom let it heat sufficiently before use—although there was evidence that, at least once, it had gotten too hot. Deep scratches gouged the iron's surface. It looked as if he'd used a hammer and chisel, rather than steel wool, to clean something off. The "something" was probably the collar of my favorite blouse.

Appliances and mechanical things were not as familiar to many Africans as they were to generations of Americans and others who grew up taking at least the more basic ones for granted. One appliance I really missed was my mixer. Thus I was delighted when my husband and children sacrificed and saved their shillings to buy me one for my birthday. Their slightly ulterior motive, expressed as a hope that the mixer would mean an increase in cakes and goodies, did not lessen my pleasure in my present.

I'd been doing some experimenting and adjusting of favorite recipes, and I was just getting the hang of some new (to me) cooking and baking techniques necessitated by Nairobi's high altitude. Higher altitudes present a cook with some extra problems. Due to lower air pressure, water has a lower boiling point and liquid evaporates faster. Generally speaking, food takes longer to cook. I found, though, that cakes and cookies benefitted from a little less baking time in a slightly higher oven temperature. This after some adjustment of ingredients. Adjustment…that often seemed a key factor of life.

With the episode of the iron still fresh in memory, I showed my new portable mixer to Okech. I asked him if he knew what it was. At his answer, I ordered him never to touch the mixer. It was difficult to keep a straight face, and my husband's face would surely have gone askew if Okech's advice were followed. Okech informed me, complete with pantomime, that Bwana would love the present I held. In Okech's opinion, that mixer was the best electric razor he'd ever seen!

A foreign language can present all sorts of problems. One is the wag who thinks it funny to tell you the wrong meaning of a word. These misguided mischief makers are more apt to be contemporaries of one's children, but there is also the occasional adult with a seemingly retarded sense of humor. I tried to teach our children never to indulge in this sort of wordplay in regard to explaining English. At the same time I taught, "Beware of saying 'yes' to anything you don't understand." Actually, I considered that good advice for anytime, anywhere, for anyone about almost anything.

But it soon became clear that Okech had no compunction about saying "yes." For him, yes was an all-purpose word he offered in complete understanding, or as a shield to hide behind. I tuned my intuitive antennae in an effort to discover the key to deciphering Yes, Memsahib.

Some of the meanings were easy to interpret. I'd been aware of them from the beginning. There was the Yes, Memsahib that meant, *What a fine idea, and I'll be happy to do it right away*. Or the Yes, Memsahib that meant, *I think it's a stupid idea, and I may have to do it, but I'm going to drag my feet the whole way*. These were easy. After all, these particular Yes, Memsahibs were similar to the Yes, Moms I'd been hearing for years.

What most concerned me was how to distinguish the Yes, Memsahib that meant, *I really do understand and will carry out your instructions forthwith*, from the Yes, Memsahib that meant, *I haven't understood a blessed word you've said, but maybe I can fake it*.

I'd already tried and failed in attempts to convince Okech he should simply tell me if he didn't understand something. Also, in an effort to improve communication, I attempted to train myself to forgo the use of slang. How incomprehensible the vernacular can be was evidenced by one of Okech's bewildered replies to Jimmy.

"Jeem. You speaking English?"

In addition to abstaining from slang and idioms, I slowed my pace of speech. This to the point where my family claimed that, overseas, I often spoke in Special English. For people who have listened to the Voice of America on shortwave radio, that phrase might recall VOA's very slow, "And now for the news in Special English." This was a broadcast of the day's news, using a simpler vocabulary and a slower speech pattern than a person really familiar with English would think of as normal. This transmission was not meant for Americans abroad. In fact, it usually set our teeth on edge with that slow pacing of words. The Special English broadcasts were geared for those people just learning English in other countries. Of course VOA had regular programming, including news broadcasts, for those more fluent in English. Radio Moscow often imitated VOA's presentation, as well as Britain's BBC. I was sometimes fooled by an American or British accent when I tuned in late. The content or slant of the news in those Cold War days fairly quickly clued me in that I was hearing Moscow rather than Washington or London. However, I did wonder sometimes how many third-world nationals got confused.

Concentrated listening paid off in sorting out Okech's Yes, Memsahib answers. After I stopped being fooled by that gap-toothed grin of his, I found I could detect the tiny tonal changes that he unconsciously orchestrated into Yes, Memsahib. I didn't bother telling him of my newfound skill. I simply employed it in promoting better understanding, and in lessening some of life's little frustrations.

Despite their longer tenure, our neighbors weren't immune to the mishaps of misinterpretation by their household help. I was a fascinated witness to one such incident. It was a rather elegant gathering of ladies that morning and included, in addition to our usual group, visitors from Scandinavia and India. Coffee and conversation flowed freely, then faltered. We all became aware of Eddisa, the young woman from Uganda who served in that household. She was carefully and slowly negotiating the obstacle course of ladies and chairs. Eddisa seemed to be headed toward me. One fact made her trek immeasurably more difficult and awkward. At arm's length, she carried a plate on which a single solitary egg rollicked and rolled. With each of Eddisa's tentative steps, the egg rolled closer to calamity.

Mesmerized at mid-sip, I peered over cup and saucer to watch the erratic approach of that desperate balancing act. To and fro in tandem, Eddisa's eyes and the egg rolled. Her sturdy hands tipped and clutched the plate tighter in a white-knuckled attempt to avert disaster.

My hostess spoke sharply, very annoyed. "For goodness sake, what are you doing?"

This caused the egg to be laid in my lap. I'd not had the chance to voice the hope that the egg was hard-boiled. It was—a part of the batch meant for the family's lunch later on. A request to Eddisa to take the eggs off the stove when done had mistakenly been translated into an unfathomed, misunderstood, but faithfully followed, command to serve them immediately.

One thing I never got used to was the servants saying, "Sorry, sorry," in a scared and nervous manner accompanied by a frightened look. This happened not only when they felt responsible for something gone wrong, but also when someone *else* dropped something or was clearly responsible for a mishap. It was almost as if the servants expected to be blamed and berated no matter who was responsible. Some of this had probably happened in the past, but I supposed too that their *Sorry, sorry* was sometimes simply an expression of regret that anything untoward had happened. I decided that I was taking *Sorry, sorry* out of cultural context, and it was simply the commiserating equivalent to *Quel dommage* or *What a pity*. But those scared looks continued to bother me.

# Shopping and Other Lessons

◩ ◪ ◩

Wherever we've lived in the world, we've been blessed with good friends and neighbors. Our neighbors in Kenya were helpful and gave me an early awareness of local customs and prices. I found that knowing, and usually abiding by, the customs and wage rates for goods or services was a help. One avoided upsetting the local economy, not to mention the neighbors.

In Kenya, this local awareness proved a boon for our budget because I could bargain knowledgeably and effectively almost from the first. This stood me in good stead whether I was ordering furniture to be made, drapes to be sewn, or doing the weekly shopping. Stores or merchants not interested in bargaining posted signs saying, "fixed price." Though even there one learned to ask for the traditional 10 percent discount on large purchases paid for in cash. For our furniture made in Nairobi, I bargained a little and got ten percent off on a half-the-money-now-and-half-on-completion deal.

Making furniture to order is often the norm in developing countries where overstuffed and overstocked is rare or nonexistent. One orders according to the ability of the furniture maker and the availability of his material. Sometimes it's best to take a whole houseful of furniture with you, if you can afford it and import regulations permit. This way one is assured of good comfortable furniture. Of course the local people will hope to buy or inherit it when you leave.

We took some larger items to Kenya—mattresses and box springs with metal frames, the dining room table. Chairs and a sofa of sorts were added there, bought from a turbaned Indian craftsman I sought out on someone's recommendation. He was as good as his word on content and quality. He and his African assistants and trainees took pride in doing a good job even though my order was fairly small and certainly not luxurious. Perhaps this accounted for delay after delay on completion dates. I suspect my group of furniture was worked piecemeal in conjunction with bigger and better orders. We certainly got tired of having no place to sit, except for our beds or the rugless floor, those many weeks of waiting. I learned patience in Africa. In this case, patience became a little easier to practice when neighbors realized our plight and loaned us some chairs.

We also took with us to Kenya dishes, flatware, pots and pans, et cetera. My extra-large cookie sheet cum roasting pan gathered dust in Kenya, but it fit into the oven in Zaire when we moved almost everything there after one year. That cute little oven in Kenya just barely held my rectangular cake pan, the lid of which became my cookie sheet. British stoves and refrigerators were traditionally small. Our children thought our maisonette was missing a refrigerator until I pointed out the compact cube under the counter.

At Nairobi's central market, bargaining was expected. In fact it was considered almost essential, whether shopping for folk art or souvenirs from the innumerable stalls, purchasing produce from the central section reserved for farmers and green grocers, or buying meat from the various butchers in their section. One bargained within one's range in the unwritten, three-tiered price structure. This divided generally into tourists, resident foreigners and wealthy Kenyans, and poorer Kenyans. As in any business deal, it helped to know the bottom line.

I sometimes saw foreigners at the Nairobi Market hesitate only slightly before paying the posted or first-asked price. Though merchandise and money quickly changed hands, an air of unease lingered at these times. The merchant might be—undoubtedly was—happy with his extra windfall. But a touch of contempt often tugged at the big smile, and perhaps a trace of disappointment. The fun had been taken out of the transaction. The game was made too easy by the free-spending foreigner who, not knowing the rules, changed them. And the foreigner, perhaps a tourist or newly arrived resident, had to be very obtuse not to be touched by that nebulous air of something wrong. Too late they might realize they'd just been legally ripped off. Some seemed to sense only the rip-off part of the atmosphere. I saw people make quick grabs to check the presence of their money in purse or pocket. This was a sure sign to a thief of available money, and where to find it. It must have been a pickpocket's paradise. I feel certain some of those unwitting victims were robbed for real on the way back to their hotels.

Some shopping lessons I learned the hard way, such as the first time I went to a greengrocer in Kenya to buy fruit and vegetables. I was used to American merchandising that always packaged products or provided sacks. I didn't realize I needed to take with me a container in which to carry away my purchases. Enroute back to the car, I performed an unsuccessful juggling act that left laughter, potatoes, and string beans in my wake. No wonder I claim a person's most essential attribute for successful overseas-living is a sense of humor, including the ability to laugh at oneself. This priority presumes that anyone living overseas already has at least a slight adventurous streak, and no major health problems. Given that and a sense of humor, the next important quality, I think, is the ability to quickly adapt to new surroundings and circumstances.

Having this ability on that balancing-act day made my next stop the basket section of the Nairobi Market. There I purchased a pliable reed basket that I could carry to the greengrocer and butcher shops in the future. Maybe I was lucky I hadn't left a trail of T-bones, though there really was no danger of that as we couldn't afford steak in those days.

I also bought, to use as a laundry hamper, a basket whose shape suggested it should come with a snake and charmer. My son, Michael, must have thought so too. I found him the next day seated cross-legged in front of said basket while he tried to coax slithery music from a toy flute. Knowing my sons, I was just a little apprehensive as I asked, "What's in the basket, Mike?"

"Dirty clothes of course."

"Nothing else?"

"No."

That was a relief. I figured I had enough to cope with in Africa without snakes in the house. It was just as well that I was unaware of what our future in Zaire, a few months hence, held on that score.

In Nairobi, I learned to get to the store (shop) early in the day to buy fresh milk in those cute, triangular liter cartons used in Kenya. If I left that stop for too late in the day, I would find the milk either sold or souring.

Rarely was milk refrigerated in a store. Most often the triangular cartons were heaped in a basket of some sort.

Oftentimes our budget dictated buying the cheaper, powdered skim-milk version made locally in Nairobi. Our children didn't like drinking this milk. So, when talking to them near the time of our move from Kenya to Zaire, I said, "One thing I know you'll like. Your father's salary in Kinshasa will be enough so we'll always be able to afford fresh milk there."

That proved to be a true statement. But what none of us knew until living there is that Zaire does not have a dairy industry. I think the tsetse fly problem generally precludes animal husbandry in most of the country. Though we could afford fresh milk in Zaire, there was none to be had. Our children learned to like Nido and Klim, two brands of powdered milk imported and available in much of Africa, in lieu of fresh milk.

For me shopping anyplace was no particular pleasure. Rather than an enjoyable pastime, I viewed shopping as part of my family job and tried to do it well while spending wisely. I enjoyed getting a good bargain. However, I didn't really enjoy the process of bargaining, though of necessity I became good at it. I can still use the skill if I deem it desirable or necessary.

One of my sons recently said, "Gee, Mom, I bet you didn't realize all that haggling over potatoes and oranges in Africa and the Middle East would someday pay off in real estate." This when my husband and I got a good buy on some property in the United States. Bargaining is a skill my husband never acquired, probably because he always considered me the purchasing agent for the family. In fact, with an unthinking comment, my husband can be downright counterproductive in the bargaining process.

My sons took after their father when it came to bargaining, but I needed them with me in Africa to see if the clothes I was buying for them fit. The boys were going through growth spurts that always seemed to catch me by surprise—as in, "But didn't I just buy you that?"

There were shops, some of them hole-in-the-wall places, near the Nairobi Market, where good buys on new clothes could be had. But one had to bargain for those buys. Mike stopped the process short one day with, "Hey, Mom, that price seems fair."

What did he know? I'm not sure who was the more startled, me the mom, or the man the merchant. Neither of us got where we were headed in the transaction. The merchant started laughing, and I too admitted the humor of the situation and joined in. Then it was Mike who was perplexed, but he got his new jeans. The merchant voluntarily took another few shillings off the price and I accepted, both of us knowing that he was still making a slightly better profit than he'd planned on. That merchant remembered me from then on and always gave a friendly grin and wave when I passed by.

Children in general seemed well liked in Kenya. There were few people too busy to spare a smile and greeting for a polite *mtoto*. Along with a greeting at my favorite greengrocer in the Market, my children always received a treat from the Kenyan lady there. Her gift was usually a locally grown banana, but it came to be not that much of a treat because we could afford to buy bananas and did so.

So did the servant of one of our neighbors in the maisonettes. About every other Saturday, with a whole stalk of bananas resting atop her head, this woman swayed past our homes enroute to the servants' quarters. The other servants, including Okech, would smile happily and nod to her and to each other. The resident women of the maisonettes, including me, would smile and nod approvingly as we thought what a good mother the woman was. She recognized the importance of fruit in the diet and provided it for her children, each of whom we'd soon see munching a banana. What a sham! The woman was the local producer and supplier of illegal hooch, made from bananas. Of course we didn't know this until the place was raided and she was arrested.

Though they liked bananas, my children really hungered for the very expensive imported apples our budget in Nairobi could not include. That I wasn't the only one who noticed their surreptitiously longing looks became apparent the day we said goodbye to our greengrocer friend, just prior to our move to Zaire. She seemed genuinely sad to say goodbye, and I know we were. Then she followed her usual custom of presenting a gift to each child—and me. Instead of a banana, though, she gave an apple to each of us. I had an inkling of how this gesture would cut into her day's profits. I fought an impulse to pay and figure out my budget later. The look in her eyes told me I shouldn't—couldn't—buy what she was giving. Our thanks was heartfelt, and for more than apples.

Nairobi's market area was interesting. In addition to the marvelous mix of people in the area—Africans, Asians, Europeans—I liked the mixture of spice smells emanating from some nearby shops. These shops contained great gunny sacks of various types of nuts and spices. I learned I could buy small amounts, usually scooped for the individual customer rather than prepackaged. This little bit of whichever-spice was poured onto a torn piece of newspaper. It was weighed, and then gathered up and presented with a deft twist that prevented spilling but left smelling.

One's olfactory sense appreciated the odor of exotic spices, flowers, or freshly ground coffee blowing on the breeze. Those good scents were in marked contrast to, and sometimes helped to mask, other odors wafting one's way in Africa. There were times when I practiced shallow-breathing exercises. I often avoided trying to identify an odor coming my way. My brain didn't always accede to my wish for olfactory oblivion. It insisted at times on sending identification signals—stale urine, rotting meat, six weeks (*at least*) accumulated body odor, or ye-gods-don't-breathe! At times my brain could have sent it all in one identifying signal because it simply added up to extreme poverty...and that kind of poverty really stinks.

Some of Africa's more unpleasant odors were caused by the lack of adequate water and sanitation. In the third world, I came to place convenient, clean, public (though clean-and-public was an oxymoron), functioning toilets on my things-most-missed list. I controlled my fluid intake if I was going out shopping or sightseeing. Still, on a trip, there was the occasional necessary stop in the middle of nowhere to answer a call of nature behind a bush or rock. A couple of times I looked up to find that I'd just squatted and performed for a silent native audience. Those missing toilets moved up on my most-missed list. I ranked them above soda crackers, one-stop shopping, and hot-fudge sundaes.

Sometimes lack of education and cultural differences entered in, or combined with, the lack of water and sanitation to make matters—and odors—worse. It was a common sight in Africa to see a man standing at the roadside turn his back to urinate.

Women seemed slightly more discreet about bodily elimination, consequently seen less frequently in the act. Or perhaps the act went unrecognized. Long skirts could conceal a lot, although they couldn't hide the telltale little yellow stream that occasionally crept from under a skirt and meandered down the gutter or puddled in the dust.

I once saw a series of poignant pictures published during the very real and terrible Ethiopian famine of the early 1980s. I mean no denigration of that disaster when I say that I suspect one picture might have been miscaptioned. To my perhaps more practiced eye, the squatting women on the hillside looked to be caught in the act of defecating rather than scrabbling for blades of grass to eat as the caption claimed. Yes, those long skirts really could be concealing.

# Observing and Learning

※ ※ ※

When we lived in Kenya, there was often an air of hustle and bustle surrounding Nairobi's main market area. I suspect a lot of that busyness was generated by us foreigners as we hurried through our lists of errands and dodged pushcarts and cars. Those two-wheeled pushcarts were sturdy affairs. In their own way they looked as strong as a lorry, and considerably less expensive to operate for the short haul.

It seems to me that muscle power has a definite place in a labor-intensive area like Africa. Not for exploitation but for employment. Not everyone considers this a viable point of view, as I found out when stopped in traffic at a road-building project near Nairobi. People in our car watched bulldozers make short work of a tall hill.

"Why not import a machine or two fewer," I wondered aloud, "and employ a hundred men with shovels."

"Oh, why not a thousand men with teaspoons?" snapped the businessman beside me.

Well, all right. We each had our own thoughts on the subject. Perhaps naively, I was thinking of the men being able to earn a living and feed their families. I grant that a thousand men shouldering teaspoons and setting off to work is a ridiculous idea. I'm not convinced it is a logical extension of the idea of one hundred men with shovels. Nor am I convinced that first-world solutions should necessarily be applied to third-world problems.

I was certainly appalled to find some first-world problems deliberately shipped to the third world. For instance, when cyclamate-sweetened soda pop was declared unsafe in the United States, cases of it shortly showed up for sale in Africa. But that seemed minor compared to more recent attempts of the first world to ship its garbage and radioactive waste to the third world. Damn such an attitude! But placing the blame elsewhere for everything wrong in Africa is too easy an answer.

Living in Africa taught me that there are no easy answers to the problems there. Africa's problems are complex and comprise intricate, interrelated involvement of people, politics, passions, and power. Perhaps a holistic approach needs be incorporated into any solution.

I had great hopes for what the Organization of African Unity might do. Then I saw it bog down in bickering and bloated bureaucracy, not to mention becoming a burlesque backdrop for some leaders such as Uganda's since-ousted ruler, Idi Amin. The OAU was conceived in the flush of freedom from colonial rule and established in 1963 in Addis Ababa, Ethiopia, still its headquarters. Thirty-two independent African countries pledged to promote unity and development. South Africa, with its apartheid of that time, was not in the founding group. The OAU grew in membership and also in bureaucracy. Now numbering around fifty member states, the OAU at least provides some employment and some solutions. Perhaps it will yet live up to its potential and promise.

While still stopped and continuing to watch the road-building project near Nairobi, I realized that modern technology had not replaced any of the women employed to build the road. They worked at very basic tasks, mainly carrying and positioning rocks.

I marvelled at the musculature of the women's necks, the strength that enabled them to carry a washbasin full of good-sized rocks on their heads. Thus burdened, every woman walked tall to the newly graded roadbed. There she carefully placed each of her rocks so their cumulative precision would line the roadbed. Nearby, a man lounged on the seat of a modern steamroller, waiting to firmly embed the tediously placed rocks. So maybe there was a machine or two fewer imported. The whole project was a blend of old and new technology.

In Africa, so much was new to us in our own lives. A lot of that new was fascinating and a little of it was jolting. There I was in the perfectly ordinary pursuit of reading the *Daily Nation*, one of Nairobi's two English-language daily newspapers. I found myself reading that so-and-so of such-and-such village was eaten by a lion yesterday. I was used to planning a menu. What a shock to realize that a human being might *be* the menu. The thought fostered a healthy, cautious respect for wild animals. Not everyone who visits Africa has this.

Some visitors don't realize how far they are out of their element or area of expertise—in game parks, for instance, where tourists might be well advised to pay attention to the advice of their local drivers and tour directors, or to at least read and heed game park books and brochures. These usually offer warnings about the wild animals and advise people to stay in their vehicles except in specified spots.

I recently heard the account of one woman from the United States. Of management level, used to making decisions and leading and influencing people, she persuaded her fellow tourists to exit their vans in an African game park. The woman was captivated by the idyllic scene of mother baboons cuddling and caring for their babies. They were so cute, and the setting was pastoral and peaceful. She was convinced it was safe to creep closer on foot in order to get better pictures—and no one was going to frighten or disturb the animals.

So the troop of tourists carefully approached the troop of baboons. The only sounds were the click of small cameras and the whir of their larger video cousins—until a galloping *ka-thunk, ka-thunk* intruded into people's consciousness. The tourists looked up to see an enraged male baboon bearing down on them, fully prepared to protect his property from these predators. The animal was as large as some of the tourists who quickly scattered, as did the mother baboons clutching their babies.

The male baboon zeroed in on one woman dashing for the safety of her van. She beat him there but had to scramble quickly out the far side door as he followed her in. Some persons in the group had the presence of mind to slam the van's doors shut. This imprisoned the large baboon and solved the immediate safety issue but was hardly a long-term solution.

Ever the picture-takers, the tourists shot film of the incarcerated baboon, even catching him behind the steering wheel of the van, seemingly set to drive off. Eventually someone opened a door and set the baboon free. He ran off into the bush, probably to find the mother baboons and babies he'd ably defended.

This group of tourists proved to be nimble and fleet of foot—and lucky.

The tourists drove away in their vans, one of which was a little the worse for wear inside. The group had a good story and cute pictures of an incident that could have had catastrophic consequences. I hope they had a realization of how narrowly they escaped injury, or even death.

It seems as if everyone who goes to Africa wants to see a lion in the wild. We were no exception. I'm not sure what everyone expects, but sometimes the king of beasts disappoints. In real life, in the wild, they don't all look like the MGM lion, or even Elsa of *Born Free*. Real life can be scruffy.

However, some of those pussy cats are magnificent, and we had high hopes as we headed for our first visit to Nairobi National Park (its official title; it is also often referred to as Nairobi Game Park). Despite being located just outside Nairobi and having the city's name in the title, there was no way this preserve could be thought of as a city park, or even a city zoo. The Animal Orphanage at the entrance gave a zoo-like impression because it provided fenced homes to young animals deserted in the wild by their parents. These animals likely would not have survived alone. At this enclave, Sebastian, of the ape family, was a big attraction when we were there. Somewhere, surely not in the wild, he acquired the habit of smoking cigarettes. These he would beg, preferably already lit, from bystanders. It seemed amusing to watch Sebastian ape human habits. With a greater awareness and sensitivity, I now wonder what his chances of getting lung cancer were.

Animals were confined at the Animal Orphanage, but those in the Nairobi National Park were free to roam and come and go. They did migrate, but the direction of migration and wandering was controlled to the extent that the park's side nearest Nairobi, and along the Nairobi-to-Mombasa highway, was fenced, as was the area near the airport.

About the only animal one might expect to see at Nairobi National Park, but won't, is the elephant—*tembo* in Swahili. Oh yes, and the tiger. Regardless of the expectation—even insistence of some tourists—there are no wild tigers in Africa. Elephants can be seen elsewhere in Africa, even in Kenya. Perhaps spectacularly so in Kenya's Amboseli Park, where Mount Kilimanjaro looms in the background.

An extinct volcano, Kilimanjaro is Africa's highest peak at 19,340 feet. This mountain does not rise to a pointed peak. Kilimanjaro actually has two peaks; its top is slightly depressed, as if by a giant hand. The logical part of my mind knows that the mountain top was shaped by volcanic action, but the poet in me easily imagines that God leaned there to survey His handiwork and say, "This is good."

Kilimanjaro is actually in Tanzania but so close to the border that it sheds its grandeur on Kenya too. Of course Kenya does have a pretty spectacular mountain of its own. Right on the equator, snow-covered year round, Mount Kenya is Africa's second highest mountain.

But no mountain peak claims attention at Nairobi National Park. The Ngong Hills are nearby, however, as is the Nairobi skyline. The park—Kenya's first, established in 1945—now has signposts and some paved roads. People are warned to stay in their cars unless a signpost indicates otherwise. The animals that frequent the park have become quite accustomed to cars and usually ignore well-mannered ones. Consequently, one gets a good look at the wild animals, and they almost seem to pose at times for photographers. The park itself is a varied landscape of savannah, forest, and hills—all of which can look lush or parched, depending on the rains. There are the "long rains" of March through June, and the "short rains" of November and December.

There is a fee for entering the park, but we were pleased to find a two-tiered price system. Residents of Kenya are charged less than tourists. We proudly proclaimed our resident status and paid that fee as we entered the park for the first time.

Just around the first bend in the road were several giraffe, *twiga* in Swahili. For me it was love at first sight. The only giraffe I had previously seen occupied cramped quarters in an old-fashioned, possibly inhumane zoo. There the giraffe looked ungainly, a freak of nature. Roaming where they belong, it is a different story. Their inherent gracefulness is immediately apparent when giraffe occupy their natural habitat.

Towering above it all seems to give the giraffe a natural dignity. Their height combines with keen eyesight, and they can be seemingly casual in their watchfulness. Seldom do they have to fight. This because they can see afar and simply avoid unpleasant encounters. The giraffe are vulnerable to attack when kneeling or splaying those front legs so as to lower their necks for a drink. Vegetarians themselves, they are apt to become a lion's dinner at this point. The male giraffe is the tallest animal in the world. When he gallops, each stride is about ten feet long.

55

The beautiful animals we saw after entering the park were feeding, not galloping. A half dozen of them eyed us nonchalantly, their bodies still, necks gracefully swaying their heads from the tasty acacia treetops to a nodding, bobbing welcome in our direction. The whole panorama was beautiful and seemed nearly unreal. Recently arrived from the United States, I almost expected some Disney animator to step out from behind a boulder to claim credit for the scene.

But on to the lions! At least that's what we hoped. And sure enough, we were soon waved to a halt by the driver of a car coming toward us. The big cats—that is, the lions, leopards, and cheetahs—were enough of a rarity that their sighting became an event. People lucky enough to have seen them usually wished to share the news of the sighting. It was almost an unwritten code of conduct in Kenya's game parks. If you knew where the big or rare animals could be found, you passed the information along.

With a wave and thanks for our newfound knowledge of where we might find a lion, we started up again. Our secondhand European car was a little low-slung, so we all—Jim and I in front, and Jimmy, Mike, and Karen in back—craned our necks for a good view. Our eyes swept over herds of zebra and graceful Thomson gazelle, affectionately called "Tommies" by the British. These were interesting, but we were searching for *simba*.

*Simba*. The very word in Swahili breathed a fearsome power.

Jim finally turned off the main road and drove along a less-traveled, but clearly discernible, track toward a distant clump of trees. Our first lion was proving elusive. We slowly bumped along in our two-door car. It was a warm day and we enjoyed having the side-windows open. Four pairs of eyes fastened on the horizon, where that looked-for lion was nowhere in sight. The fifth pair of eyes—mine—suddenly saw it. *Simba!* Blending with the dried grass, the lion was just a few feet ahead along the side of the track. My side. Talk about fear. But that was the trouble, I couldn't talk. I was the only one aware of possible danger, aware of the lion. It was sleeping, but its tail and a paw flopped across our path. If we continued, our tires would roll right over portions of that lion's anatomy. The adage *let sleeping dogs lie* popped idiotically into my head. I felt certain the maxim must doubly apply to sleeping lions.

With one hand I rolled up my car window, and with the other I jabbed my husband. My vocal cords finally said something profound like "aagh-

aagh." It seemed appropriate to the situation, and it got my husband's attention. One glance at me caused him to stop the car and ask what was the matter. I pointed toward the lion while wagging shushing motions toward the kids. We stopped about five feet from the lion. Though we stopped just in time, I felt there might still be danger if we woke Africa's biggest hunter. We didn't know what the lion's reaction might be. I was afraid that if awakened, the lion might be a real bear. Though there are none of those in Africa either.

My husband gently depressed the car's clutch and caressed the gearshift, trying to find reverse without a whisper of grinding gears. He succeeded and stealthily tiptoed the car backwards to safety. We never saw our first lion awake. I, for one, did not feel cheated.

# Quirks of a Common Language

A long with the occasional report of someone eaten by a lion, Nairobi's daily newspapers fairly often reported people being killed or injured at zebra crossings. I grew up in the western United States. I'm familiar with cattle crossings and deer crossings. Signs along highways in the United States warn of these, so without giving the subject much thought, I saw nothing unusual in Kenya having zebra crossings. After all, I supposed if the animals migrated, they probably had to cross a road somewhere. Luckily, I made no public gaffe over this. In Kenyan-British English, a zebra crossing is a pedestrian crosswalk. It is usually well marked with diagonal white lines painted on the dark tarmac—hence, the zebra reference.

That brings to mind the question of whether a zebra has black stripes on a white background, or white stripes on black. Perhaps it remains a perennial question, or maybe each of us supplies our own answer. The pronunciation of the word "zebra" is determined by whether one is speaking British English or American English. It's a short *e* for the British, a long *e* for the Americans.

Of course one doesn't have to move to a different country to find language differences. Radio and television have smoothed some of the edges off regional accents, but the media have also made us aware that some of life's ordinary objects are multiple choice. Is it a soda or a pop, a sack or a bag, a bucket or a pail?

In Kenya's British English, we found our American wastebaskets and garbage cans translated to slightly more elegant trash baskets and rubbish bins. Other words were almost, but not quite, the same. It took me months to comfortably curl my tongue around aluminium instead of aluminum.

One of our sons still remembers that word as the bane of his existence in science class in Kenya. *Aluminium* was simply incomprehensible to Michael every time his science teacher spoke of it. At each use, the word aluminium retained its garbled character for Mike. He didn't know whether the teacher was talking animal, vegetable, or mineral. In answer, finally, to a direct question about its properties, Mike offered a bewildered, "I don't think we have that in the United States."

"Of course you have it in the United States," snapped an exasperated classmate. "It rolls out of a box, it's shiny, and you wrap food in it!"

Mystery solved.

The mystery word for me one day was "pavement." My British friend was clearly upset, that much I understood. But why she was upset about the neighbor children riding bicycles on the pavement was unclear to me. Repetition proved no help. To my mind, the pavement (street, and maybe driveways) was where they *should* ride their bikes. This little episode evidently hid in my subconscious as something unsolved, something that didn't compute. Years later it came forth to claim clarification. When my husband and I lived in England for eighteen months, I became aware that pavement there does not mean the street but rather the sidewalk. No wonder the British and Americans have been described as two peoples separated by a common language.

At times in Kenya, the quirks of our common language caught us and our British friends by surprise. Our best friends were also our next-door neighbors. One social evening, the husband offered to knock me up at nine o'clock the next morning. Since the proposal seemed in the nature of an appointment made in the presence of my husband, I wasn't sure what that made him, but it made me laugh. I knew it simply couldn't be what it sounded like to an American ear. I was right. Our car was broken down, and John was offering me transportation to the market for shopping. He expected to leave about nine a.m. and would knock on my kitchen door to indicate he was ready to depart.

So the British have problems too with our so-called common language. One faux pas was confided to me by an ambassador's British wife. When she was a very newly married and completing an errand of mercy—visiting a sick American man in the hospital—she left him with a pat on the hand and a cheery, "I'll see you again soon, Dick. Keep your pecker up."

It was a phrase she had grown up with and never given any thought to. She simply wanted him to keep his courage up. She had his spirits in mind, not a portion of his anatomy. The British woman hurried out of the hospital room realizing from the look on the man's face that she had probably said something open to American misinterpretation. The incident happened early in her husband's career, but diplomatic immunity doesn't necessarily spare one embarrassment. She still blushed years later as she shared the story with me.

Speaking of hospitals, I noticed we Americans say someone is "in the hospital," while the British shorten it to someone being "in hospital." It's one of the few instances I can think of where the British say something in fewer words than Americans do. And in the medical line, I noted another phrase. Americans usually reserve "seriously ill" for someone suffering from a disease. We tend to refer to accident victims as injured, seriously injured, or critically injured. If someone is knifed or shot, the American media say the person is wounded slightly, seriously, or critically as the case may be. I never quite got used to a British, or British-trained, news person announcing that someone was "seriously ill in hospital from bullet wounds." Lead poisoning, perhaps.

I almost came to think of myself as bilingual in Kenya: British English and American English. Unfortunately, I didn't succeed in being bilingual in Swahili and English. The official language of Kenya is now Swahili, which replaced English in 1974. But there is no doubt that English remains strongly entrenched as it is taught in the schools and widely spoken. Perhaps the two languages have simply switched places in East Africa.

Swahili evolved as a lingua franca, a means of diverse peoples or tribes communicating with one another. English seems more and more to be taking on the lingua-franca role worldwide. This fact doesn't deter me from wishing I were better at languages. I'd love to be able to speak several languages fluently. I'm impressed by persons who do. Some people seem to have a special faculty or facility, a gift, that enables them to "pick up" a language. For me it's heavy going. Learning even a little of a foreign language can be hard work. However, I do make the effort to learn some of the local language when I live in foreign countries, if for no other reason than to be a polite guest.

While learning some Swahili was a rewarding labor, I considered comprehending British English a delightful challenge. The dry British wit also delighted me, and one day in Kenya I wasn't sure which I faced—wit or words, or maybe both.

One neighbor's hobby was the restoration of antique cars. We in the neighborhood were appropriately admiring of one such gem on which the man had worked long and hard. The car was shining and beautiful, and I asked him if it was nearly finished.

"Yes," he replied with a smile. "I just have to put the wings on."

*Hmmm. Sure you do.* Wings? As an avid Agatha Christie fan, I knew that a proper British motor vehicle has a bonnet over its engine rather than a hood, and that the boot is the space we Americans refer to as the trunk. I even knew that one works on mechanical parts with a set of spanners rather than wrenches. But to me wings were for flying and I'd never heard of them on cars. Had I missed some subtle sense of British humor, or humour as the case may be? Was he gently ragging me? I wouldn't blame him.

This was the same man who asked me what I thought of the design of our maisonettes, and I told him. I particularly commented on what I thought was the inappropriateness of the steep-pitched roofs. I said they looked out of place on dwellings near the equator, that they looked as if they should be shedding snow in a Swiss alpine village. Live and learn—I learned he was the architect of our dwellings. So, if this man wanted to put wings on his car, it was certainly all right with me. I played it safe with just a smile and sidled over to my husband nearby. From him I quietly learned that indeed British motor cars have wings. American cars have fenders.

There were differences in celebrating some holidays too. The British still held to their traditions in Kenya and firecrackers sounded on the English Guy Fawkes Day, not the American Fourth of July. We celebrated Mothering Sunday in March instead of Mother's Day in May. However, I was determined that our family observe, in some way, our American Thanksgiving Day. This even though it would be a normal work and school day in Kenya. I figured at least we could eat some of the traditional menu for dinner Thanksgiving evening. For this holiday, my family counts on turkey, stuffing, mashed potatoes with gravy, and pumpkin pie. Cranberry sauce, sweet potatoes, olives, et cetera—even the hot vegetable I insist on—are considered nice but not necessary to the occasion.

I concentrated on the basics and knew I could make pumpkin pies from fresh pumpkin or squash, as my mother and grandmother had done. Then I eliminated pumpkin pie from our basic menu because neither pumpkin nor squash were available at market. Whether out of season or not grown in Kenya at all, I didn't know. I did know that Nairobi's shops carried no canned pumpkin. Thanksgiving pumpkin pie would be missed, but potatoes were no problem, nor was gravy. Gravy-making was an art that I'd mastered. The turkey proved to be a problem, though—scrawny-looking at best, but with a fat price. No way could I afford it, even if I thought its gaunt carcass appealing. Production-line poultry was unknown there. Even chicken was a high-priced treat in Kenya, where fowl roamed more or less free so as to scratch out their food. No wonder they were tough. I figured I could afford one small chicken for Thanksgiving and found where I could buy some extra giblets. These would enable me to make lots of extra stuffing, which my family liked so much. The small chicken would hold very little stuffing, but the extra would still be tasty baked in a pan.

Okech was unaware of my plan when he returned to work that Thanksgiving Thursday afternoon. His greeting grin fled, to be replaced by a look of disbelief at the comparatively huge bowl of stuffing beside the little chicken I'd just begun to fill. Shaking his head in utter rejection of what I was doing, Okech looked at me as if I'd taken leave of my senses. Then he took a step forward, held out a remonstrating hand, and burst out with, "Too much, Memsahib! Chicken little! Chicken little!"

"And the sky is falling, the sky is falling," I laughed in reply.

This literary allusion held no familiar meaning for Okech, and he gave me a strange and wary look. I hastened to explain what I was doing and was rewarded with Okech's look of relief and joy. I think he was immensely relieved to find I wasn't demented. Later I heard Okech telling the neighbor servants what a clever idea I'd had.

In the category of weights and measures, our family went metric. We learned that a kilogram is about 2.2 pounds, and a kilometer is a little less than two-thirds of a mile. For easy remembering, we thought of a meter as roughly three inches longer than the three-foot yard, and a liter of liquid as being a shade more than an American quart.

Somewhere along the way of weights and measures I must have encountered stone. Thus I understood when a British friend concluded her story about her husband with, "He was so sick the first three months here. He lost two stone."

"Oh, the poor man. Did it hurt terribly?" asked an empathetic, if uninformed, American newcomer.

The storyteller and most of our group looked British blank. Me? I absolutely broke up. When I could stop laughing at my mental image of a fourteen-pound kidney stone, I tried to recover a little decorum. I also tried to be diplomatic in setting straight that other American in our group. The sick man had simply lost weight, twenty-eight pounds over a period of three months.

# Cars and Commentary

▨ ▧ ▨

Our second trip to Nairobi National Park was Roxanne's first, and as if to welcome her to Kenya, we seemed to see everything possible in the park. The animals that day ran the gamut from almost A to Z…baboons to zebras.

We had a good view of everything from the high-perched seats of our new Land Rover—new to us, that is. Jim purchased it secondhand, or third- or fourth- or fifth-. Sometime in its career, our Land Rover belonged to a movie company that filmed wild life. Personally, I think they chased pink elephants. That's the only thing I can think of that would cause them to "camouflage" that Land Rover with purple stripes and pink polka dots. A subsequent owner painted it over with an inadequate supply of conservative blah. This dimmed the effect long-distance, but up close our Land Rover was still colorful enough for comment. My own, at first sight, was a disbelieving, "Oh, no."

I hated driving that Land Rover, not so much for its color scheme, but because I felt I just barely had control at the wheel, which took tremendous strength to turn. The driver's seat had long since frozen into one position that really required longer legs than mine, which barely reached to work the brake and clutch. Fortunately, I didn't have to drive the beast very often because my husband enjoyed tooling around in his new toy. And I had to admit, that day in the park, our Land Rover was great for game-viewing.

With the Land Rover. From left: Michael, Marilyn,
Karen, Jim, Jim Jr., Roxanne.

We got that off to a great start just inside the park gates, where a cheetah was stalking a waterbuck, for all the world like a pussycat stalking a mouse. Something alerted the waterbuck to the presence of the cheetah, and just as the cat poised to spring, the waterbuck bounded a few yards away. The cheetah then unwound and strolled off in the opposite direction, trying to look as if she hadn't been really serious about having a meal in the first place.

We saw the usual herds of zebra and Thomson gazelle. The gazelle were such pretty, graceful little animals that seemed to have the need to constantly twitch their short tails, as if to dispel an excess of energy. We watched herds of hartebeest and wildebeest, the latter also known as gnu. We spied a secretary bird and plenty of marabou storks, scavenger birds. We had a very close-up view of an ostrich as one left its group and paced alongside us as we drove along. It kept turning its head to look at us, as if to make sure we were still there. Or maybe the ostrich too had trouble seeing and believing our Land Rover's colors. We saw a few impala and several wart hogs. These last are as ugly as their name implies, yet they're almost cute.

We parked and got out at the hippo pool, one of the few places people were encouraged to get out of their vehicles in the park. We hadn't seen a thing there on our other trip, but this time even the hippos cooperated and obligingly surfaced. I was just a little nervous strolling down the bushy path to their pool because we passed a sign saying, "Beware of crocodile."

The place was alive with monkeys that day. They tended to congregate around the cars because they could smell food. Of course there always seemed to be a few tourists who ignored the warnings to not feed the animals. They didn't seem to realize these were wild animals in the most literal sense. I was anxious at the risky behavior of one woman who stood holding a small child in one arm, the child eating a cookie. With her other hand the woman fed biscuits and bananas to a group of monkeys, one of which was quite large and aggressive. I had visions of the child being hurt as those animals were inclined to snatch all the food they could get. Luckily, the child finished her cookie before the mother ran out of goodies. It was the mother who was scratched when the most aggressive monkey got tired of having the food doled out and grabbed the whole supply.

With some difficulty, we managed to get back into our Land Rover, sans monkeys. However, they were all over our vehicle as soon as we started to eat our lunch inside it. Those monkeys tried to reach through even the smallest opening. We were the focus of a lot of cameras, particularly when one mother-monkey and her child perched on the spare tire mounted on our bonnet, or hood. This simian mama nursed her little baby and looked hopefully at us through the windshield. Finally despairing of our generosity, or lack thereof, she seemingly commented on our stinginess by urinating all over our vehicle. Thus relieved, she bounded away with her baby.

While parked there at the hippo pool, we got a good view of five giraffe who came within a few yards of us to browse on the foliage and get a drink. Again I marvelled at how lovely and graceful they were in their natural habitat.

We were so lucky to see everything else, we figured it was too much to hope to see lions too, but our luck held, and we saw a pride of two lionesses and five cubs. The five were darting about and keeping their mothers busy keeping track of them. As a mother of four, I could identify with that.

Shortly before leaving the park near the 7:00 p.m. closing time, we saw a herd of gazelle almost surrounded by cars. It was the herd of cars that attracted us because cars usually gathered in a group only if it were the big cats or a kill to be seen. Sure enough, at first we couldn't see anything, but then we spotted a leopard or cheetah. By that time it was too dark to distinguish exactly which of these big cats was stalking the herd of gazelle. There were too many cars, though, and the cat seemed to get annoyed. Suddenly it headed right for us. I wasn't taking any chances and quickly rolled up the window, but it wasn't after us. We could see then it was a cheetah, and it wanted the escape route offered by the culvert a few feet from us. The cat slunk through there and sprang off through the bush. Perhaps the cheetah remained hungry that night, but at least it was free of its nemeses...the four-wheeled, stalking beasts.

Cars seemed to hold a fascination for many people in Kenya. That fact may account for the popularity there of the East African Safari, an internationally known road rally whose route can be dictated by political circumstances as well as road conditions. So far as I know the rally has always run in Kenya, but its itinerary has not always included Tanzania or Uganda. In Nairobi, we lived just off Ngong Road, which was usually part of the rally route. Sometimes it seemed to me that drivers on that road thought every day was race day.

To learn to drive—that was the ambition of many young Kenyan men. A number of them approached my husband or me with the idea that we should do them a favor and teach them this valuable skill. Okech's oldest son and also our young friend, Mathew, were among those asking to be taught to drive. We provided them transportation sometimes, and I tried to be helpful if they asked for advice or help with schoolwork or filling out papers. But on learning to drive, we always said no, repeatedly, because one no was seldom enough to deter a second or third request. The young men figured they could get great jobs if they just knew how to drive. Maybe they were right, but I kept thinking of all the accidents and near misses caused by excessive speed and new drivers around Nairobi. Besides, we had enough trouble with our vehicles and paying for repairs.

Our secondhand European car had a defective clutch that periodically needed repair. Someone finally explained to us that the next year's model of that car had a redesigned clutch that eliminated the problem. I was glad to hear it. It didn't help pay the repair bills, but it made me feel better since it eliminated any thinking that the problem was caused by the way I drove.

Actually, neither Jim nor I had any trouble driving in Kenya. We both had driven stick shifts before, though it was strange at first to be shifting gears with the left hand and sitting behind the steering wheel on the right side of the car. One drove on the left side of the road of course. The roundabouts, circular junctions for several streets or roads, were new to us but caused no problem. This was unlike one new driver we heard about who entered one of these vehicular whirligigs and then froze at the wheel—mentally and physically. There he went, round and round the roundabout, until his vehicle stopped when it ran out of petrol.

What one had to watch out for was driving on automatic—not the car's transmission but one's brain. Preoccupied and pulling out onto a street with no other vehicles around could be dangerous. One could then easily revert to driving on the wrong side of the road. More than once, on days when I was especially tired, I drove along muttering, "Think left, think left," so that I wouldn't get myself in trouble. Some people put a sign on the dashboard to remind them.

One day I was running on automatic, running late, and not even in the car yet. I grabbed my purse and car keys, ran out to the carport, and jumped into the car, ready to pick up the children from school. Just one little thing was wrong. There was no steering wheel in front of me. What a silly feeling to realize that I'd hopped into the wrong side of the car. It had bucket seats, so I couldn't even slide over unobtrusively. In fact, there was nothing unobtrusive about it because, at that moment, I glanced up to see my neighbor watching me as she washed her kitchen window. I knew, from the look on her face, that she had witnessed my performance but was doing her British best not to laugh at me outright. I also knew how funny the incident must have looked, so I got out of the car, accompanied my embarrassed grin with a shrug, bowed a curtain call, and exited stage right to the correct car door. As I waved and drove away we were both laughing.

Another time the situation was reversed, at least to the extent that it was my neighbor at whose expense a laugh was shared. Our families joined forces for a day's outing to the remoter Kenyan countryside. Several times as we drove along, we saw an official-looking road sign proclaiming, "Polepole." Invariably we rounded a bend just afterwards, and there would be a small town or settlement.

"For goodness sake," my friend finally exclaimed. "Why in the world do they name all these little places the same thing? It's not very original."

At that time in Kenya, a lot of street and place named in colonial times were being replaced by Swahili names. But I guess languages weren't my friend's forte any more than they were mine. Though even I knew that, contrary to my friend's thinking, *polepole* would be quite an original name for a town—*polepole* being the Swahili word for "slowly." We enjoyed a good laugh as we went *polepole* 'round the next bend.

It was good to have friends next door with whom we could share trips. Together our families straddled the equator at the sign near Nanyuki, Kenya, and entered a pub there to quaff a beverage. We sat at the pub's counter, which boasted a jagged line across it of different-colored wood. This reputedly indicated that it, too, stood astride our earth's great imaginary circle.

At the equator. From left: Karen, Marilyn, Roxanne, Michael, Jim Jr.

Most of all it was nice to have friends next door with whom we could share a good laugh. Sometimes being next door to each other occasioned the laughter. Our maisonettes, all together in a row, looked remarkably alike. I doubt there was a resident, child or adult, who had not, in some preoccupied moment, found himself approaching his neighbor's door instead of his own.

But our son Jimmy's preoccupation may have been the most prolonged. "Hi, Mrs. Farmer, what's for dinner?" he asked as he entered.

"Stew," Anne replied in surprise as she stirred the contents of the pot on her stove.

"Good," said Jimmy as he passed through the kitchen to the rest of the house. He saw nothing unusual in Anne lending a hand and assumed that I'd stepped out for a moment. Poking his head back through the doorway, he asked, "Where's Mom?"

"Isn't she at your house?"

"Oh, God, *I'm* not at my house!" In a rush of anguished embarrassment, young Jim bolted back through Anne's kitchen and out her door, muttering a hasty apology enroute.

# Combining Cultures

Iloved Nairobi and its surrounding area. When we lived there, a few years after Kenya's independence, there was an exciting atmosphere of new commitment—an aura of purpose and determination, an air of hope amidst change. An amalgamation was going on in Kenya at that time. I found it fascinating, that blending of old and new.

People reflected the era of change. That a person could mix two very different cultures, and be proud of both, seemed embodied in two men I saw walking through downtown Nairobi. Both men were dressed in well-cut western business suits. Both men exuded success and self-confidence. Neither seemed bothered by ear trouble. Yet, one man wore his earlobes unfurled and draped on the shoulders of his impeccable, well-chosen suit. You could have driven a toy truck through the tribal-decreed aperture in each of his earlobes. They had been punctured at an early age, with progressively larger discs inserted over the years to achieve the final desired opening in each lobe.

The other man's earlobes also had endured this procedure. He chose, however, to create a new style. His earlobes were neatly rolled up and secured with what looked like a diamond-headed stickpin in each. I averted my eyes in passing, but I couldn't help thinking what I'd just seen gave new luster and flair to cauliflower ears. And it certainly gave a whole new meaning to "got his ears pinned back." I thought too that these men's coping skills, their courage in combining cultures, probably augured well for Kenya's future.

I liked the colorful cotton caftans some of the women in Nairobi wore, and of course the beautiful saris of the Indian women. The occasional goatskin cloak was interesting, but not personally appealing to me as something I would like to wear.

Kenya's life those few years after independence was history in the making. There was an undercurrent of vitality inherent in changing times. I felt that spirit in our own lives as we recovered from a year of unemployment. I liked being a part of Kenya at such a hopeful time.

*Uhuru*—freedom. *Harambee*—all pull together. These vital concepts in Kenya were energized in large measure by one man, Jomo Kenyatta, Kenya's president when we lived there. He was Kenya's first president and led his nation for fifteen years before he died in office of old age. That last was still somewhat rare then in African politics. Perhaps it spoke of more than his predilection for longevity. Kenyatta's philosophy of hope tempered by practicality was espoused and paid more than lip service by Kenya's leaders. I wondered if that might give the country its greatest chance of success.

The practical blend of diversity that I saw in Nairobi swept across the whole spectrum of life in Kenya to forge a new nation. Independence from Britain had been achieved, but forming a unified nation of diverse tribes was still in progress. During the European partition of Africa in the 1800s, arbitrary borders were slashed across the continent, cutting through original tribal nations and territories. The long-ago caprice of colonial powers now seems incredible.

I wondered if England's Queen Victoria thought of Mount Kilimanjaro as a mere birthday bauble. She "gave" that magnificent mountain to her first grandchild, Kaiser Wilhelm II of Germany. Some borders in Africa look as if they might be the result of a royal game of darts, played blindfolded with someone later drawing lines to connect the resultant dots. These borders became fixed in the colonial power's share of African history, and having gone pretty much past the possibility of change, were accepted almost in totality by each African country at their time of independence.

Despite the fixed borders, many Africans did not wholly identify with the country decreed by the colonialists. Some Kenyans explained to me that for many of them their first and deep-seated loyalty remained to their tribes, of which there were forty-eight or so in Kenya. Consequently, even at independence, most Kenyan natives identified themselves first as Kikuyu, Luo, Masai, et cetera, rather than Kenyan.

Forging a national identity, tempered by proper pride and patriotism, is an ongoing process in countries the world over. Of necessity it receives a high priority in newly emerged nations. A measure of Kenya's achievement in this respect was thought by some to lie in the fact of presidential succession. On Jomo Kenyatta's death, he was constitutionally succeeded in office by his vice-president, Daniel Arap Moi.

The Kenyatta Conference Center was built in memory of Jomo Kenyatta. It stands in Nairobi as an embodiment of his blending of old and new. Once jailed by the British as a reputed Mau-Mau leader, Jomo Kenyatta carved a place in history to be remembered as an African statesman, as well as Kenya's first president.

Nairobi seemed the hub of change for Kenya when we lived there. This transition time was epitomized for me by the sight of a modern skyscraper abuilding, with its attendant scaffolding made of slender tree trunks tied together with bark thongs.

I don't know what kind of trees provided the scaffolding, but some of the trees in Kenya—such as the flattop acacia or thorn tree, and the enormous baobab tree—were decidedly different from any trees I'd encountered before. The baobab sometimes looked as if it were waving not its branches but its roots in the air. I thought the appearance of the baobab fit so well the smiling explanation of one local—"Perhaps God planted it upside down."

One didn't have to go far from Nairobi's center to find villages and huts in the old tradition. There I felt as if I was driving through my childhood geography books. A different culture came to life as no teacher had ever been able to call it forth. I learned that one could often tell tribal affiliation by the shape or architectural feature of the hut, except I could never remember which meant what. Just about the time I thought I had it figured out, I'd discover that even in some of the villages things were changing to incorporate new ideas.

I had an opportunity to visit a new Kikuyu village—mud huts and thatched roofs—when I accompanied a European friend taking her *ayah* home for a vacation. An ayah was employed to care for the small children in a family. She was sort of a cross between a nanny and a babysitter. The home of my friend's ayah was in a very large village—government-sponsored, yet still with no water facilities.

Village residents carried water for a mile or more after buying it from a local entrepreneur. We saw small donkeys with large steel drums of water strapped to their sides. We also saw women, each carrying a large barrel of water on their backs, a strap attached to the barrel and then around the forehead in the traditional Kikuyu way. A woman can carry only one barrel at a time. Maybe that's why, in some parts of the world, I've sensed that the women of the local culture seemed to rank somewhere below the donkey in status.

In Africa, women are often the real beasts of burden. This fact causes me, to this day, to keep in my kitchen two miniature replicas of the heavy pottery water and grain jars carried by some village women. These little pottery jars are not especially good art, but they are excellent reminders for me to count my blessings and give thanks.

In the same manner as their mothers, the girl children of the Kikuyu village carried smaller steel drums of water, one each. The girls reached their arms backward to help handle the heavy load. Those girls strong enough to spare a supporting hand waved at us. Most also gave us a smile, which my friend and her ayah and I returned. I was surprised to see that the girls' faces usually reflected pride rather than drudgery. Helping with the work was part of growing up, and they seemed proud to do it.

Lots of locals—men, women, and children—were walking that day. Of necessity, shank's mare is the most common mode of transportation in Africa. People often walked long distances to work, to shop, even to hospital when they were very ill.

I was glad when my friend slowed down on the dry dirt road so that her car cast only small clouds of dust on the parade of people trudging that last mile to the village. I wasn't happy causing any discomfort to the people walking, but I knew that slowing to a dustless crawl might envelop us in a tide of people wanting rides in or on the car. That was a potentially dangerous situation—for instance if someone fell off and was run over.

It was a situation far better avoided for lots of reasons—among them the fact that a foreigner's life could become unimaginably difficult if one got involved in an accident that killed or injured someone. Apart from one's conscience-inflicted guilt or sorrow, and in addition to court-decreed justice, tribal customs might need to be satisfied. If that last applied, one could find oneself saddled with a lifelong commitment to provide for the wealth and welfare of not only the injured party, but also the person's extended family.

In Africa that could add up to a considerable number. No wonder that embassies and foreign corporations may find it simpler to transfer their people after a serious incident or accident, though they sometimes might try to satisfy obligations incurred by giving a onetime settlement of funds.

But for Jim and me in Kenya and Zaire, there was no corporate umbilical cord. Trouble bad enough to put Jim out of the country would also put him out of a job. I was glad we were both good drivers, but even so, we had some heart-blipping near misses during those years. My nearest miss occurred in daytime, when a young woman afoot darted across the road in front of my car in order to escape the man chasing her. But I think I worried most about hitting someone when driving on a moonless night. Darker-skinned people in dark clothing are not easily seen when they are walking in unlighted areas, and that describes the larger part of Africa. There were times when I would have liked to have dispensed an unlimited supply of reflective tape.

My friend was a good driver too, and so we delivered her ayah safely to her village. When we got out of the car, we were surrounded by friendly, curious little children. The inquisitive village youngsters were delightful, but oh, those runny noses! I suppose the children were lucky to have enough cloth to cover their backs. Sometimes they didn't have even that. Certainly there was no leftover cloth for handkerchiefs even if it was their custom to use them. But unwiped runny noses are repugnant to me. It was all I could do to resist the impulse to pull out my supply of tissues and indiscriminately wipe every nose in sight.

I gathered that a woman tourist from California felt much the same way. I was told she gave a goodly sum of money to a bush minister and specified it was to be used to buy Kleenex for the villagers. The minister accepted the money but had visions of the Ngong Hills festooned with tissues, so he later wrote and received the lady's permission to spend the money on towels and bars of soap. It was a much better purchase for the village children—and the environment.

We weren't invited inside the ayah's home, but the door was open and the glassless windows uncovered. My quick glance inside showed the hut to contain little furniture. The household help in Kenya usually took their beds home, or at least the fold-up mattress, as had this ayah. This was done when their visit required sleeping over. Having a good bed enhanced their status as well as their comfort in the home.

The mattress could also serve a purpose totally unrelated to any envisioned by the manufacturer. Some unscrupulous individuals turned the mattress into a burglary tool—and not to steal a maiden's virginity. In African cities, affluent people's homes were often surrounded by stone or concrete walls topped with firmly embedded glass shards. This jagged topping effectively discouraged even nimble burglars. That is, it did until some agile, clever crook took that defense of property as a challenge. He tossed his mattress up to cover the broken glass atop the wall and gained easy access for robbery. Then his mattress, rolled up and tied again as usual, became a handy hiding place for his loot. With the mattress riding easy on his head, the thief could carry stolen goods from the crime scene in a seemingly natural manner.

I heard about one burglar who needed a refresher course in knot tying. Stopped by the authorities for questioning, the man's story of lies unravelled along with his poorly tied knots. The burglar's mattress unrolled and presented his plunder to the police.

# A Masai Village

❖ ❖ ❖

All things being relative, the Masai village I visited a short time later made that Kikuyu one seem a shining example of civilization. At Kenya's independence, many of the Masai still lived and wandered much as they had done for eons. With civilization and its attendant regulation creeping in upon them—plus the fact that Kenya has one of the highest birthrates in the world—the Masai's nomadic way of life will be limited.

They have always owned large herds of cows and goats. The animals were their wealth. In fact, so I'm told, the Masai believed they originally owned all the cattle in the world. Therefore, if they took a cow from here or there that seemed to belong to someone else, it wasn't really stealing… merely taking back what belonged to them in the first place. Be that as it may, when one area was grazed and the water holes dried up, the Masai and their animals moved on.

A Christian volunteer group from the United States was helping the Masai in one area about an hour's drive from Nairobi. The Masai Rural Development Center comprised a small church, dispensary, farm, cattle dips, and water projects. One of the latter was an ambitious scheme to build a small reservoir and then pipe water to it from a spring in the Ngong Hills. The work was being done by the Masai themselves, the very ones who would benefit and be able to stay put if they could avail themselves of a constant water supply. If they could be prevailed upon to remain in one place.

Strongly encouraging this group to stay put and help with the beginnings of a new way of life was one enlightened elder of the tribe. He worked in close cooperation with the director of the project, a volunteer from the United States. Neither knew more than a few words of the other's language yet their obvious trust and respect for one another, and their shared enthusiasm for the reservoir project, spoke volumes.

I had lived in Nairobi several months before I joined the American Women's Association there. This time lapse was due to partly our limited budget and partly my reluctance to move halfway around the world only to surround myself with other Americans. However, most American women overseas tend to be an adventurous lot who find absorbing things to do and interesting places to see. On an organized level, the two concepts often combine in an effort to help some local charitable projects. This was the case with our visit to the Masai Rural Development Center, my first outing under AWA auspices.

After a brief tour of the Center, the American project director acting as our guide decided to detour to a Masai village enroute to the reservoir. We got out of our cars some distance from the village and waited to see what the reaction would be. We were not expected, and a short time before in Masai history, we would have been driven off with clubs and spears.

The elders of the village came out because they recognized our guide. Through our guide's interpreter, the elders welcomed us after it was explained that we were friends of this American. As a rule these people didn't allow outsiders into their village, so being invited in was a rare privilege for us. The chief elder apologized and made clear that if he had only known we were coming he would have had some refreshment prepared for us. In view of the fact that the Masai considered cow's blood and milk mixed together a fine drink, I don't think there was one among us who didn't give thanks that the gentleman was unprepared for our visit.

The Masai village was built in a circle. The outer ring was of thornbush, thick enough and high enough to keep out any intruder, be it animal or human. Thornbush is just what the name implies, nature's barbwire. There were two entrances to the village. These were closed off with thornbush at night. Just inside the outer circle of thornbush was a circle of small, igloo-shaped huts. These were constructed of twigs and branches plastered with cow dung. There were no windows, but a small opening permitted entry and exit. At the top of the hut was a hole about three inches in diameter to let out smoke from a small cooking-fire inside. We were allowed to look inside, but it was so dark we couldn't see anything. We were told beds were the skins of animals.

Inside the ring of huts was another ring of thornbush, which surrounded the large area of open ground in the middle of the compound. This space served as a corral for the cattle each night. Each morning it was the job of the women to gather the manure and carry it "outside." There it was saved for various uses, including building material and fuel for a fire. I wondered if the children ever borrowed a cow chip to use as a flatulent Frisbee.

If the Masai village was unprepared for us, so we too were unprepared, in a sense. We women had been warned about the flies and some of us had seen pictures, but absolutely nothing could have prepared us for the actual experience. Etched in my memory is the cute little toddler running toward us as we approached the village. Her teeth were so white in her dark face, and her welcoming smile was adorably crooked. Then horror hit my heart. I saw the delightfully curved smile was crooked because it was defined by the swarm of flies in and around the child's mouth.

In the village flies were everywhere, swarms of flies, hordes of flies, extensive, enveloping clouds of flies. The sheer number of flies and their pervasive presence was incredible. It was impossible to wave them off. The Masai didn't expend vital energy on futile fanning and wriggling. They stoically got on with surviving such a hard life. But, oh, the unthinking "kindness" of some of our group of ladies. Generous and well-intentioned, but incredibly thoughtless, they gave pieces of hard candy to the children. When the Masai children licked the candy, it instantly became a black, swarming, wriggling mass of flies, which each child so honored continued to lick.

It was not a village for tourists, but this fact didn't prevent some of our group from behaving as tourists. They asked to buy jewelry the Masai were wearing, though they could have purchased this stuff at regular shops elsewhere. I thought it out of place to buy it here. Our visit probably changed the economy of the whole village, not necessarily for the better. It wasn't extra trinkets that our resident tourists were buying. To be obliging, the Masai took off the earrings, necklaces, and belts they were wearing. They would sell them because these "friends" wanted them.

Some of their jewelry indicated the Masai could adjust to modern means, or rather adjust the modern means to suit themselves. I'd heard about the difficulty of keeping the underground telephone lines to the airport working. It was first thought that wild animals might be digging up the cable, but investigators decided some of the breaks were too neat and tidy to support that assumption. All sorts of human motives were considered—perhaps a disgruntled employee, or maybe a primitive provoked about progress. Actually, there was no annoyance involved. Eventually it was discovered that some of the Masai were delighted with this new resource material. They were able to make vivid new jewelry from the little plastic coated wires. Those colorfully coded communication cables to the airport provided a prime supply.

In the Masai village, I stood back from the bargaining, not wanting to be part of the impromptu bauble bazaar. I smiled at the children and shook hands all around, but I was careful to not smile too broadly lest the flies get in. I carried a red and white sweater over my arm, and the Masai seemed to love the color red. All the little children had fun coming up and patting my sweater and feeling its texture. One little chap got brave and smelled it, then a couple of others followed suit. However, that foreign odor of cleanliness was obviously awful to them. They grimaced and voiced what I took to be the Masai equivalent of "yech."

One curious, brave little fellow did the sweater-patting bit, and he even reached down to touch my shoes. But something else was obviously on this child's mind as he walked around me, stood beside me, and looked me up and down. Suddenly his hand darted out and lifted the hem of my overblouse a tiny bit. It then dawned on me. He wanted to find out if I was that same, strange, whitish color all over. We were probably the first white women these children—and many of the adults—had seen, at least in such close proximity.

My village visit and descriptions of life in general went into my letters to our families back in the United States. I knew my mother and aunts would be interested in all facets of our new life, so after describing the village visits, I added:

> In contrast to much of the preceding, I've also been to tea at
> the American Embassy Residence, along with the rest of the
> women in the American Women's Association—which, by

*the way, I was pleased to find has associate members of other nationalities. The tea I attended is an annual affair given by the Ambassador's wife.*

*Jim and I also attended an American potluck supper where my chocolate cake, made from scratch rather than a mix, was a big hit. Our Ambassador also attended, and we were fortunate enough to meet and chat with him for a few minutes. Hobnobbing with ambassadors was never part of our suburban social scene prior to Africa, so in its own different way, teasing the Ambassador about his fishing stories seems almost as much an adventure as visiting that Masai village!*

Yes, Africa certainly gave greater scope to my letter writing. I tried to capture and transmit to our families my enthusiasm for Kenya and our life there.

# "Why Do You Kill Old People?"

☒ ☒ ☒

I liked it when I sensed enthusiasm in the air of our household. I tried not to squelch any of it as I became aware of a cooperative project my children were working on during a school break.

"Can we put on a show?" they asked. "Our drapes are perfect for it."

"Sure," I replied, "I don't see why not." I'd heard songs being practiced and a lion-taming act put together over the past several days. Some of the neighbor children were enlisted. It seemed a good channelling of energy.

I had to admit to myself that the comment about the drapes had some validity. The living room drapes indeed looked as if they might frame a stage. I certainly hadn't intended that effect when I designed them, but we were stuck with them since there was no money to change them. The elegant blue drapes with matching valance framed the patio doors. A Nairobi shop had made the contrasting drawdrapes to cover the glass. I wished my mind's eye had seen the theatrical effect that would be created. The trouble was, I fell in love with that material and how well it looked next to the blue drape sample I took with me to the shop. My shortsighted look at the colors and fabrics next to each other didn't take into account the overall picture. Oh, well, maybe one goof out of six was not bad. I'd always made those blue drapes work before, and in Nairobi they were hanging in their sixth house. They sort of doubled as our family's security blanket: "This is really home now. The blue drapes are up."

Something else I didn't foresee was that my children would go out and sell tickets to their show. Charging admission was not, to my way of

85

thinking, implicit in, "Can we put on a show?" But to my entrepreneurial sons, it went without saying that if one put on a show, one charged admission. I cringed inwardly when I found out about the ticket sales. I found out from a neighbor who let me know that it seemed a bit of crass Americana.

What are the neighbors going to think, I silently wondered, when they find themselves seated next to one of the neighborhood servants at the grand performance? My children had sold tickets to one and all. But that's what American democracy was all about, I decided. And I knew I was going to back my children's democratic decision.

At least they weren't charging much. Then I found out they expected to make most of their profit from selling popcorn at the performance. That too was typically American, but I thought it might be going too far with the multinational, multiracial, multicultural group involved. Inviting these people to our home and then charging them for refreshments?

"No. I'll pay for the popcorn, and it will be given free to each ticket holder."

"Yes, I know you'd rather sell it but I don't think it's right."

"No, it's not exactly 'wrong' either. I just feel it's not quite appropriate here."

"Look, enough already. I'm not too keen on those ticket sales either. I could have had you refund the money instead of just limiting sales to those already sold or in this complex."

The show went on, and if it wasn't an artistic triumph, neither was it an international debacle.

Our younger children had little contact in Kenya with other Americans, but they managed well and made friends among other nationalities. However, they wouldn't have minded finding another American family in our Nairobi neighorhood, and one day Karen thought she had. She came running to find me, and her eyes sparkled with excitement as she said, "Mom, there must be other Americans around here. I hear 'My Country, 'Tis of Thee'!"

I listened, and sure enough, someone was playing a flute. How I hated dimming that sparkle in my daughter's eyes, but it was past time for her to know the history of that song. I explained that though it was the same tune she was familiar with, the British had it first. Same tune, different words—very different. I told Karen that our homesick British neighbor was really playing "God Save the Queen".

For good or ill, we are all ambassadors abroad, whether we have any official connection to our government. There are still parts of the world where a person or family might be the only representative of their nationality the locals will ever meet. Or perhaps a handful of one's kind will have preceded one to those parts. Maybe they left a lasting impression, right or wrong, good or bad, about one's country.

Such was the case in Kenya with young Mathew, a village youth in his teens. I encouraged his inclination to lean on the bottom half of our kitchen door and chat with Okech and me. Mathew and Okech weren't of the same tribe. This fact, as they verbally compared notes, made for some interesting listening on my part. I think they knew this, and for this reason they spoke most often in English. It was also their chance to practice a language they had in common but weren't proficient in. With me there, they had someone willing to explain a word or add some to their English vocabulary. In addition to each one speaking his tribal language and a modicum of English, Mathew and Okech both spoke Swahili, the lingua franca of East Africa. Anything they thought too delicate for Mamsahib's tender ears was discussed in Swahili. Memsahib learned to butt out at that point.

I learned that lesson the day Mathew came limping along after a several-day absence. He did not look at all well, and the limp made me wonder if he'd had an accident. In a misguided attempt to help, I insisted on knowing what was wrong. That was not one of my more intuitive days. If I understood them correctly, Mathew and Okech said they didn't want to discuss the tribal rite of male circumcision with Memsahib.

Another day my intuition was working better, at least to the extent that I knew the increasingly heated Swahili discussion had something to do with me. Okech seemed somehow to be defending me in the discourse. Yet I didn't really detect a verbal attack from Mathew—it was more of a sad, but firm, insistance on some point. I overruled Okech and encouraged Mathew to tell me what was bothering him.

Overcoming his initial reluctance, he blurted out, "Why do you kill old people?"

I swallowed a squeaky, "Who, me?" and managed a calming, delaying tactic—"Would you please repeat the question?"

"In America," Mathew insisted, "why do you have to kill people when they get old and can't work?"

"But we don't!" I replied in utter bewilderment.

Years of mental leapfrog with my own children hadn't prepared me for anything like this. My brief, bewildered denial didn't convince Mathew of anything, except perhaps my own personal ignorance of such a practice. I felt I had to get to the bottom of this. Like a surgeon excising a cancerous growth, I started probing.

I learned it was a longstanding belief in Mathew's family, passed from one generation to the next. Mathew's father himself had witnessed the agonizing admission of the existence of such a practice. As a young man, Mathew's father worked very hard building a road. The boss of the road gang was an American. Maybe it was even an American company. The American boss was a very nice man, a very good man. He didn't want to have to kill anyone. The old grandfather of one of the local workers kept hanging around, pestering the American boss for a job.

"No, old man, the work is too hard."

"No, old man, I can't hire you. You're too old."

"Please go away, old man. I don't want something to happen to you."

Finally, the American boss went to the worker and told him to make his grandfather stay away. The American boss explained it all to Mathew's father's friend. How he liked his old grandfather. How he himself, the American, would like to give the old man a job. But the work was too hard—he needed to hire strong young men who would be sure to do the job. The old grandfather would never be able to keep up with the other men. And the big, Big, BIG American Boss who was coming soon would see this.

"So you see," the American boss said to the worker, "I just can't give your old grandfather a job. If I did, I'd have to get rid of him. My boss, who is coming here soon, would make me get rid of him. And don't you see, please, I don't want to have to do that."

"So you see, Memsahib, is true. In Ameri . . ."

But my look of radiant, relieved comprehension cut short Mathew's earnest explanation.

"Is *not* true, Memsahib?"

"Oh, Mathew," I said, "most definitely it is not true! You see, in America, when we say 'get rid of'. . ."

# Church

We couldn't give much money to our church in Kenya, so we tried to give time and energy instead. Plenty of opportunity for these sorts of contributions were presented, particularly when we learned a new parish was being established in our area. A rectory and then a church were to be built across the street from Adam's Arcade, the small shopping center about a mile from our maisonette. This was a project of missionary priests from Mexico. One or two of them would spearhead the Nairobi building plan, while the others in their group went to serve the people of Kenya in outlying areas.

The priest appointed to pastor the new parish was about as new to Kenya as we were, so maybe that explained why we were drawn to friendship. I think too he liked the fact that Jim and I could usually understand his heavily accented English, and if he resorted to Spanish, we'd sometimes understand. This priest studied Swahili and English and was trying to improve his knowledge and pronunciation of both languages. He knew far more Swahili than we did, but I think we helped his English. He could celebrate Mass in either language and give short homilies. Occasionally he checked the draft of a sermon in English with us. It was casual, conversational English that more often tripped him up, though.

Perhaps more amusing than any of our pastor's *lapsus linguae* was the potential social slipup made by one of his fellow priests. This priest insisted on conversationally laying out all the diplomats by repeated reference to the diplomatic "corpse." Finally, in a spirit of helpfulness, I corrected the priest's pronunciation. So far as I know, the diplomatic corps remained unaware of their brief demise.

Our pastor had a collection of tapes of parts of the Mass sung in Swahili. One day an errand took me to the rectory, and I found the pastor and some young Kenyan women clustered around a small tape player. They listened briefly, and then the priest directed them as they sang a fair facsimile of what they had just heard. As I applauded their efforts, Father was called to the telephone. Clergy had more clout than we did in acquiring a phone. Father showed me how to work the tape machine and asked me to keep the girls at it until he returned. Practice time was almost over when he came back. He asked me to return in a week to help with the next practice. I agreed.

I was there the next week, and so were the girls, and Father stopped in just long enough to leave the tape player and tell me he'd be in his office tackling a mountain of paperwork while we practiced. Tea and biscuits (cookies) were served in the dining room by the houseboy an hour-plus later. Our pastor joined us and assured the girls that practice had sounded fine. He told me he'd like to talk about the music, if I could stay a few minutes after the girls left.

". . . so, Marilyn, I want you to take the tape player, learn the music, teach it to the girls on Saturdays, and maybe in about a month, start leading them at Sunday Mass. The congregation will learn it that way, and soon everyone will be singing."

"Father," I exclaimed in dismay, "I can't do that. I can't get up as the leader in front of God and everybody and sing!"

"Of course you can. God will help you."

Just like that. Simple. Well, I thought, maybe that's what faith was all about. Could I do it? I'd sung in school choirs. I loved to sing. But still, God and I both know what my voice was like. My singing voice was untrained and seemed to be the kind that, when it was good, it could be very good; but when it was bad, it was horrid. I still remembered, from very early childhood, the time I'd been asked not to sing in the Christmas Pageant because I was off-key.

"Father," I said, "there must be someone else. Someone better qualified."

"No, I don't think so. You can sing. I heard you. And you're good with the girls, and I can count on you."

Yes, but could I count on my voice? If I got too scared, I'd sound like Minnie Mouse, or even Mickey. But God would help me—and there wasn't anyone else. And I was flattered by Father's confidence.

"Okay, I'll do it, but I'll need written words, a copy of the Swahili lyrics."

"No problem."

Easy for him to say. With a written copy, I'd be able to pronounce the Swahili words all right, even if I didn't understand a good many of them. At the priest's suggestion, we moved practice to the nearby school, which was kindly allowing us to use their auditorium for Sunday service. We still adjourned to the rectory for tea and to report progress to the pastor each Saturday. Our singing debut at Sunday service came and went without notable mishap, despite the lack of instrumental accompaniment. Our repertoire increased and so did my confidence—a good thing because I found that the singing didn't work well unless I got up in front of the congregation and waved my arms in some semblance of direction and encouragement. Sometimes I felt like God's cheerleader.

The long rains of spring often covered the school yard, which doubled as a car park for church events. One Saturday I wheeled our car in there in a hurry, eager not to be late for choir practice. I completely forgot about the open, foot-deep, concrete drainage channels lining the perimeter. They were full and invisible because most of the parking lot was hidden under a couple of inches of muddy water. Just as I parked, a front wheel dropped into one of the drainage ditches, and there was no way I could drive out. There was also no one in sight to help. *Well, first things first and that's choir practice.*

Afterwards I showed a wandering custodian my car problem, and he responded by wandering off. Oh, great. I wondered if I was going to have to walk home in the rain and present the problem to my husband. I'd sure rather tell him about it after the fact—preferably after the solution. Tears of helplessness and frustration welled up and over. It had been a long, hard week and I was annoyed with myself. Life in Africa was difficult enough without my own carelessness contributing to the problem. I sat in the car, my head bowed, trying to decide what best to do.

"Is okay, Memsahib. Is okay."

At this worried tone of reassurance, I looked up to see the custodian and several other men. At his direction they clustered at the car's front corner and proceeded to lift. My sprits lifted too, and there were smiles all around as I drove off. The men had waved off my movement toward my purse. They didn't want money for their good deed. One of them said something about my helping the children.

On the way home I mused that "manpower" took on a new, perhaps old, certainly literal meaning in the third world. I'd seen another demonstration of manpower when our household goods arrived at our maisonette. One large wooden crate was particularly heavy, perhaps four hundred pounds or more. That weight hadn't seemed excessive in the United States, where there was access to mechanical lifting devices. Without even a hand truck or dolly, it was a different story. I realized our mistake when I saw consternation cross the faces of the Kenyan men unloading the lorry that contained our last box of goods. Did I also detect a hint of disgust at our thoughtlessness or lack of awareness? I quickly offered to unpack that box while it stayed on the truck, but this suggestion was totally unacceptable to all but me. My husband told me to let the workmen work the problem, and they did, finally getting enough men gathered to move the box. But none of them refused money that time. Quite the contrary.

Prior to Mass one Sunday, our pastor told me he hoped everything would go especially well because Mexico's Ambassador to Kenya was attending the service. I figured the priest lowered the odds of things going well just by telling me that because I experienced instant fright. Somehow, all did go well (God *will* help you…?), and I was introduced after the Mass to the ambassador. She was kind enough to say that she thought Father fortunate to have an American family to help in the new parish. She said that in her experience, Americans brought energy and organization to the projects they tackled.

Perhaps this was somewhere in my mind as Christmas approached, and I attended a meeting called by some parishioners, with the pastor's blessing, to discuss and plan the parish's first Christmas. There would be a midnight Mass, and music would be a mainstay. By then I was aware of voices better than mine and good musical talent in the congregation, much of it present at the meeting. There was clearly a core group of people willing to give of their time and energy for extra Christmas music practice. Therefore, I figured it might be time for me to stay in the background and let others lead. We were certainly a mixed lot—Kenyan, Indian, and British predominately—but there were a number of other nationalities too, including the lone American, me.

I listened as the meeting progressed to the point of standstill—or standoff. Christmas should be peace on earth, goodwill to all, but that spirit wasn't apt to well up from dissension and indecision. What was needed at the meeting was a unifying force. I looked around and didn't see any. What I did see were a number of people looking back at me expectantly. I knew I didn't have the best voice, but I thought perhaps I had the best chance to smooth out difficulties, reduce tension, and influence unity if I volunteered to organize and lead the Christmas music. I could pull together the various suggestions, so there would be music representing all. And I was already doing Sundays. A British expression came to mind as I stood up—in for a penny, in for a pound. I also sent up a silent prayer—I wanted all the help I could get.

At our newly formed church in Nairobi. From left: Jim Jr., Michael, Marilyn, Jim, Roxanne

It was going well, our Christmas Mass in Kenya. The Christmas spirit prevailed when, a little ways into the service, I sang out loud and awful on an opening note. What a clunker! Maybe God's way of helping was to make sure I didn't break my arm patting myself on the back. The congregation gamely tried to follow my bad lead, and instead of making a joyful noise unto the Lord, we sounded like a chorus of caterwauling cats. Voices started dying, and so did I, on the inside, of embarrassment. Oh, how the little girl in me wanted to run, but the adult in me couldn't think of any place to hide—not from myself at any rate.

I wigwagged everyone to a halt and we started over. Thank God I got the right note the second time, and there were no more musical mistakes—at least not bad ones. Still, I was glad when it was time to announce the closing hymn. The congregation joined in, and we all sang heartfelt and full voice to our God.

At the end I called out, "Thank you all for coming and singing. Merry Christmas! Happy Christmas! *Feliz Navidad! Krismas a Furaha!*"

Everyone promptly sat down and looked at me expectantly. *Oh, sheesh, what have I said? Did I tell them to sit down? I must have mixed up my Swahili again.*

I glanced around for help. The priest had left the auditorium-cum-church during the last hymn, but my husband had stayed at the lectern after reading the announcements. He smiled at me and said, "I think they're hoping to hear more Christmas music."

I rarely credited Jim with being more intuitive than I, but sure enough, I turned back to find three hundred heads nodding agreement. We sang for another half hour. It was one of my best Christmases ever—despite that clunker.

# A Wedding and Goodbye

▨ ▧ ▨

At our pastor's request, Jim and I discussed the happiness and hazards of married life with an engaged couple from our new parish. Our priest explained that his limited knowledge of married life made giving a course on marriage difficult, and his limited English made it impossible. Paul and Mary were both Kenyan, but of different tribes. They were professional people who met at work, but mingling in the workplace was one thing— mingling to the point of matrimony was breaking new ground for them and their families.

Jim and I were invited to the wedding, which was a blend of traditions, theirs and ours. We had no church building yet, so the wedding was held in another Catholic church, which was part of a complex comprising a hostel, kindergarten, and more. The ceremony was overseen by nuns, and one of them tried to be helpful by playing a phonograph record from the movie, *The Sound of Music*. Her selection for the recessional was the magnificent organ music from Maria's marriage to the Baron. It sounded great as Paul and Mary were walking out, except Sister didn't lift the phonograph needle in time, and out blared, "How do you solve a problem like Maria?"

We were also invited to the reception, and in fact felt honored when, after the wedding, the best man came to us to reinforce the written invitation. He told us they would very much like us to join them if we had no other plans for the evening, and if it wouldn't inconvenience us. Heavens, we were eager to join them! As far as any inconvenience, I think I was secretly worried that we might be putting *them* out as we were the only Europeans, except for a girl friend of the bride.

So we went to the reception at a modest house in Kabete, a suburb of Nairobi. When we arrived, we could see the house was decorated for a party, but no one was inside except for the families of the bride and groom. This togetherness seemed to augur well for the marriage. Everyone else waited outside, and the wedding party hadn't arrived yet.

Despite being only sixty miles south of the equator, Nairobi can get cold because of its mile-high elevation. Outdoor entertaining is seldom done in the evenings as it gets too chilly for comfort. It can even feel cold during the daytime if the weather is overcast. I hadn't planned on being outdoors after the wedding, so I had only a light stole for a wrap. I concentrated hard on trying to not look half frozen. Jim wanted me to have his suit jacket over my shoulders, but I could just imagine the furor that might cause. I'd be besieged with offers of coats or wraps, and people would be uncomfortable and upset at the thought that I was cold. I certainly didn't want discomfort on my part to mar or disrupt the occasion.

The wedding party finally arrived, got out of the cars some distance away, and walked in procession to the lawn across from the house. A line of ladder-back chairs waited there, with two overstuffed chairs in the middle for the bride and groom. The families came from the house to sit with the happy couple.

The wedding cake, traditional as we might know it, was assembled on a table in front of the group. The cake was cut, and the maid of honor presented a piece in turn to the groom, the bride, the groom's mother, and so forth. As each piece of cake was accepted, a trilling African chant broke out from the assembly. After the group in the chairs had each been served, the maid of honor filled a plate with slices of cake and turned toward the rest of us. There were at least a hundred people standing around, and I would have liked to have been just one of the crowd. But I somehow knew she was going to head straight for us. Sure enough, the maid of honor offered the cake first to me and then to Jim. As each of us accepted a piece, the trilling chant broke out as before. She then offered cake to the rest of the people, but there was no more singing accompanying it.

Next there were the speeches, of which we understood hardly a word. There was an interpreter, but he was translating from a tribal language into Swahili. When the speeches ended, those of us who had brought gifts formed a queue and presented them, along with our best wishes, to the seated bride and groom. The wedding party then proceeded inside the house, followed by the rest of us.

The place was jammed, and the chairs lining every wall were filled by the time we got inside. At our appearance, however, people alongside one whole wall jumped up and insisted that we be seated. We tried to protest but quickly realized we would make everyone uncomfortable if we didn't gracefully accept the honored-guest treatment. After being seated, we were offered our choice of drinks and chose beer. The groom's mother, sitting one person away from me, soon honored me by offering me what she was drinking, indicating I should pour it into my beer. My polite refusal was overridden, so I gamely combined our drinks and sipped the new concoction. Thank God she wasn't drinking whiskey. It was something like flavored sparkling water.

Plates of cooked meat chunks were passed, no napkins or forks. We each took a piece of meat with our fingers before passing the plate to the next person. The piece I chose proved particularly tough, and I chewed, and I chewed, and I chewed. I saw a look of concern start on the face of the groom's mother as she watched me. I felt I should swallow that chunk of meat to prevent her concern but it took a mighty—I hoped unobtrusive— effort. For one awful moment I thought I might choke on my good manners. The groom's mother beamed approval as she watched my throat reflex. I beamed back in relief, knowing that persistent piece of meat was gone, I could breathe, and I was no longer in danger of choking. I firmly refused seconds.

The party was going strong, and I was glad our presence didn't seem to inhibit it. We had to leave early, however, because our pastor had another appointment that night and he'd come with us in our car. Normally, at home in the United States, we would have quietly thanked our host and hostess and slipped away as inconspicuously as possible. Here, as soon as we made motions to leave, we intuitively knew that a grand exit was expected of us.

We thanked our host and hostess and were then escorted to the bride and groom, where we again expressed, to all within hearing, our reason for and regret at leaving early. Paul asked someone to get his mother, as he wanted us to meet her. The groom's mother obviously held the top place of honor at the gathering. With Paul interpreting, we chatted with his mother. I said I felt I already knew her a little as we'd shared a drink and some sign language of sorts. This had augmented the Swahili that was in short supply for both of us. She blessed Jim and me and wished us eleven children. This was her way of honoring us as she herself had ten children. In Kenya, large families were traditionally considered a blessing, thought to contribute to one's happiness, well-being, and prosperity. Jim managed to wait until we were in the car to comment that being wished eleven children seemed more a curse than a blessing.

During our goodbyes, someone in our crowded vicinity accidentally knocked over a bottle of beer. It was a large, full bottle, which splashed over Jim and me and poured into one of my shoes. I naturally glanced down and when I looked up...I'll never forget the look of frozen horror on the faces of the people around us, or the look of relief when they realized we weren't going to turn into stereotypical, irate, berating, colonialist types. Other than saying, "It's all right," and meaning it, we ignored the accident and squished through the rest of our goodbyes.

More goodbyes were soon in the offing. My husband's salary was based on the British system, but we'd come to realize that most, if not all, of our children needed to continue their education in the American school plan. We acknowledged to ourselves that the two concepts were, for us, destined never to meet on a financial level if Jim stayed with East African Airways. So, despite our love for Kenya, we made plans to leave for Zaire and a higher-paying job for Jim.

The Kenyans we knew seemed genuinely sorry to learn that we were leaving. When I filled our car's gas tank for the last time and said goodbye to the petrol-station man, he expressed real regret about our departure. I knew many whites were getting a sort of muted goodbye, good- riddance reaction to news that they were leaving Kenya. Impulsively I spoke frankly to the gas-station attendant.

"You know, I thought maybe you would be pleased to hear we are leaving. Often, lately, Kenyans seem to want whites to leave."

"Yes, but not the good kind," he said earnestly. "You are the good kind."

"Thank you," I said. "I certainly hope so." I knew I would treasure his words.

We'd poured a powerful lot of living into our year-plus in Kenya. It seemed as if we'd been there much longer. I regretted not having mastered more Swahili but realized I'd learned the important words: *Jambo—Habari—Mazuri—Mazuri sana—Asante sana—Rafiki*...Hello—How are you—Good—Very good—Thank you very much— Friend.

And then it was *kwa heri*, Kenya—goodbye.

# Language

I hoped our moving to Kinshasa, Zaire, on April Fool's Day was no kind of omen. We settled into the Memling Hotel in downtown Kinshasa. Air Zaire paid for rooms for their expatriate single staff and staff whose families did not accompany them. My husband had been there a couple of months without us, settling into his new job. We were allowed to stay at the hotel too until we could find housing.

Altogether there were five of us. Roxanne had again been left behind with friends because she was due to graduate from Nairobi International School in a little over two months. I would return for her graduation and escort her to Zaire. By then I hoped we'd have a house. As it turned out, we didn't, and she arrived in time for a little hotel living.

We were allotted two rooms at the Memling. It seemed simpler to divide up into His and Her rooms so as to better supervise the kids night and day. I'd hoped for at least adjoining rooms, but that was not possible, so Karen and I— and later Roxanne—were down the hall. Not ideal family living conditions for sure, but we thought it would be for only about three weeks—not three months.

The Memling had been the number one hotel in Kinshasa until superseded by the newer and nicer Intercontinental. The Memling was nice enough, perhaps a trifle faded in glory, but it wasn't geared for children. There was no swimming pool or game room or any place for them to work off exuberant spirits. Nor were there hotel grounds for walking and exercising in. We did go for walks to the small park nearby but were surrounded there by insistent souvenir vendors. In walks around town, we were fair game for beggars and thieves, so that wasn't too relaxing. It would have been nice to have had a quiet place to get our exercise. We had books and games to exercise minds. But what got exercised most was my patience and ingenuity as I tried to keep the natural exuberance of my children—the teenage boys in particular—under some semblance of control.

The Memling was a difficult deal for our children. Being resourceful, they soon discovered that the hall outside our rooms offered possibilities with its long length and highly polished floor. I vetoed anything that made marks or noise, the first to keep the cleaning staff happy, the second to keep the other guests happy—some of whom were pilots trying to sleep before a flight. I'm sure there were times when my children felt I simply vetoed all fun. That they cooperated as well as they did, which wasn't always, was good. That we all survived seemed a great accomplishment.

It felt good to drive a car on the right side of the road again. Still, there were things to learn, such as a line of greenery placed in the road was a warning there was an accident or disabled vehicle ahead. This was a better cautionary device than the line of rocks sometimes found in more barren places. We learned too that a driver ahead of us, with an arm out and uplifted and with fingers and thumb rapidly flicking together, was not giving us a rude gesture but rather a message that we'd left a turn signal on.

None of the traffic lights in Kinshasa, formerly Leopoldville, worked. I don't know whether the damage was done during the Leopoldville riots in 1959 or amidst the power struggles that followed the Belgian Congo's independence from Belgium on June 30, 1960. The country was renamed the Republic of the Congo, later Zaire. (It is now again Congo after the ouster of President Mobutu in 1997.)

In the 1970s it was my impression that Kinshasa's traffic lights, for whatever reason, hadn't operated in years even though they were mostly still in place. So, though the traffic lights weren't removed, their function was performed by Zairean traffic policemen. And sometimes "perform" was the operative word, particularly at one roundabout where several streets converged.

The center of this roundabout contained bushes and greenery, and in their midst was a wooden, laddered pedestal, which the policeman climbed to reign supreme at the top. The way he stood on that traffic tower, the poses he struck, all indicated the direction the traffic should move, or not move. For each signal—"go" (green light) and "stop" (red light)—the policeman had distinctive stances immediately recognizable to the initiated, and he took seriously his job of substituting as a traffic signal. None of the policemen took kindly to having his directions ignored or misinterpreted. Understandable, since a chaotic traffic jam could result.

Such was the case in the story that made the rounds of Kinshasa's expatriate community. It seemed traffic snarled when an expatriate driver moved ahead when he should have stayed put. The traffic policeman was not happy. He climbed down from his pedestal and stalked toward the culprit car. Reaching it, he gave the driver a withering look through the open window. The policeman flung out his arms and demanded, "What color am I?"

The freshly arrived expatriate, who happened to be white, was startled. Color could be a sensitive issue in newly independent African countries. The expatriate didn't want to offend, but he wasn't sure just what he should say. Brown? Black?

"What color am I?" indignantly demanded the policeman again.

"Black?" said the expatriate tentatively.

"No, no, no!" raged the policeman. "I am green. Look! I am green. Green! And now I am red." He changed posture and position. "Red! Did you not see? I was red when you tried to drive through!"

The policeman's conversation was conducted in French, as were most conversations in Kinshasa. This was due to the earlier years of Belgian control when Zaire was known as the Belgian Congo. Among locals, a conversation might be in Lingala, the trade language along the Congo River. Or the Zaireans might converse in a tribal language. There are over two hundred ethnic groups in Zaire, but ethnicity didn't seem to be an all-consuming, all-controlling factor of life or conflict when we lived there. At least in Kinshasa and the surrounding area, people of various tribes seemed to get along all right.

My husband was fortunate that English is the universal language of airline flight operations. Jim finds learning another language even more difficult than I do. Thankfully, no matter where in the world my husband's job took him, he could carry on his work—in English. Though there was the occasional difficulty. In Puerto Rico, his bilingual secretary telephoned him at home, and I overheard Jim say, "Wait a minute. You know I don't speak Spanish. Please speak English." After a slight pause, I heard him utter a chastened, "Oh," as his secretary informed him that she *was* speaking English.

It is true that at least some English is now spoken in much of the world. But I can vouch for the fact that English is not spoken or understood in a good many parts, particularly on the shopping or housekeeping level of life.

In Zaire, I frantically studied French books. If I'd thought languages a problem in Kenya, it was really rough in Zaire. French has gender requirements and all those different verb tenses—present, past, future, and many more. I concentrated on present tense for the most part, figuring I could always add yesterday, last week, soon, or something to move my statement into its proper time frame. I felt the main objective was to communicate, even if laughter did sometimes ensue.

The textbook told me that French has two different forms of "you," the familiar *tu* and the formal *vous*. The familiar form, according to that book, is used with very good friends, children, animals, or sometimes people of inferior status. I don't like thinking of people as inferior, so I knew it would be a problem for me if I had to decide who might or might not be of inferior status. I quickly solved that problem by deciding to always use the formal form of the French you, *vous*. That way nobody was inferior, and I figured I was less apt to offend anyone if I erred on the side of formal rather than familiar.

My French vocabulary grew, but I had trouble in any conversation that went much beyond, "Hello, how are you?" And somehow I was never able to work in any comment about that prevalent instruction-book phrase, *the pen of my aunt*. I could manage a brief discussion of the weather, with perhaps the addition of my husband's occupation, how many children I had, and when we had arrived in-country. But I learned, many times, just how fragile was my French comprehension. For instance, while waiting for the assistant bank manager who spoke English, I successfully negotiated all the above subjects in French with his secretary. A quiet time followed as she went back to typing and I sat lost in thought, English thoughts—until the secretary's sudden, rapid-fire French directed at me blew me away. At least it blew away all my French, or most of it. The only thing I could remember was,

"I'm sorry, but I don't speak French." I knew it was an idiotic statement the instant I uttered it, even before I saw the look on the secretary's face. After all, we'd just conversed in quite a bit of French. I was rescued, in English, by the assistant manager.

It is said that one sign of facility and fluency in a foreign language is if you dream in it. My foreign-language dreams were always variations of, "I'm sorry, I can't speak the language."

We moved from the Memling Hotel, but not without one last incident on the penultimate day. Our children had accompanied me on an afternoon shopping trip to buy housekeeping supplies. Returning to the hotel, I saw my husband in the lounge area having a drink with a business friend. Jim motioned for me to join them. I handed a broom and other stuff to our kids, who were helping me carry things, and directed them to take everything upstairs to our rooms.

"This is a lot of stuff. Can we take the elevator?" asked Michael.

"Sure," I replied. Our rooms were only one flight up. I had long since banned most elevator riding because neither hotel staff nor guests took kindly to having the Memling's one elevator tied up by children.

I joined my husband and was introduced to the other man. A drink was set before me, and I relaxed and thought how pleasant it was to be with grownups. The interval was short lived.

I looked up to see Michael approaching with concealed urgency. His face reflected a look of concern that tried to masquerade as nonchalance and failed. I excused myself and met Michael halfway. He told me his brother was stuck in the elevator. Well, not his brother exactly. The broom was stuck in the elevator and his brother couldn't let go of it.

"The elevator?"

"No, the broom. Jimmy poked the broom at the side of the elevator shaft and it's stuck on something and we can't get it loose. We've been riding up and down trying to."

"All this time?"

"Yes."

I'd barely begun my drink, and for that the time seemed short. But it seemed a pretty long time to be riding in an elevator. I looked around the lobby and no one seemed unduly concerned, though there was one impatient couple waiting for the elevator. Michael told me his brother was holding the elevator for us on our floor, one flight up. We hurried upstairs, but not before I looked back at my husband in a mute appeal to join us if he could.

The Memling's elevator had no interior door. The elevator was a three-sided box. When this box raised or lowered beyond the level of the fixed door on each floor, one saw the side of the elevator shaft. There was a two- or three-inch gap between the elevator floor and the side of the elevator shaft. It looked as if the broom was stuck in this opening, probably on the elevator itself just under the floor. This seemed confirmed by the fact that the boys had been able to ride up and down with it. The girls had gone directly to our room and were not involved or aware of their brother's stupid stunt. Smart girls.

"I'm sorry, Mom. I'm really sorry." Young Jim looked frantic as he clutched the broom and tried to maneuver it loose. He was afraid to let go for fear the whole broom would plunge downward into the elevator shaft.

"Yeah. Me, too," I said. Being sorry wasn't going to fix anything. The broom was upended and the handle seemed well and truly stuck. I was somewhat relieved to see that the broom still seemed its normal length. I wasn't worried about the broom, but I'd had a brief vision of it being chewed up and gumming up the elevator works. So far at least, that hadn't happened.

As I assessed the situation, Jim Sr. arrived. My husband took one look and ordered us out of the elevator and out of his way. Then he grabbed the broom and applied brute force. The broom suddenly came free. Except for a slight nick it was intact, a fact I was relieved to see. Jim Sr. stepped out with the broom before the elevator doors closed. The look in his eyes suggested it was a good time for everyone to be quiet. He handed me the broom, picked up his briefcase, and stalked down the hall to his room.

In the silence, the elevator purred past us in a perfectly normal way, except for the annoyance of its occupants who'd been made to wait. The normal sounds of the elevator running seemed music to my ears. Thanks be, it wasn't broken or damaged.

"Mom, I'm really sorry. Don't be mad at me, please. I was just…"

"Spare me, James. I really don't want to hear it."

Slightly subdued, the boys headed after their father, and I went to join the girls in our room. I decided to be grateful for the peace of the moment. I was thankful Jim Jr.'s playfulness hadn't progressed to peril. I also decided not to waste any energy wondering what unusual situations the future might hold. I hadn't a doubt there would be some. It seemed to be that kind of a life.

Jim Jr. redeemed himself more than slightly the next day. He volunteered to spend the night alone at our house with our just-delivered household shipment while the rest of us spent the last night in the hotel. I was assured, by someone my husband knew in the area, that our son would be safe enough. He was unlikely to be harmed, but someone's obvious presence was needed as a deterent, else half our belongings might walk off in the night. It was brave of young Jim to do it. I felt a little brave in letting him—and very relieved to see him alive and well when we arrived the next day to join him.

The two men I hired as household and garden help proved helpful in many ways. Neither spoke English but they helped me with my French. Victor and Joseph used their Christian names, pronounced in the French manner with the accent on the last syllable. I addressed them by name and with the more formal you (*vous*) of French, though I did hear some servants addressed with the familiar form (*tu*) used with friends or children. To me it seemed out of place. They were not, at least not yet, my friends, and I detested the notion that they be treated as children. Again I opted to forget the familiar in French. We Americans have a bit of a reputation around the world for being too familiar, too fast. I wouldn't add to it.

Victor

Joseph and Marilyn

How much Victor and Joseph helped me with my French was evidenced when I spoke with a Frenchman who taught French in Kinshasa.

"Madame, you speak French like a Zairean."

"Oh, thank you."

"Madame, that was *not* a compliment."

Oh, well, at least I'd understood him. Perhaps it wasn't surprising that the French I learned from my household staff wasn't quite up to par. French wasn't their first language either.

My not knowing enough French was a problem I dealt with daily in Zaire. On the other hand, a friend there told me that fluency in French can present a problem too. She and her husband are British but both fluent in French. While living at a hotel in Kinshasa, her husband had to leave on a business trip. He expected to be away at least a week, and my friend was a bit nervous at being left alone. She double locked the hotel-room door and felt fairly safe as she had the only key, as was customary. The key was usually attached to something large and heavy so that a guest going out would leave the key at the hotel desk, rather than pocket it or put it in a purse and walk off with it. Nor was the key easy for anyone else to pocket.

Three days went by and my friend began to relax and think she could handle being alone, even though she had several more days of it. That third night she slept soundly, only to be awakened by a soft, insistent knock on her door.

"What do you want?" she called out fearfully in French.

"I want to come in," answered a gravelly, deep voice in French.

"No. Go away!"

"Let me in!"

"No."

"Cherie, I am your husband. Open the door."

"No. My husband is not in Kinshasa."

"I tell you, I am your husband. Let me in."

"No. You don't sound like my husband. And besides, my husband is away on a trip."

"Cherie, I have a cold and I am back. The trip was cancelled."

"If you are truly my husband," said my skeptical, puzzled friend, "why are we speaking French?"

"Dearest," came the laughing, raspy reply in English, "please open this door now and let me in."

Language problems can come at one from all angles. A friend of mine, an erudite American teacher living in a non-English-speaking African country, left her apartment to go out for an evening. As she was leaving, she heard her neighbors' raised voices in the local language but didn't know what was being said. She noticed the neighbor's door ajar, and the loud language continued. Just then the lady of the house put her head out and, a tad distraught, said, "Tiff, tiff." My teacher friend thought she was describing a minor domestic dispute, so she gave her a tight little smile and marched resolutely onward. No way did she want to get involved in someone's family arguments. Only later did my friend find out her neighbor was telling her, "Thief, thief," in hopes she would notify the nearby police before the prowler fled with his loot. My well-educated friend was not too smart in this case. *Tiff* might be an ordinary word for her, but it was unlikely to be in the vocabulary of someone just learning English.

"Sounds like" may help in the game of charades, but in real-life language-learning it causes confusion—or maybe comedy, depending on one's point of view. For instance, a young man learning English became part of a student-exchange program and lived with a family in the United States. An elderly grandmother was part of the American family, and her reaction to anything unusual was to say, "For heaven sakes."

The young man would tell stories of his homeland, and grandma's invariable reaction was, "Adam, for heaven sakes."

After a time, an agitated Adam sought out the father of the American family and said, "Please, I don't understand. I am a young man. Grandma is an old lady. Why then is she always asking me for having sex?"

For heaven sakes.

# Water

⧅ ⧄ ⧅

O ur problems in Zaire included more than language difficulties. Some of the homes in Mont N'Gafula, about 30 kilometers from Kinshasa, were connected to a main source of water. Ours was not. When we agreed to rent the house, I was under the impression that the landlord intended to use our rent money to pay the sizable fee necessary to hook up to that water main. I was wrong.

For the duration of our stay there, we bought black-market water. We had an underground cistern, which we bribed a tanker-truck driver to fill on his way to sprinkling President Mobutu's flowers. About once a month, he would divert to our place in Mont N'Gafula with this water from the Congo River. If we were lucky and the whole family had practiced conservation, the water truck would arrive in the nick of time. Sometimes we weren't lucky. A time or two, when the driver needed cash, he arrived well ahead of time and couldn't put the whole load of water into the cistern. I had to pay for it all anyway so as not to jeopardize our water source.

Our water cistern had a large, more-or-less square block of concrete covering its opening. Tremendously heavy, it was all Joseph could do to move it aside when the water truck came. This weight assured that nobody could accidentally nudge it aside and let any critters or creepy-crawlers in to contaminate the water. The water still had to be boiled and filtered to make it potable. The problem with the concrete block was that it fit the cistern opening all right, but just barely. It needed to be exactly aligned.

The time it wasn't caused one of those lessons learned from experience.

111

But it was certainly a novel experience. How often does one turn on a tap and find tadpoles running out?

The cistern had to be drained, cleaned, and refilled—all easier to say than do. Despite the tadpoles, I saved some water in available containers and then proceeded to waste the rest. People passed by and looked askance at my generous watering of every flower, bush, and tree in the yard. Those brave enough to ask "why" enjoyed the humor of my froggy explanation. Our balky water pump threatened to pack up at being expected to run for such an unusually long period of time. We shut the pump off and borrowed a ladder to go down into the cistern. Strange, I'd always thought of a ladder in the context of reaching up to something. A two-man bucket brigade formed, and we learned Joseph had a fear of either a confining space or falling into the water. He and Victor traded places. We also learned the cistern had a crack in need of repair. A dirty several days ensued.

I longed for that three or four inches of bath water I usually allowed myself. The bathtub had no shower, not even a handheld telephone-type. Once I did have an unexpected shower. That was when the Italian-made hot water tank above the bathtub sprang a number of simultaneous leaks. Fortunately for me, the tank had refused for some time to actually heat the water. During that time was when I concluded water temperature is really relative to its use. If I brushed my teeth with the unheated water, it was plenty warm, but if I sat in it to bathe, it was definitely cold.

The tub drain worked well. It drained directly outside and watered the flowers. I was relieved to find the toilet did not. Of course I did worry a little about that tub drain. I pondered the thought that if the water ran outside, what was to prevent something from running (crawling?) inside? The pipe was unscreened, but so were all our windows and doors and the gaps under them. I decided the tub drain was very minor overall, but it didn't hurt to keep the tub's plug in place most of the time.

Our cistern was finally refilled, its lid precisely fitted, and it was good to have water again. The family had been great about the minuscule amounts of water we had to use during the cistern repair. Now I wanted them to cooperate again in the usual water-saving methods, such as turning off the tap while soaping their hands. My family preferred to cooperate in this water-saving measure by simply skipping hand washing a good part of the time. Hand washing was my thing, not theirs. I was concerned about germs; they weren't.

"Oh, Mo-o-o-om." I marvelled at the length to which they could drag out the word. I also marveled at the lengths to which they would occasionally go to avoid doing something they were told.

I'd sent young Jim to wash his hands. He was back too soon but cut my protest short with, "Mom, you may not believe this, but I was shocked when I went to wash."

"Maybe you should do it more often and it wouldn't be such a shock."

"Sure, Mom. Funny. I mean I was zapped. When I went to turn on the faucet I got a shock. Like an electric shock."

It was evening, and Victor and Joseph were gone. So was my husband, away on a trip. At Jimmy's behest, I checked the shocking bathroom faucet, and it zapped me too. I also found the kitchen taps in a shocking state, as were the sides of the refrigerator when I brushed by.

"What's happening, Mom?" By now all the kids were gathered.

"I'm not sure. Just don't touch any metal, and don't go barefoot. Wear shoes. Your father will be home tomorrow, and he can fix it. There's nothing we can do tonight."

I didn't know if wearing shoes was relevant to the electrical problem. The thought had popped into my head. I figured it might be a good idea, and if not, wearing shoes wouldn't hurt. This problem was definitely out of any area of expertise I might have. I didn't even understand what was happening, much less how to fix it.

The whole house seemed to have become electrified. I wondered if the heavy rain I heard had anything to do with it. Perhaps a power line was down on the house? I took a flashlight and gingerly waded around the outside of the house flashing the torch up and down to check things out. Everything seemed normal. The power lines were in place. I hoped my flashing torch wouldn't seem like a signal or bring anyone to ask what I was doing. I didn't have a clue in English—I'd never be able to explain in French.

My husband and our pilot neighbor arrived home the next morning. They'd been on the same flight from Kisangani, formerly Stanleyville. It took the two of them to trace our electrical problem to a downed and drowned wire in the attic crawlspace. They fixed that wire, but one problem led to another. They also had to rewire and rebuild an antiquated fuse box.

All that was simpler than trying to find a qualified electrician to come repair things soon.

Although our cistern water-system was an uncertain way to supply one of life's necessities, we were better off than many Zaireans. I think I will forever retain the memory of an incident along a river road in Zaire.

I was driving behind another car driven by a white man. He was no one I knew, and perhaps the fact that he was white was not pertinent. So am I, and I feel that we are all human beings together. Sweeping around a bend in the road that followed the contour of the small river below, we came upon a tall Zairean woman. She had just negotiated the steep climb from the river and was about to cross the road. She held one toddler by the hand, and two others clung to her long skirt. With her other hand, she gracefully balanced the large pan of water on her head. This picture-perfect scene disintegrated before my eyes. Our cars' sudden appearance startled the children, who jostled their mother and the pan went tumbling. All this sent the man ahead of me into gales of laughter.

How dare he laugh? Had he seen no more than the antic empty pan bouncing down the jagged, barren slope? Didn't he know how precious water was? Hadn't he seen that statuesque woman shrink before our eyes?

People don't come to their lives preshrunk. To see them diminish, as if to die a little, is a shattering experience. From statuesque to shrivelled, the woman sat huddled in hopelessness, her hardscrabble life and her children surrounding her. More than water was drained away—her spirit seemed gone too.

The man in the car ahead saw slapstick comedy and laughed. I saw human tragedy and wanted to cry... though I would have been hard-pressed to say whether my tears sprang from rage at the man in the car or compassion for my Zairean sister.

I would have liked to have stopped my car, gotten out, and helped in some way. I settled for slowing down as I passed and tried to convey all the compassion I felt, one woman to another, in the single glance allotted when her bleak gaze met mine. For an instant, I felt the emotional tightrope across the cultural chasm was traversed. I would have liked, somehow, for that tightrope to have been a lifeline, but one follows the custom of the country.

I'd been warned over and over never to stop my car to help in Zaire when something happened. Not only my husband, but even our Zairean servants worried about me regarding this. They extracted my promise to not let my tender heart be the cause of losing my head. They assured me they meant this literally, Victor pointing to Joseph's machete for emphasis.

In a crisis in Zaire, all sorts of factors might, and occasionally did, combine to cause the emotional excess in which the concern of a stranger could be misinterpreted. The stranger was apt to become simply a target for all the pent-up passion and frustration of a lifetime. I hoped I'd never be put to the test of coming upon or being involved in a car accident where help seemed needed. I might have lost my head and stopped, or vice versa.

▨ ▨ ▨

Victor suggested to Joseph that he employ his gardening skills to raise a few vegetables out in our yard. Certainly there was ample space, but a lot of it seemed pretty barren, and I wondered how good the soil was.

Joseph worked hard at the project in his plodding way and built up the soil. With what, I wasn't too sure, but I decreed there be no human waste used for fertilizer and hoped that would suffice for food safety. Two plots took shape side by side. They looked to me like mounded graves. I resisted the impulse to go out and place Rest-In-Peace markers.

The garden project was not a huge success, though we enjoyed the flavoring of some sauces with a bit of watercress, which I'd always thought of as just decoration. We also used the green tops of the shallots. Victor would go out and pinch off these tops, explaining that by leaving the bulbs in the ground they would continue to send up green shoots.

I was unaware that we had another herb garden growing at the far back corner of our yard. Or can marijuana be classed as an herb? That was not an attractive area of our property, faced as it was with our garbage burn-pit. The only time I remember actually approaching that corner, ever mindful of snakes, was when I sneaked a forbidden copy of a newsmagazine out to burn. Wouldn't you know it, the rare time we acquired a copy of that publication from the outside world was when it contained an article President Mobutu considered derogatory. His word was law, and having that banned magazine on hand might be detrimental to our well-being or Jim's job. We didn't know of any disgruntled people in the area who might report us but thought it best not to take unnecessary chances.

Joseph tended the burn-pit with a long-handled hoe, poking at this or that and making sure the fire didn't spread. Even when the flames died down, he kept a good eye on it while scratching around the plants that grew in that back corner. Most of them, my older son informed me years later, were marijuana plants. I do remember wondering at young Jim taking a sudden interest in horticulture and occasionally helping Joseph with yard work. I also remember naively thinking it was good to see Jimmy taking an interest in something productive. He tells me that marijuana also grew wild on the grounds of TASOK, the American School of Kinshasa.

Use of this drug, we were told, wasn't encouraged in Zaire, and justice, or that perceived as such, could be swift. My husband told us soon after our arrival in Kinshasa that he'd heard of one case at the airport where a uniformed gendarme was discovered sneaking a marijuana smoke. His uniformed and booted buddies kicked him to death. Now that I'm slightly less naive and a tad more cynical, I might wonder if it was because he didn't share.

This was what I thought of when I accidentally discovered a stash of marijuana in young Jim's bedroom in Zaire. At least I assumed it was marijuana, and I was horrified. Young Jim confirmed it was marijuana, and he was contrite. I hoped his remorse arose from true regret and not just from the fact that he was busted. Only part of me was naive. I suggested a large helping of cold turkey seasoned with prayer and contemplation, plus the joining of a teenage study group counselled by a young doctor who volunteered his time.

There were no trained counselors to contact. For better or worse, one took care of one's own problems, sometimes with a little help from friends. But some problems didn't lend themselves to easy sharing, particularly with friends who might have no more expertise than I. Jim Sr. was out of country on an extended trip, and besides, I was sure his expertise in this matter was as limited as mine.

At the time, I didn't make the connection between the bag of marijuana I held in my hand and Jimmy's earlier gardening efforts. As time went on, I did notice a slight rift between Jimmy and Joseph, but I remained unaware of its cause. Consequently, Joseph remained in my good graces and went about his work. He kept the whole yard neat and tidy and cleaned out a small ornamental pool. When the rains filled it, he put in a fish to raise for food. I'm not sure where the fish came from—perhaps from the Congo River along with our water supply.

There are crocodiles in the Congo. Stories seemed to abound about this or that hapless person caught in their jaws. Some longtime residents of the area, expatriates, seemed to delight in regaling us with these real-life horror stories. Though anxious to learn all I could of our new environment, I found these stories upsetting. I told one man that I thought being caught by a crocodile would be a horrible and, literally, bloody-awful way to die.

"But Marilyn, you don't understand. The crocodile doesn't chomp you up like hamburger and eat you right then. He takes you under water to drown, and then down to a cave-nest where he stashes your body to ripen for future snacks."

I was supposed to find that comforting?

# Social Times

❚ ❙ ❚

When we lived in Zaire, there were few opportunities to meet Zaireans on a social level. Their government was partly responsible for this. Zaireans weren't encouraged at the time to mix socially with foreigners. This applied particularly to the women. Their husbands might have business reasons to attend a social gathering, but rarely did they bring along a wife even if she was included in the invitation. There were probably a raft of reasons for this, including man's-world syndrome and language barriers.

In Kinshasa's foreign community, we English-speaking women of various countries found ourselves naturally drawn together. Often included were women whose first language wasn't English but who spoke it and wanted to practice it. Shortly after settling in Mont N'Gafula, I learned there was to be a meeting in Kinshasa whose purpose was to draw together interested bridge players, particularly English-speaking women. I made a point of attending. It seemed a good way to meet people with a common interest, plus I felt the need of some regular recreation that I enjoyed.

About twenty women, most unknown to one another, attended the meeting. It was quickly decided we'd actually play some bridge that day rather than just talk about it. Our American hostess rummaged for decks of playing cards, uncertain that she had enough. She raided her children's supply and suggested we count the cards in each deck to make sure her children hadn't lost any. Some of the women set to work at this task, and the hostess handed me a deck to count. Not really thinking, I immediately handed it back to her as I said, "This one isn't a full deck." I hadn't checked it other than by heft.

Counting and conversation around me ceased as the hostess gave me a strange, quizzical look. "Are you sure?"

"Yes," I replied as she began to count the cards in question.

"You're right," she said when she finished. "There are three cards missing."

Strange looks were directed at me, as if maybe I'd arrived in Kinshasa via Las Vegas or Monte Carlo. Someone muttered about not being sure she wanted to play cards with someone who knew a card deck that well.

I laughed and hastily dispelled the notion that I was a cardsharp. I explained that I'd just lived months in the Memling Hotel, where I'd played endless games of cribbage with my children. The card deck in question was of the same brand, and I knew what that deck felt like.

I and my explanation seemed accepted, and we settled in to play bridge. Still, when we cut the cards at my table to see who would deal first, I was relieved not to win.

The bridge meeting, where I didn't know anyone, led to good things— most of all, to good friends. One woman extended a quiet invitation to me, and to two or three other women, to play bridge at her house the following week. She said she knew a few other ladies who might join us as well. From the first I liked this lady, with her pleasing manner and unassuming dignity. I was glad to accept her invitation. She was from Europe, and her English was probably better than mine. I asked where she lived, and she gave me directions and said there was a sign on her garden wall, that I couldn't miss it.

"What does the sign say?" I asked.

"Embassy of ------," she replied. "My husband is the ambassador."

So serendipity opened the door to the diplomatic world in Kinshasa. Our social life and eventual circle of friends there had an international flavor that I found very interesting and enjoyable. In at least one respect, I finally became bilingual. I played bridge in both English and French.

It took French to extricate me from one of life's embarrassing moments in Kinshasa. I was delighted to be invited to play bridge by the wife of an African ambassador. I was enjoying my first time at the embassy residence. The place was actually a little rundown, and the next ambassador would insist that it be renovated and refurbished. But the company and cards were good that morning as I excused myself to go to the lavatory. That duty done, I found I couldn't open the bathroom door. Left, right, up, down, and around—nothing made the doorknob work. I waited a little, thinking someone might come to look for me, and then I realized that was unlikely for a while. It was Africa, where intestinal upsets are common. The ladies would politely guess I needed extra time in the bathroom, though they might not be happy at missing a bridge partner.

At least I wouldn't get claustrophobic—the bathroom was a good-sized room with large curtained windows. I contemplated climbing out and running around to ring the front doorbell. However, this struck me as undiplomatic and certainly undignified. Besides, I found there were bars on the windows. I stood at the door again and directed a few phrases through it in both French and English, but the bathroom was well-tucked away, and there was no one on the other side of the door to hear me.

My mind raced around solutions, and I rejected the idea of calling out loudly and making noise. That would embarrass my hostess. As for me, I already felt embarrassed, and maybe a little more wouldn't hurt. Through the window I'd noticed several gardeners at work. Why couldn't there have been just one? I wondered. I swallowed my pride and found that, unlike the door, the window opened easily. Through the bars I called out quietly and explained my predicament in fractured French. I asked them to tell someone inside the house to open the bathroom door from the other side. The men tried to hide their grins as one of them went to the back door. I thought it just as well that I didn't understand their comments to one another. Red-faced but more or less calm, cool, and collected, I waited for rescue, which soon came from the kitchen. So far as I know, my hostess remained unaware of the incident, though I later shared it with the wife of the next ambassador who lived there when she spoke of renovation. I felt that the story of a guest locked in the loo might bolster the argument for repairs.

When it was my turn, I hosted our international group in Mont N'Gafula. It was a bit of an extra drive for the ladies but none seemed to mind. Some had chauffeurs and shared their good fortune by sharing the ride. One time the determination of one lady to attend our bridge gathering at Mont N'Gafula surprised and amused us all. On arrival she recounted the lengths to which she'd gone to get there.

Part of the job of an ambassador's wife was to pay and receive calls within the diplomatic community and within a strict order of protocol. My friend was annoyed that her husband's secretary hadn't checked with her before scheduling her to pay a visit this morning to another ambassador's wife. My friend had scheduled herself to play bridge with us as usual. She decided to do a bit of playacting in order to resolve the conflict in her favor. She arrived at the other ambassador's house about 8 a.m. to find him and his wife, still dressed in robes and pajamas, having breakfast. Our friend swept in and out with profuse apologies of having gotten her appointment wrong. Duty done, she left the bemused ambassador with, quite literally, egg on his face.

I found it fun to be on the fringes of the diplomatic world, to be invited to the occasional party or gathering at that level. The conversation was often stimulating and the food usually good. I enjoyed the opportunity to meet interesting people of various nationalities. Of course, having my hand kissed in greeting by the occasional gallant or Old World diplomat took some getting used to. Startled and a bit gauche the first time it happened, I grew to accept the gesture with some measure of aplomb.

A bit of humor was provided for our children by one of our new friends who drove a fairly unassuming car for his status. Our children watched for his expected arrival so they could run in and say, "Here comes the ambassador in his Ambassador."

Friends liked to visit us in Mont N'Gafula, leaving for a while the hustle and bustle of Kinshasa. Mont N'Gafula was quieter and still had trees, though for how long was problematic. I winced whenever I heard the crashing sound of another big tree cut down to be made into charcoal. The locals needed charcoal to cook food, and some considered trees a never ending, God-given resource. I suggested to Victor and Joseph that men who cut down a tree should plant one to replace it. They laughed and told me God planted the trees. I thought of Joyce Kilmer's words about who makes poems and Who makes a tree. I doubted if God minded a little help, and I wished success to the struggling, United Nations-sponsored, tree-planting research effort nearby.

# Bugs

◪ ◙ ◪

Kinshasa and its environs were devoid of the kind of animal life that made an ordinary Sunday drive outside Nairobi, Kenya, extraordinary. No big game competed with cattle for forage. I suspect the tsetse fly was to blame for there being neither game nor much livestock in that part of Zaire.

When we first moved to Zaire, we found ourselves a little "homesick" for Kenya. In our collective mind's eye, we couldn't help but compare things in the two countries, sometimes to the detriment of Zaire. I didn't encourage any of us to make a habit of this. The two countries were totally different. And besides, vocalizing complaints was a bad habit to get into.

"Remember that we are guests in this country," I reminded our kids. "We chose to come here, and it's not polite for a guest to criticize."

"So all right. Your father and I chose to come here, but we tried to take your best interests into consideration. This job pays your father more money, which in turn provides better for all of us—like paying for your education. Think positive."

I tried to practice what I preached but couldn't help noticing Kinshasa's abundant bug life. I remembered a letter my husband had written from Zaire while we were still in Kenya. Jim had commented there seemed to be less of a bug problem in Zaire. Was he remembering the evening in Nairobi when the top half of our kitchen door was accidentally left open and the light left on? Hordes of termites swarmed in and dropped their wings and then their bodies all over the place. And there was the time when the

123

luscious big strawberry in that good, made-in-Kenya jam turned out to be a large, well-preserved fly. That seemed pretty minor stuff as I mused the matter in Mont N'Gafula.

There, outside Kinshasa, we needed to shake out our shoes to make sure we didn't share them and wear them with something that had crawled in during the night. When we relaxed with a cold drink at hand, we learned to glance at the glass before sipping so as not to ingest something unpleasant. We inspected our beds before retiring to make sure they weren't already occupied by snakes, bugs, or lizards. But that didn't save me from a fright the night a lizard chose to do a free fall from the ceiling onto my bed—while I was in the bed.

When the mosquitoes were bad, we pulled mosquito nets around each bed and slept the night through unless a persistent mosquito found a hole. If the insistent mosquito medley outside the net woke me in the night, I borrowed a phrase from my children and went back to sleep. "Nyaa, nyaa. You can't get me." One takes life's little triumphs where one can.

We knew some people who kept their toothbrushes in their refrigerator so the nocturnal ramblings of cockroaches wouldn't contaminate them. We didn't bother doing this ourselves—perhaps because I held somewhat to the theory that we needed a few germs to build up some immunity. For that reason too, I didn't insist on boiled water at tooth-brushing time, though I did emphasize that tap water was to be spit out rather than swallowed. Perhaps too I wasn't positive the refrigerator's seal kept it roach-free, though I certainly hoped it did. Once we moved in and cleaned up, I never saw any roaches inside our refrigerator. However, I remembered opening that refrigerator on our house-inspection trip to Mont N'Gafula. The refrigerator was empty except for the dead body of the largest roach I'd ever seen in my life.

Roaches rivalled snakes as the bane of my existence in Zaire. Some of the roaches were huge, several inches in length. To come unexpectedly upon a score or more of these together as if in a nest, and then to have them begin clacking and darting at me—it sent shivers up and down my spine. I felt as if I was facing a malignant, prehistoric presence. Maybe I was—cockroaches have been around a long time.

We could never completely eliminate them from our household in Zaire, though we tried. The presence of roaches, to a greater or lesser degree, was simply a fact of life there. Our reflexes became honed to dispatch them on their darting forays if we saw them in the house. I could face a few at a time without my spine getting the creepy-crawlies, but I certainly never learned to like cockroaches, quite the contrary. Thus I was hard pressed to express proper appreciation to Victor for his particular parting gift to me—a beautifully-carved, roach wall-plaque. He was so proud of having acquired this special gift to give to me. I could tell he'd rehearsed his speech to go with it, probably simplifying some of the French so I'd be sure to understand. And there was Joseph beaming over Victor's shoulder. That carved cockroach was a special gift—unique, perhaps, as I've never seen another before or since. And I did appreciate it. I still do appreciate that carved roach and hope there was no tinge of dismay in my thanks.

I still have that plaque. It's just that I've never been able to bring myself to hang the cockroach and look at it every day. Yet, though the roach plaque isn't enshrined on my wall, the sentiments and goodwill with which it was given me hold a place of honor in my heart.

I awoke one night in Zaire to strange noises coming from the living room. Upon investigating, I thought at first glance that our roach population had flipped out—literally. Here were these things flipping and jumping all over the place. Closer inspection showed them to be overactive crickets the size of mice. A window had been left wide open.

A few hours later Joseph didn't seem to mind the extra work corralling the crickets. In fact, he seemed quite happy about it. He even saved some of them in a bucket that he covered with a torn piece of netting and set on the veranda. I thought maybe the insects were being saved for bait—perhaps Joseph was going fishing.

Our inquisitive chimpanzee soon found the cache of crickets. A yell from Joseph caused me to look up to see our chimp happily munching what sounded like a crunchy cracker. An unhappy Joseph arrived on the scene to scold Sam for freeing and feasting on his, Joseph's, dinner. I swallowed hard as I contemplated crickets as comestibles.

It was easy to observe Mont N'Gafula's kind of animal life—snakes, lizards, bugs, and bats. Some of the lizards lived in the house. We welcomed this to a certain extent because they ate some of the bugs. We even named and became fond of two or three who took up residence behind pictures on the living room wall. The lizards seemed to be territorial. As we came to

125

recognize some of them, we noticed that each staked out its own area. More than once we watched a lizard defend a section of wall or chase off another lizard who encroached on his area. We didn't have television to watch, but sometimes nature provided a show.

I'll always remember my butterfly day. I was absolutely enthralled when I looked out and saw clouds of butterflies. All alone, I regretted there was no one to share the sight with. I stood entranced and watched the winged creatures fill the sky. They were gorgeous, of varied hues. I was struck by the wonder and beauty of the scene. Victor and Joseph arrived to find me marvelling in awe at those butterflies. I was all but ecstatic at their beauty. Victor and Joseph marvelled more at me and my enthusiasm than they did at the butterflies. That sight they'd seen before. It happened every year, and they told me most of the butterflies lived only one day.

"What a shame. How sad."

"No, Madame. That is how the good God made them."

From clouds of butterflies to swarms of bees at a neighbor's house. When I heard about the bees, I kept a wary eye out and told Victor and Joseph we must run to close windows and doors if there was any sign of the bees swarming toward our house. Our younger son, Michael, had a life-threatening allergy to bee and wasp stings. He'd finished three years of desensitization shots before we left the United States for Africa. However, since he'd not yet been stung again, we weren't sure of the effectiveness of that course of treatment. I was sure that subjecting him, or any of us, to a swarm of bees was not a good thing. The bees kept the neighbor a prisoner in his house until nightfall. Then various knowledgeable Zairean men smoked and captured the bees and transported them elsewhere.

Sometimes our children showed an interest in the biology of bug life in Mont N'Gafula, calling out the characteristics of a newly discovered bug and usually ending with, "Hey, Mom, you gotta see this."

"No, I don't"—but I usually answered the call. Occasionally one or more of the kids would insist on performing a descriptive autopsy on a bug. They found this fascinating. I did not.

But some bugs were fascinating. They came in all shapes and sizes and weren't always what they appeared to be. There was one bug that looked for all the world like a six-to-twelve-inch-long dry twig that had fallen to the ground. Another was nicknamed the "acid bug." Its bite was bad enough, but if one smacked the bug, it could cause a very unpleasant, itching, stinging rash, which was sometimes accompanied by a fever.

More pleasant in memory is the relaxed hour I spent one afternoon observing a praying mantis. This was up close and personal as it perched on the coffee table to share my cold cola. The praying mantis was a beautiful green color, delicate and deliberate in its movements. I took care not to frighten it in hopes it would stay until the children could see it. It did. So there were rewards to living in Mont N'Gafula if we were open to seeing them. Where else could we have encountered our bat story for instance?

I was apprehensive at the sight of a bat flying into our house through the open veranda doors. Even in Mont N'Gafula this was not normal, and I was afraid the bat itself might not be either. I'd heard of rabid bats and I wondered about this one. I thought bats liked the dark, so what was it doing flying around our lit living room and dining room? Maybe its sonar sense was sick. Whatever, I wanted that bat out of there and without anyone touching it.

A neighbor was visiting us that evening. He looked around and spied the badminton racquets, grabbed two of them and tossed one to my husband. And yes, before going after the bat, our friend actually said, "*Batminton* anyone?"

# Play It Again, Sam

▨ ▧ ▨

T he beat of the African drum sounded tentative, half-hearted. Perhaps the drummer lacked conviction, or maybe he was unsure of the message to be sent. Then the rhythm picked up. Intensity and volume increased too. Now there was no doubt the drummer had a definite message. That pounding became an upsetting sound. I could decipher the communication, but I didn't like it.

I covertly watched for signs of understanding between the African servants. At first they pretended not to hear, but now they were muttering, recognizing the beat's urgency. There seemed to be some indecision—whether to continue their household tasks or respond to that compelling call. The message throbbed loud and clear...impossible to ignore any longer: our chimpanzee wanted his tea.

In his cage, he was thumping a sturdy wooden box about two-feet square. The box was empty, and sometimes the little chimp liked to jump into the box to play, or curl up in it for a nap. Now the animal had turned the box upside down to make a good drum, and the noise got our attention.

It hadn't taken long for our chimpanzee, Sam, to train us all. It began as a joke when I let him out of his cage to join me on a stroll around the grounds of our home in Mont N'Gafula. He let go my hand and scampered up the steps to the veranda to greet Victor and Joseph, who were taking a break from their duties. Victor laughingly offered his tea mug to Sam, who promptly accepted and drained it. He spilled more than a little but obviously enjoyed the taste of tea and appreciated the brew.

A couple of mornings later Sam went to considerable lengths to escape from his cage at teatime. He sneaked up behind the servants and snatched a cup of tea at the first opportunity. From then on Victor made extra tea, filling a bowl for Sam to enjoy in his cage. Sam was hooked.

He soon became undisputed boss of the timing of each day's tea break. Should the fellows try to delay it unduly, Sam would start an insistent drumming on the empty box inside his circular, heavy-wire enclosure. This was a pseudo African hut-cum-cage. From there in the back yard, he could survey the house and know whether anyone was reacting to his message. If Sam felt ignored, his box-thumping increased. If he continued to feel neglected, he augmented the drumming with his full range of chimp vocabulary and volume. This was considerable. Sam was a type of dwarf chimpanzee, but his lung power seemed inherited from his larger cousins. It may have been some of Sam's relatives who took part in the American space program. Their participation predated the manned space flights.

Certainly some of our mornings in Zaire took on a *Planet of the Apes* quality. I would hear Victor and Joseph pleading with Sam to be patient. Sam would listen as they called out explanations to him for the delay— they just wanted a little more time to finish the ironing, the dishes, et cetera, before fixing tea. The men requested his understanding. Sam would consider only briefly before berating them with renewed vigor. Lovable most other times, he became the tyrant of the tea break.

This was never more evident than on Sundays, the servants' day off. We squeaked through Saturdays because the fellows worked a half day and were there to fix Sam's morning tea as usual. But once a week, and on a few holidays, it fell to some family member to make and serve Sam's tea. There were enough of us to share the job, but it fairly quickly fell to the lot of the two younger children. Partly because the rest of us managed to hand the job down, but mainly because Mike and Karen drank their tea with milk and sugar. The rest of us preferred it straight. They therefore had a better chance of coming up with the correct combination to satisfy our chimpanzee connoisseur.

Sam set very demanding standards for his tea. Each of us took a turn as his hopeful, hovering waiter. No wine steward ever waited more anxiously for the first sip to be approved. Should the tea not meet his expectations, Sam was quite capable of shattering the Sunday quiet indefinitely with his screeching rage. Or he might opt for calm and calculated cunning. When our attention was held by his droll display of disdain, which included a clumsy attempt at folded arms, we'd suddenly find ourselves drenched with the offending tea, having forgotten to watch Sam's facile feet. Running a catering service for a cocky chimp had not entered my wildest imaginings about what life in Africa might bring.

Sam was brought to us as a complete surprise. For that reason my defenses were down. If I'd had the chance to think about it, I could have— and probably would have—mustered a long list of reasons as to why we should not, would not, keep the animal. For the fact that I did not do so, my family and I are forever grateful.

Sam walked into our house and straight into our hearts the first night we saw him. Our neighbor accompanied him to our home. Our neighbor's intention, or so he said, was simply to show the animal to our children before taking it to some other friends in Kinshasa. These other friends were unaware of what largesse was about to be bestowed. However, our neighbor seemed certain of his and the animal's welcome there. Psychological ploy? Perhaps. Certainly I was all too unsuspecting as we listened to our neighbor relate what he knew of Sam's history and how he, our neighbor, came to acquire him.

Our neighbor friend was a pilot for Air Zaire, and on his most recent trip to the interior had visited an elderly Belgian friend. He found his friend to be ill and preparing to leave Zaire for good. The man's one remaining worry, other than his health, was what to do with his little chimpanzee companion.

I don't like the idea of taking animals from the wild in order to turn them into household pets. However, my disapproval abated somewhat as I listened and learned this little chimp's background.

The old Belgian fellow felt he rescued this chimpanzee from almost certain death in the jungle. He found the little chap, just a baby, wandering near its mother's body. She was evidently the victim of a poisonous snake. There are many kinds of snakes in Zaire, almost all of them deadly.

Capturing the confused little animal wasn't difficult. Whether it was necessary remains a moot point. Chimpanzees are not usually solitary creatures. It is quite likely there was at least a small group of them hiding nearby, frightened into frozen silence by the approach of upright two-legged

131

predators. Sam's father, brothers, and sisters, or even his aunts, uncles, and cousins may have watched his "rescue," choosing instinctively to allow the silent sacrifice of one of their members rather than to endanger all. That the old Belgian fellow felt he was doing the right thing is not in doubt. What will never be known is whether his actions precluded Sam's rescue and rearing by his own kind.

This was something that bothered me throughout the recital of how Sam came to be sitting across from me in our living room that night. He was too far from his own kind, not only in distance but in manner. There was an uncomfortableness about him, an uneasiness...sort of an embarrassed sadness that seemed to well from some inner, knowledgeable but inarticulate source. To me the animal's unease seemed totally unconnected to the fact that the little fellow had just been uprooted from his most recent familiar surroundings.

Part of his discomfort seemed to be with his clothes. He was dressed like a little boy, or an organ grinder's monkey. And he wasn't a monkey. Monkeys have tails, chimpanzees don't. They more nearly resemble humans.

Perhaps the chimp's inner being wasn't so inarticulate after all. He had been staring at me with those big brown eyes for quite some time. Yes, he was communicating all right and knew just the approach to use on me. He was a creature in need, a need I instinctively felt I could fulfill or at least alleviate. And if I didn't, would anyone else? Maybe. I couldn't help but see the hopeful look on my children's faces. Maybe there was a need there, too.

I made a feeble effort to fight the rapport that animal seemed to wrap around me. I am not an animal lover, per se. However, I've had a special rapport with one or two dogs and several cats in my lifetime. One of those dogs, Twinkie, belonged to my brother-in-law's family. Because we usually lived far away, months or years might pass between our visits to that family. But each time we arrived, Twinkie greeted me with joy and a heart-to-heart "talk." It truly seemed as if she was telling me all that had happened since we last met. And of course I encouraged it with appropriately placed comments: "Is that right. Really?" and "You don't say." No wonder I was once introduced to guests there as, "My sister-in-law who talks to the animals." But, in Zaire, it was no dog or cat communing with me. What did I or any of us know about caring for a chimpanzee?

Our neighbor finished telling of the trip back from the interior. The little chimp had ridden in the cockpit, shades of his space-age kin. He had been forcibly restrained from touching anything vital to the aircraft's operation, but, at the chimp's insistence, was allowed to wear the captain's hat. The captain even pinned his shoulder boards of rank on the chimp.

Our friend, the captain, was tempted to send this comical caricature strolling down the main cabin's aisle. Fortunately his common sense prevailed over his sense of humor. He realized his passengers might well misinterpret the whole scene. The captain also realized he might lose his job. The airline was transitioning from European to Zairean pilots. This chimpanzee caricature might be misinterpreted by some as race commentary rather than general comedy.

At a break in the captain's conversation, our children made it plain that they dearly wished to keep this comical creature. Then they became strangely silent. I felt my children were holding their collective breath.

My husband made his stance plain with, "It's up to your mother."

"Oh, I just can't say yes to keeping him," I burst out. "I have enough trouble rearing four children. I most certainly don't need a fifth, be it child or chimp! Besides," I added weakly, "I can't even pronounce his name."

"We can change it," came the children's chorus, as if on cue.

The chimpanzee was introduced to us with a French name that my brain refused to register. I sensed the animal wasn't overly fond of it either. Maybe that was rationalization on my part because my tongue had trouble trapping that French pronunciation.

"It's probably just as well (unpronounceable name) doesn't stay here," our neighbor interjected. "He is not used to women. My Belgian friend maintained an all male household, including the servants. That's why I can't keep him. This little fellow likes me but not my wife and daughters. He didn't care for the stewardess either. In fact," our neighbor concluded, "he doesn't seem to like women at all."

At this the animal cocked his head to cast a skeptical look at the speaker. I tried to sort out my mixture of emotions, which mainly seemed to be a kind of disappointed relief at being off the hook. After all, I couldn't be expected to take on the care of a misogynist male chimp. Before I could really get used to this theory, the maligned male in question disproved it.

Leaving our friend's lap for the first time, the chimpanzee very deliberately walked over to stand in front of me. His eyes held mine in that pleading, bleeding-heart gaze he had employed on me periodically since his arrival. Then he gently reached for my hand and held it.

"Hello, Sam." I said.

"We get to keep him," exhaled the children.

I had no idea where his new name sprang from. It just seemed to fit. Sam seemed to like it too. Name and animal became one, and both stayed.

His clothes did not. That was the first order of business. And while I was getting those ridiculous garments off him, I began to talk to him. As if he could understand me. I never became convinced that he could not. Quite the contrary, and my conviction was shared by others. Maybe we raised a bilingual chimp. He was talked to in English and French and seemed to understand both.

This first time though, I think I was talking to the children as much as to the chimp. I had a feeling my children and I had different ideas about this little animal. So I proceeded to lay down some ground rules. My first conversation with Sam was in English. Everyone watched and listened.

"My little friend," I addressed him as I undressed him. "The fact is you are a chimpanzee. If this is to be your home, that is what you will be. You will not wear clothes nor dine at our table."

This last elicited a disappointed groan from the children. I suspect they had visions of disproving the statement, "Mind your manners. This is not feeding time at the zoo."

"Forget it, gang. I'm not teaching table manners to a chomping chimp."

They let that round go to me without much argument, but the next one was not to be so easy.

"Where is he going to sleep?" Karen wondered.

"With me," said Jimmy.

"In my room," said Mike.

"Oh, no," said I.

"Why not?" came the chorus.

Being a family man, our neighbor figured it was a good time to leave. For similar reasons, my husband indicated he would see our neighbor out and stroll to the gate with him.

Our old friend and new friend said goodbye to each other, and I watched to see if this parting was going to present a problem. Other than leaving me on my own to face children and chimp, it did not. Sam looked slightly apprehensive but made no move to leave with the men.

Jimmy, our man-sized teenager, must have seemed a reassuring substitute to Sam, who sidled over to him and took his hand.

"See, Mom, he likes me."

"Good, but he's still not sleeping with you."

"Ahhh, Mom. Just see, will you? He really does like me." By this time, Jimmy had the animal in his arms. Sam looked quite content to be there.

"I'm delighted he likes you," I acknowledged. "And because he does, I hereby appoint you his number-one keeper. But, as managing director of this menagerie, I repeat, he is not sleeping with you!"

"We could take turns," Mike interjected hopefully.

"Yes, but as keeper, not sleeper," I replied.

"But where is he going to sleep?" little Karen persisted.

"I don't know where he is going to sleep," I admitted. "I just know where he isn't."

"Maybe he could sleep in your room," Karen offered.

"No!" I was emphatic. "Believe me, our room heads the list of places where that animal is not going to sleep."

I noticed she was not offering her and her sister's room. Roxanne was away at college in Spain. It might have been natural for Karen to offer her sister's bed. She didn't, and I wondered if she might be having mixed emotions about our newly acquired pet.

If she wasn't, I certainly was. Where in the world was that animal going to sleep? I wondered and pondered. Disjointed thoughts bounced around. A cage. Yes, of course. But there was no cage this night. We must build one. And as soon as possible. But that doesn't help this first night.

"Most certainly not!" I definitely vetoed locking the animal in the kitchen until morning. There were enough germs to cope with in African living without inviting them to invade the food-preparation area via an animal.

The bathroom was also out as a holding pen. We were a one-bathroom family. It was difficult enough to get one's turn in there. I couldn't see complicating the situation further by letting the chimpanzee take up residence in that small but vital room.

In fact, I didn't want him taking up residence in the house at all. But without the safe sanctuary of a cage outside, there seemed no choice. The African night is full of things that go bump, and worse. The poor little fellow's first night with us would be traumatic enough, perhaps for all of us, without having him terror-stricken.

So, having eliminated the great outdoors, there was nothing to do but reconsider the house. And I had already eliminated most of that. If I wasn't going to allow the animal to sleep in the kitchen, bathroom, or bedrooms, we were left with the room in which we were standing.

This was a very large, long room comprising the living room at one end and the dining room at the other. By continuing the process of elimination, because he most certainly was not going to be allowed to curl up on the couch, we came to Sam's final resting place that first night. The bare, dimly-lit corner of the dining room was it. The other corner contained the china cabinet, and I didn't want him rattling around it.

I was surprised this corner hadn't come to mind immediately. If not perfect for the purpose, it would certainly do nicely. It would leave the animal in somewhat familiar surroundings, since this large room was all he yet knew of our establishment. That should be of some comfort to him. More comforting to me was the thought that the corner could be easily cleaned the next day. No rug covered the tiles in the dining room, and, as a matter of routine, it was swept and mopped daily by one of the servants.

*Oh, Lord, the servants.* What would they think of the newest member of our family? I would have to have an explanation of this animal's presence thought out in French by tomorrow morning.

*Please, God, let them like him.* I silently sent up the plea.

The children, even my husband, might think I was the final authority in this matter. However, I knew better. I wasn't going to volunteer this information, least of all to Victor, but the fate of this chimpanzee rested on Victor's approval or disapproval.

Joseph could be replaced. In fact, I was sorely tempted on more than one occasion to initiate the process. He was always saved by the fact that he did try hard to please and, at least some of the time, worked hard. I really liked that—and him—which always outweighed my annoyance at Joseph's slow-motion work pace.

Victor's position was another matter. He was sometimes my second-in-command. I valued—and at times was guided by—his good judgment, helpful suggestions, and knowledge of the local scene. We liked and trusted each other. We had a good working relationship. It was a good thing we did because it took the hard work of both of us to keep our house and household running smoothly. In short, Victor came close to being indispensable. In consequence, so was his good opinion of the chimp.

I reminded myself of part of the reason I had originally hired Victor. My judgment had proved sound. The twinkle I'd detected in his eyes had, as I'd suspected, proved the harbinger of a good sense of humor. I would just have to hope it would stand us all in good stead in this situation.

I also reminded myself that I'd better get my priorities straight. Though Victor's good opinion would rate the highest priority the next morning, getting the chimp settled for the night was of immediate importance. Judging by his now droopy-looking eyes, maybe it wasn't going to be too difficult.

There was a stack of burlap sacking on the veranda, and I sent Mike for some of it. Instinct told me the animal needed something soft to snuggle into this night. Instinct spoke truly. That burlap became Sam's Linus-blanket for some considerable length of his life with us.

Mike made a soft nest in the dining room corner with the burlap. When Jimmy moved to take Sam to it, I stopped them.

"No, I have to do it." This brought forth Jimmy's loud protests, which I cut short.

"Hush, you're scaring the animal." In a soothing voice, for both Sam's and Jimmy's benefit, I went on to explain.

"You and the other kids are not home a good many hours of each day. You're in school or wherever. Your father's work takes him to the office or even out of the country. And the servants come and go."

"Yes, of course. I come and go too, but of all of you, I am most often here. And though, believe me, I fully intend to delegate the care of this animal, he has got to realize that I am the boss. Particularly since he's not used to women. So, to establish my authority and impress it upon him, I will take him to his bed tonight and tell him to sleep there."

"What if he doesn't?"

"He will," I said, a trifle grimly.

To my relief, he did. I remembered having a lot more trouble settling our children to sleep at a tender age than I had with our somnolent Sam.

137

# Victor and Joseph Meet Sam

※ ▨ ※

As day follows night, so too did the morning arrive—and the servants.

"Bonjour, Madame," Victor called cheerfully as he entered the kitchen from the veranda.

I figured that cheerfulness augured well for the cause. "Bonjour, Victor, Joseph," I replied.

Victor and Joseph were not yet aware that anything was out of the ordinary this morning. It was their custom to arrive together, though they lived in different villages. If, as on this morning, my husband took the children to school before going to work, he'd already unlocked our gate, and the servants had no difficulty entering the grounds. The same applied to the kitchen door at the end of the veranda. It was Victor and Joseph's habit to enter there, call a greeting, and close the door opening onto the dining room. On the back of that door hung their uniforms, into which they changed. Their reopening of the door signified they were dressed again and ready to begin work.

Sam and I stood hand in hand, well back from the veranda doors. We had quietly watched the servants arrival. I had a feeling this subdued manner, which Sam had exhibited since his arrival, was too good to last forever. Nevertheless, I counted on it continuing awhile longer. *It had better if he wants to keep his newly acquired happy home,* I thought sternly as we faced the closed kitchen door. We waited as Victor and Joseph conversed in Lingala while they changed clothes. Suddenly the language changed too.

139

"What was that?" came Victor's startled French.

Sam, apparently wondering what was going on, had voiced a quiet, questioning, "Woof?"

"Madame is there." Joseph, with his placid pragmatism, answered in French.

"That wasn't Madame I heard." Victor was emphatic.

"Maybe she has a cold."

"That's stupid! She didn't have a cold two minutes ago when she said good morning, did she?" To confirm this and more, he called through the closed door, "Madame, are you all right?"

"*Oui*, Victor, *merci*."

The sounds of their changing had grown progressively hurried. Understandable. I doubt that any man in any society wants to face the unknown with his pants down. Victor was still buckling his belt as he yanked open the door.

The sudden movement startled Sam. He let out more than a quiet woof and took about a half step forward. The fact that it was all done while clinging tightly to my hand assured me the act was mostly bluff and bluster.

I felt reassured, but Victor felt threatened. He jumped back. Joseph felt scared and looked rooted to a spot well behind Victor.

I overcame the urge to laugh at this incongruous tableau. Given that the men had been caught unawares, it was perfectly natural. But it was also funny. Here was this tiny, timid little chimp intimidating two grown men. It was an act Sam would repeat, in varying degrees and with varying degrees of success, during his time with us. Unsuspecting people had no way of knowing they were witnessing a totally false display of confidence.

Victor retreated halfway behind the kitchen door. He peered around it, ready to slam it shut. Joseph, being taller but perhaps even more afraid, stared over Victor's shoulder from a safe distance. He kept behind the barricade of the sturdy kitchen worktable.

All the while, there was Sam—a towering two feet tall, doing his *I'll huff and I'll puff and I'll blow you down* bit. The chimp blustered and bounced. However, his bladder betrayed his bluff. It was either so full or he was so frightened that urine spurted with every jiggle. Being a bouncing water spigot in the dining room was not apt to win him friends at that point, but it did detract considerably from his ferociousness.

"Ça va, Sam. It's all right." I quieted him down. Then I turned to the servants. "Ça va, Victor, Joseph. This is *mon ami*, Sam. I hope you will like him."

"But, Madame, your friend is a chimpanzee." Joseph pointed this out quite seriously.

I tried not to laugh as I wondered if he thought I hadn't noticed that fact. By this time Sam was his subdued self again, quite content to let me handle the situation. I thought I now detected the familiar twinkle in Victor's eyes. I suspect Joseph's stolid observation of Sam's genus had piqued Victor's sense of humor as it had mine.

Hurrying to take advantage of this lightening of the atmosphere, I marched out my arguments. I explained as best I could in my limited French. I'm sure the clinchers were what a good pet he would be for the children, and the fact that he was not going to live in the house. As to the animal's history and how he had arrived to take up residence, I finally gave up and recommended they approach our next-door neighbor for the full explanation.

Victor had let go his hold on the door and was standing hands on hips, foursquare in the doorway. I felt he'd not yet given his wholehearted approval. Exactly what I expected from Victor indicating his acceptance and approval, I wasn't sure, but—like shopping for a new dress—I felt I would know it when I saw it.

Sam too seemed to know from whence to look for official sanction. He had been favoring Victor with a rendition of his woebegone-waif look. Sam certainly didn't look threatening now. He was scared and didn't leave my side. But with a weak grin and outstretched arm, he made his submissive appeal to Victor.

That did it. Victor's heart melted, and he came forward to gently take the proffered hand of friendship. Bending down, though not too far since he himself was fairly short, Victor shook Sam's hand and said in French, "You are a friend of Madame? Me too. Say, 'bonjour.'"

Sam and I both grinned from ear to ear. We all delighted in the relieved and relaxed laughter.

The next few days passed with nimble novelty. Sam was all over the place exploring his new domain. So was I trying to keep up with him. I feel that pet owners have a responsibility not only to care for their pets, but also to see that those pets don't bother others.

When we lived in Puerto Rico, we found the houses built very close together. This promoted a degree of neighborly nosiness when voices rose. The windows were always open to the warm weather and often were unscreened. Decorative grillwork kept out burglars, at least the human kind. Feline felons were another matter.

As with French, my Spanish was limited. However, one dinnertime in Puerto Rico, I knew from the next-door senora's sudden screeching that she was upset. I caught the words for *look, cat,* and *chicken.* My vocabulary lacked the word for thief.

A few days later a friend a block away confided his perplexity about a recent incident. He was used to the rodents and reptiles his large cat insisted on bringing home to prove her hunting prowess. Recently though, the cat had come racing in carrying a chicken. Yes, it was most certainly dead, but he didn't think his cat had killed it. In fact, he was quite sure of that because it was a ready-to-eat, roasted chicken!

With this in my memory, I kept a wary eye on Sam in Africa. God knows what a chimp could cart off. Dwarf he might be, but he was still considerably bigger than that Puerto Rican cat who had dined so well.

My husband promised to build a cage for our chimpanzee but not until the following weekend. I would have preferred Sam's immediate incarceration. However, in retrospect, I think those days of relative freedom were good for him. He came to know all of us very quickly since one or more of us was with him every waking hour. He learned the boundaries of property and behavior—and the limit of my patience.

My physical stamina was also taxed. It had been a few years since I had chased preschool children. I hadn't always kept up with them either. Burned in my memory was the image of our younger son at age three after he managed to turn on our garden hose, and then pointed its nozzle down the furnace-oil-intake-pipe of the neighbor's house.

I shrieked a horrified, "Michael! What are you doing?"

He looked up in angelic innocence before sweetly and logically replying, "Me playing oil man."

Those neighbors in New York were very forgiving and understanding.

I wasn't at all sure how neighborliness in Zaire would work. After a move from the West Coast, New York had sometimes seemed like a strange country, but at least I never had to worry that some innocent infringement of the rules would get us deported.

In Zaire, one of the first stories I heard emphasized the difficulty and potential problems inherent in cross-cultural communication. It seemed—so the story went—that an expatriate professor in Zaire was counselling one of his students. This young man, judging from his grades, simply had no aptitude for the difficult major he'd chosen. The professor noted the Zairean's enthusiasm and wanted to encourage him to continue his higher education. The teacher suggested the young man change majors and switch to another, easier branch. The teacher meant branch of learning, but within forty-eight hours the well-meaning professor was given half that time to leave the country. Apparently he had insulted a relative of a high-ranking government official. This by suggesting the young man was the same as a monkey in a tree swinging from branch to branch.

As for Sam, we tried to keep him from climbing the trees and swinging from branch to branch—at least those trees near the fence, because we were afraid he would swing over and get himself in trouble—maybe us too.

Sam could scamper and move quickly and really kept us hopping. I longed for the promised cage to confine him, but there seemed no movement on that building project—no time, no material. The chimpanzee was impacting my life more than I expected. Looking after Sam all the time because he didn't yet have a cage was confining *me*. I couldn't go to my weekly bridge games with women friends. Fortunately—for again we had no telephone—I was able to send advance warning of and apologies for my absence via the children at school. However, I missed more than the mental exercise and good company. A bridge game was also an opportunity to hear the latest rumors, if any, of unrest or danger in the country.

This helped me decide when to be more watchful, and whether I should say yea or nay to unnecessary comings and goings in our family. More than once in those troubled times, a child of mine, in order to participate in some extracurricular school activity, stayed in town overnight with a friend. My children were pleased when I gave this permission and generally remained unaware of why it was granted. I didn't always tell them of trouble I'd heard of, and that I feared for their well-being if they were out and about then. I tried to give them enough information for safety but also tried to beware of horror stories. I saw no reason to burden them unnecessarily, though if they asked, I gave honest answers. Sometimes their reaction was, "Oh, Mom, you worry too much." I hoped they were right.

Sometimes we heard stories of army deserters, or alleged army deserters. These people were also alleged to be gangster types in stolen army uniforms. They were said to be armed and dangerous. And they had attacked some isolated homes in the countryside.

Though not exactly isolated, I figured Mont N'Gafula qualified as countryside. Therefore I was scared, but not surprised, to be awakened by gunshots at two o'clock one morning. What surprised me was that Michael, our younger son, slept through all the excitement. The rest of our family ran to each other and met in the living room. We remained there awhile, hunkered down and watchful.

Later that morning, from Victor and Joseph and neighbors, we learned more of the incident, which seemed to be unconnected to earlier rumored events. This one was thought to be an attempt to settle a private score, perhaps by a disgruntled former employee. No one was killed, no one was caught. The exchange of gunfire occurred at a Belgian household. There seemed general agreement in Zaire that, in the time before independence, some Belgians were harsh taskmasters. Stories abounded on this theme.

I remember one small international gathering of ladies that happened not to include any Belgians. Perhaps this allowed the conversation to range freely over pre-independence horror stories of harrassment in Zaire. The tales escalated until one of my younger Nigerian friends, married to a diplomat, burst out with, "Well, all I know is that ever since coming to Zaire, I've been glad it was the British who had us!" I thought it a wonderfully undiplomatic statement.

I got quite good at gauging the tenor of the times in Zaire. I was fortunate to have a wide circle of friends and acquaintances. When I started hearing the same stories of danger and distress over again, I could be fairly certain things were quieting down. Otherwise, some new report would be quietly making the rounds.

All these bits of news or rumors found their way among friends by word of mouth. In any country governed by a dictator, things that can be construed as criticism, or in any way against the regime, are usually said or done quietly—if said or done at all. Free speech there might be dearly paid for with loss of a job, or worse.

So talk of danger or anything even mildly critical of President Mobutu's government was discreetly done in Zaire. Just how discreetly was illustrated the time I found my hostess a tad distraught as she greeted her friends with the usual kiss on each cheek, and an unusual warning whispered in the ear. "Be careful what you say. I just learned our servant speaks English." It may have been bridge, but there were times when a poker face was a distinct asset.

In addition to rumors and relaxation (it was most relaxing if there weren't too many rumors), those social get-togethers with other foreign women provided an exchange of information on food. It would have been nice to have some Zairean women in our social groups, but in those days there seemed to be an unwritten rule of the Zairean government against easy intermingling. Meanwhile, we foreign women gathered in various settings such as instruction or learning groups, cards, whatever. There was the occasional recipe exchanged, but more often it was knowledge of food sources that we passed along.

"Sedec, near the American Embassy, has some sugar. At least they did yesterday." This was automatically assumed to be white sugar, though in reality dirt would cause it to be varying shades of grey or brown. Real brown sugar hadn't been seen in Kinshasa's shops for nine months.

"This morning I saw a few tins of margarine at Le Grande Marche." This was the very large sprawling outdoor market in Kinshasa. I was never sure whether its size should be measured in square blocks or square miles. It was one very big site for lots of small entrepreneurs. In good times, if one knew where to look, almost anything necessary could be found there. It even had some things one might not feel necessary, such as fried caterpillars.

"Does anyone know where I can buy salt?"

There was definitely a food shortage in Zaire. Even the basics like flour, sugar, and salt were missing from the grocery shelves much of the time. One of the recent rumors was not about mayhem and murder, but it worried me almost as much. The rumor claimed the country's bakeries would soon close for lack of flour. What would we do then? I wondered. My own supply of flour was getting very skimpy. I grabbed the chance to be included in a group ordering one-hundred pound sacks of flour via someone who knew a wholesale source. But if the bakeries couldn't get flour, I wasn't very hopeful of results for us from some nebulous, unknown source. Besides, I had never baked bread in my life. Oh, well—the thought occurred to me—I had never had a hand in raising a chimpanzee before either.

# Lessons Learned

▨ ▨ ▨

Lack of building material delayed it, but the weekend for building the promised cage finally arrived. I figured it was more in my husband's sphere of expertise than mine. Jim's father had been a carpenter. The son hadn't followed in the father's footsteps, having instead pursued his dream career in aviation. However, I knew my husband hadn't forgotten the trade he was taught in his early years. With help from his father, Jim and I built our first house a year after we married. Admittedly that was almost twenty years earlier than our time in Zaire, but necessity over the years had dictated a number of do-it-yourself projects for Jim and me. My own role at such times was Jill-of-all-work, occasional idea-person, and number one go-fer.

This time I opted to go-fer groceries. Having to watch Sam all the time had prevented any shopping excursions, so the larder was pretty lean. I regretted not getting an earlier start though. It was Saturday, and the stores would all close for the weekend by one o'clock in the afternoon. I wouldn't have time to go to many places. I hoped the one or two stores I'd get to would have something worth buying and at a price I could afford. Ready-to-eat breakfast cereal had already been elevated to gift status in our household, though we felt lucky if any could be found for birthdays or Christmas. Too many things were going missing in the shops, and nothing seemed in abundant supply. The grocery stores in Zaire had row upon row of empty shelves.

Young Jim and Michael stayed home to corral Sam, while Jim Sr. built the chimp's cage. Karen elected to accompany me to Kinshasa—whether in hopes of a special treat such as a package of Smarties, or simply for lack of something better to do, I wasn't sure. I again wondered if she was having mixed emotions about our new pet.

Her opinion of her brothers seemed straightforward enough as we drove along. "The boys hog everything!" Karen burst out. "I can't even get near Sam."

*Do you really want to?* I wondered. I'd detected earlier that she might be afraid of Sam. However, I felt that to focus now on her fear might make it worse. She hadn't yet had much chance to play with Sam. Her brothers really had monopolized him, now that I thought about it. Moreover, I was sure her fear would diminish, and she would deal with it better, when she had the chance to find out for herself that, deep down, our chimp was a pussycat.

Maybe Karen just wasn't enough bigger than Sam. He had already discovered he could intimidate her. Despite his small size, he would sometimes turn on her threateningly. I think it was as much a game as anything for him. Sam liked getting a rise out of her, much like a bored, bullying brother. Most of the time she could handle both brothers and chimp, but occasionally she yelled to be rescued.

For now, I tried to calm Karen by pointing out that perhaps the youngest in a family needed to practice an extra measure of patience and forbearance. I had felt this way growing up as the younger of two. I thought it might be doubly applicable to the youngest of four. And I agreed it wasn't necessarily fair but that there were also advantages to being the youngest. Name one? Being able to learn from the older ones, even from their mistakes. Though that's not to say one doesn't go on to make one's own errors.

One of mine that day was trusting the young man selling potatoes outside Sedec. I knew the price was a little high, but we had to eat. Besides, Victor made good French fries, and they were my kids' favorite food. Maybe they would finally get their fill. There were a lot of potatoes in that container.

It was tightly bound with a flexible vine rope. Through the open weave of the square basket, I could see good looking potatoes on top and around all four sides. A canny shopper, I tilted the basket to have a look at the bottom, halfway expecting to find some rotten potatoes there. So much for my suspicious nature, everything looked fine. I bargained the price down a bit and felt quite pleased about the whole matter. I didn't know my potato-purchase satisfaction would last only until Monday morning.

Karen and I continued our Saturday outing, and when finished, I considered it a fairly successful shopping trip. True, I was too late to buy any bread at the bakeries. Those days, their meager production sold quickly. However, my timing was excellent at another shop. A small shipment of imported cheese was being put on display just as Karen and I walked in. Zaire itself produced no cheese because it had no dairy industry.

In the same shop, I stood in a crowd milling around the sparsely stocked meat counter. I watched as the butcher sold meat cuts I wanted to other people who had arrived later than I. For a long time I couldn't seem to get my turn. Assertiveness training later became a regular business in the United States. I had a do-it-yourself course each shopping trip in Kinshasa. My main trouble was that I found it difficult to be assertive in floundering French.

Nevertheless, I finally managed to buy a piece of beef that I would be able to cut up for stew. It seemed a good choice to go with our bonanza of potatoes. The butcher's supply of pork consisted of a few large ham bones. I chose the one with the most meat attached as it would nicely flavor a pot of bean soup. I moved on to the small produce section, where the head of cauliflower I saw was a rare sight. It seemed almost too good to be true. In a way it was. There was no way I would pay that price, the equivalent of several American dollars. I put the cauliflower back and settled for the withered carrots because they were cheaper and would taste fine in the ragout I planned.

On the drive home we were glad to see our favorite grandmotherly crone selling *pistolets* by the side of the road. These ten-inch-long bread rolls would go well with the cheese and olives we had found. All in all, the family food situation was in pretty good shape for the coming week or so.

As we neared home, I hoped the same could be said for Project Cage. The boys and Sam greeted us at the gate. Until the hinges started to sag, thus hampering its opening and closing, our kids liked to step onto the gate to ride as it swung open and closed. Jim repaired and oiled the hinges, and we forbade any repeat acrobatic performances on the gate. Now I saw the children had taught the trick to Sam. It wasn't likely his lighter weight would damage anything, so I saw no reason to spoil the fun.

What I was really interested in was the cage. Was it finished already? I didn't hear any sawing or hammering. I drove the car to the far side of the house to park. Where was the cage? There—it was by the fence. My heart sank. Yes, the cage looked finished. And it would make a great little rabbit hutch. Damn!

My husband strolled out of the house onto the veranda. He had a pleased, welcoming look on his face. That quickly changed when he saw the look on mine. "You don't like it," he said.

"I haven't really had a chance to look at it." I stalled as I supervised the unloading of the car. How was I going to handle this? I didn't really know, except I had a feeling it wasn't going to be very well.

"I told you she wouldn't like it," Mike muttered as he passed his brother.

The inevitable can only be delayed, not stopped. I had to walk over and examine the cage. Defying the law of physics, it seemed to get smaller the closer I got to it. In effect I was looking at a duplex. Our parrot occupied the right side. The left and slightly larger side—but only slightly—was for Sam.

*Perhaps my husband thought to kill two birds with one cage,* I thought inanely. *Yes, and Sam might very well die if kept confined in this glorified chicken coop.* My silent conversation with myself went on.

"What do you think, Mom?" My family had followed me.

"I think Sam is a very active chimpanzee, not a damned rabbit or rooster!" With that I stalked off toward the house. I was right. I wasn't going to handle the situation at all well.

It being Saturday afternoon, the servants were gone for the weekend. Consequently, I had the kitchen to myself. I hoped it would stay that way for a while. I needed some time to myself. I started putting away the groceries the kids had carried inside and dumped on the floor. I stopped short of slamming doors and drawers, but just barely. I found myself slam-banging things into place as I tried to vent my annoyance and frustration.

It hadn't been a very big shopping trip, so things were all too quickly put away. The fact that I was wishing for a few dozen more groceries just so I could continue banging things struck me as childish and silly. I decided to calm down and work the problem. Indulging my annoyance would just delay a solution.

My husband was reading in the living room.

"I'm sorry I got upset," I said.

"And I'm sorry I didn't build the cage to suit you, but I'm not a mind reader."

Obviously I wasn't the only one upset.

"I didn't really have anything specific in mind," I said placatingly.

"Oh, really? From the way you acted I thought maybe you expected him to have his own house, a two-story mansion perhaps."

"That's it!" I said excitedly. My husband's sarcasm had triggered an image in my mind.

"Well, I'm sorry but I think you're being ridiculous. That cage is plenty big enough for him to sleep in, and during the day he's got the whole yard to roam around in."

Oh, brother! I thought about the recent past and the merry chase that chimp had led all of us. Well, not quite all. Obviously my husband had remained oblivious to any difficulties.

Jim didn't like being unduly bothered by problems at home and counted on me to take care of things, or else to clue him in if I thought his concern and attention was warranted. Since my husband's job often took him away from home, he wasn't always around to handle our problems, even if he were so inclined.

For the most part, I took as a compliment Jim's unbounded confidence that I could handle anything and everything. Only occasionally did I fight down feelings of being overworked and underappreciated. Jim tended to tune in mostly when there was a problem around home. Consequently, our system didn't get me many pats on the back for a job well done. However, life was interesting and far too busy to allow any of us the indulgence of more than brief self-pity. Besides, to me seriously indulged self-pity seemed so unproductive and such a waste of time and energy.

Therefore, I proceeded to explain to Jim that the chimpanzee had to be confined during the day as well. The servants and I had more to do than constantly watching Sam to keep him—and us—out of trouble. However, being such an active animal meant he needed an enclosure large enough to allow him to work off some of that energy.

"I know you were joking about a 'two-story mansion,'" I said, "but it's given me an idea. Why not a sort of modified version of an African hut?"

"What do I know about building an African hut?" exploded my husband.

"Absolutely nothing, dear." And I smiled semisweetly. "That's the part you'll like best. I won't expect you to do it. After all, who better to build an African hut than an African?"

"Victor?"

"No. Actually I was thinking of Joseph, though I imagine Victor will get into the act with ideas and supervision."

"He'll very likely have to. I don't think Joseph can do it by himself."

"You may be right," I agreed. "Certainly I doubt if he could do the design part, but I've got that fixed in my mind now. I bet if I can just explain it to him, Joseph will be able to do it."

"Maybe." My husband remained skeptical.

# Sam Is Lost

▨ ▧ ▨

Since Sam's arrival, we had curtailed our evening social life. Not that evenings out were all that frequent before his advent, but Sam's living with us sans cage meant that chimp-sitting chewed up an enormous amount of our time. However, there we were with a Saturday night and a cage for Sam—albeit one neither he nor I was happy with. Since Sam was incarcerated, we no longer had to be.

Our family decided on a night out at AERWA, the American Employee's Recreation and Work Association of which we were associate members. The facility had a snack bar, and on most Saturday nights a movie was shown outdoors at the site in Djelo Binza, a suburb of Kinshasa. People supplied their own seating, and we felt fortunate to have folding chairs to take along. We had only three or four of them, so not all of us could sit at the same time. However, the boys were usually wandering, or in motion anyway, or else perched someplace with their friends. Sitting on the ground was not considered a good idea given Zaire's abundant bug life.

We prepared for some of the bug life we'd meet at the movie by lining up on our veranda to spray with whatever bug repellant we had available. From past experience, we knew AERWA moviegoers were number one on the mosquitos' snack list.

Sam sadly and silently watched our departure ritual through the chicken-wire mesh of his jail cell. Chocko too was quiet as he watched from his perch next to our little primate. The parrot's silence was nothing new. That bird never did learn to talk. It's only verbal trick was the imitation of the guinea fowl it heard next door. Maybe the bird used up its vocal cords on that one accomplishment. Our parrot sometimes managed to sound like the whole guinea-fowl flock.

Facing off: Sam and pal Chocko

Despite this feat, that bird was a disappointment to me. I hadn't expected to carry on erudite conversations with the parrot. I would gladly have settled for brief discussions of Polly and her crackers. This bird rarely even mentioned cocoa. And those two syllables, I was told, came naturally to this species of parrot. Quite naturally too, this accounted for the fact that most parrots of our acquaintance were named Cocoa.

"See how the bird says its own name," boasted each proud owner.

I wanted our bird's name to be just a little different. With a somewhat humorous play on words in mind, I mentally ran through my favorite cocoa-candy bar list. Hershey, Nestle, and Ghiradelli were rejected. I thought these might be too difficult for the bird to enunciate, if indeed it tried to proclaim its name to the world. The parrot occasionally made clicking sounds, which I thought might enable it to easily begin another name on my cocoa list. Cadbury didn't fly with my family though, and we argued to a compromise: Cocoa, Chocolate, and finally...Chocko.

Chocko liked to perch on the veranda railing or on the backs of chairs. Early on I didn't think about how painful a bite from his powerful beak might be. I was comfortable enough when the parrot perched and peered over my shoulder as I pecked away at my typewriter. He seemed fascinated by the clicking keys. Later I wondered about the staccato bursts of clicks that Chocko let loose with. Maybe that was his imitation of my best bursts of typing. The parrot also liked to perforate paper. He once got hold of a letter I wrote to my mother, and it looked as if someone had added swear words in Braille. I sent it off anyway but first scribbled an explanation.

We all tried, and then gave up on, teaching that bird to talk, each of us reduced to the same muttered phrase, "Stupid bird, stupid bird." I started expecting the parrot to repeat that to us sometime, but it didn't.

However, the bird had some smarts after all. We learned this on our return from that Saturday night movie. The children were first to see that Sam's section of the cage was empty. Sam was nowhere around, but we saw how he'd gotten out. The wire mesh was neatly snipped, and Jim wondered aloud if someone had stolen Sam. We'd recently turned down an offer of three hundred zaire for him, which was then equivalent to five or six hundred U.S. dollars. A closer look at the cage, though, eliminated that theory. It was obvious Sam's friend Chocko had lent a hand, or rather a beak, to the escape.

The wire separating parrot and primate was cut in a neat, vertical line. The parrot had evidently begun at the top and methodically snipped each little piece. Then Chocko must have repeated the process for the front of his cage, thus allowing Sam into his side of the cage and then out into the night. As if to prove the accuracy of this theory, which we were discussing in front of his cage, Chocko stretched his neck and snipped a few wires to show us how it was done. His beak made a great pair of wire cutters. I doubted I'd ever again be comfortable hand-feeding him. Or what about when I'd lean my head back as Chocko perched on my chair? Maybe I was lucky he hadn't pierced my ears.

So far as I know, Chocko never bothered to leave the cage that night. It was as if he'd simply done a favor for a friend. Or maybe he'd gotten rid of a bothersome tenant, one who ruffled his feathers, literally.

We searched high and low for Sam, but he seemed to have vanished. How quickly that chimpanzee had captured our hearts. We were saddened to think he'd left us so soon. I wondered what had so frightened him that he'd run away after breaking out of his jail. I knew that dogs and cats were known to trail after their humans. I wondered if somehow Sam had attempted to follow us. Whatever the reason for his absence, I thought it unlikely we'd see him again. The animal was worth money. If found unhurt he'd likely be sold or kept for a pet. Being a pet would probably be best for him as he lacked the skills to survive in the wild. I hoped he wouldn't end up in a stew pot.

Early the next morning, while my family still slept, I pondered our loss over a cup of coffee. Standing just outside the kitchen door on the veranda, I stared toward the empty cage and wished I would see Sam appear. In answer to the thought, there was movement nearby. Under the ironing table was a basket of clothes to be ironed. Sam had burrowed in and bedded down, completely hidden from view. He must have slept through our search the night before. It hadn't occurred to any of us to give more than a cursory glance to the basket, which looked as if it contained only clothes.

Hand in hand, Sam and I went to tell the family it was a good morning. I suspected young Jim would be pleased to have the chimp as an excuse to skip church. Mike would be annoyed that he couldn't be the one to stay home and chimp-sit, but at that time, he was Father John's only altar server for the Mass in English at St. Luke's.

By Monday morning I had looked up the French words to explain to Victor and Joseph my brainstorm about Sam's "house," and my notion that Joseph would build it. Victor was as skeptical as Jim of Joseph's ability to handle the project. However, I was sure I remembered Joseph saying he had helped build his one-room hut in the village where he lived. What I was mainly concerned with was whether he knew how to thatch the roof. With a yes answer to that question, I quashed Victor's teasing skepticism and affirmed my confidence in Joseph's skill.

I made it clear to Victor that I expected him to be supportive of this primate-house project. I also pointed out to him and Joseph the benefit of a properly built hut-cum-cage. It would free the three of us from tripping over and traipsing after that little bundle of energy, our chimp. We all agreed on that good thought, and then went about our Monday morning duties.

Victor soon called me back to the kitchen. He'd unpacked my Saturday potato purchase, and they were good potatoes—what there were of them. Then he showed me how I'd been swindled. It was a uniquely constructed basket. It had a top, bottom, and sides, all of which I had carefully examined.

What it didn't have was a middle. This area was taken up, not by potatoes, but by a mass of sticks and stones and tangled vines. *Caveat emptor*, buyer beware. In spite of my wariness and thorough examination of that basket, I hadn't been aware enough.

The incident spurred my learning of French. I made it a point to learn the French word for thief and enough others on the subject, so that when I next saw the young man who had deceived me, I could give full measure for the short measure I had received. I considered it a most satisfactory encounter two months later when I had the opportunity to fire a fixed salvo of French at that trickster. Some of his potential customers were warned away by it.

Sam continued to be a source of entertainment for all of us and our guests. Sometimes the chimp's antics proved embarrassing. He seemed a lecherous little animal at times. The chimpanzee sometimes sneaked up on the ladies to lift their skirts for a lewd look.

"Ah, Mom, he's just curious." Yeah, right. I let myself be convinced until the day our chimpanzee mounted the leg of a woman guest. It was a decidedly sexual act, and it took two of us, at some risk, to pry him loose. Henceforth, Sam was banished to his cage the instant guests arrived.

Consequently, I felt no qualms the time a guest sat in Sam's chair. Sam was in his cage and wouldn't even know. We'd taken to calling this particular living room chair Sam's because, in desperation, I'd allowed Sam on that one chair in hopes of keeping him off all the other furniture. The bargain worked.

We even managed to potty train Sam, at least to the extent that he bounced onto this chair, then up to the open window, where he pointed outdoors to urinate. He could also slip through the window bars to get in and out if he were so inclined. Sometimes in passing through, Sam gave a tug to the blue drapes if he noticed me watching and wanted some action—or reaction.

Sam made his objections known a time or two when someone occupied "his" chair. So rather than have an unsuspecting guest upset, and on the theory that the animal chair might be dirtier than the others, it became standard practice for one of us family members to sit there. But one day when a guest beat us to that chair, I knew Sam was in his cage and wouldn't bother the man. And the chair was clean enough. It seemed one of those lazy Sunday afternoons, a time to enjoy the afterglow of a good meal with good company.

Partway into our relaxing time, Cat jumped up from the outside and sat on the inside of the window ledge. Felines too found it easy to slip through the bars if the window was open. Sitting a few inches from our guest's head, Cat surveyed the living room scene. I made a slight move to get up and do something about Cat, but the man's wife indicated with a motion of her hand that I was not to bother; the cat was fine. As time went on, I think we all thought the man was aware of the cat's presence and that he chose to ignore it.

Our desultory conversation turned to talk of snakes, and each interesting story prompted another. It was then that Cat chose to stretch forth a paw with gentle claws to tap our guest's neck. The gesture caused our friend a near heart attack. In the context of snake stories, the cat's claws must have felt like fangs. After the smelling salts worked, we learned the man was totally unaware of the cat's presence.

Cat and our chimpanzee were friends. They seemed to have a gentle rapport and often spent time together. I never saw them upset with each other.

Not so the relationship between our chimp and Chocko the parrot, whom Sam loved to plague. To promote a squawk of protest, Sam tried to pluck a tail feather. He never succeeded but the parrot always squawked on cue. Also on cue, the parrot retaliated and used his powerful beak to nip Sam. Someone asked if that was how our chimp lost part of a finger. No, though that could have been possible. Sam was missing that finger segment when he came to us.

The interaction between chimp and parrot convinced me that, in at least some instances, the chimpanzee had a clear concept of cause and effect. He knew he'd get nipped, and Sam screwed his face up in painful anticipation each time he edged close enough to dart a hand at the parrot. Evidently the screeching squawk made Sam's painful nip from the parrot worthwhile.

Sam also knew how to get a rise out of me. If bored, he deliberately sat by one of the blue drapes and waited to make sure I saw him. Then, looking straight at me and grinning, he reached out an arm to tug gently on the drape. If I didn't react to this cue for a game of tag, Sam forced the issue by yanking on the drape until I went to its rescue.

Sam loved to play with our children, and they with him. Michael and he played many a game of hide and seek. Jimmy tried to teach Sam to toss a Frisbee and had some measure of success, though none at all in teaching him to catch one. Sam either fled from the oncoming Frisbee or sat and cowered with his arms covering his head.

Though the boys monopolized Sam, he and Karen became friends too. Sam liked to push Karen on the old tire swing in the yard, sometimes hopping aboard to share the ride.

If any of the children cried or whimpered when Sam was out and about, his tender heart came into play. At such times he dispensed long-armed hugs, soothing chimpanzee grunts and woofs, and clumsy, but encouraging, pats on the back.

Victor and Joseph continued to like Sam, despite the slight addition to their workload he created. Joseph would scold Sam when he purposely dumped his water dish. I don't know whether it was the dry dish or some dietary need that caused our chimpanzee to occasionally recycle his urine. I thought drinking one's own urine a decidedly distasteful act. I still think so, despite its reported recommendation as a health aid by Prime Minister Morarji Desai of India in the late 1970s.

Victor sometimes liked to test our chimp's reaction to something new in his environment. For instance, what did Sam think of ice? Who knows? The ensuing conversation was pretty one-sided. It was fun, however, to watch Sam's cautious investigation of the large icicle Victor put in his cage. So much so that Victor made it a tradition each time he defrosted our refrigerator. Sam seemed puzzled to see the ice melt. He always poked at it with an exploratory forefinger and gave ice and water a tentative taste test.

# Snakes

Snakes were the bane of my existence in Zaire. I was someone who fled from harmless garter snakes in the United States. Actually, I wasn't sure what a garter snake looked like because I'd never stayed around one long enough to find out. If something slithered, I was out of there.

In their early years, if my children insisted on visiting the zoo's reptile house, they at that point became solely my husband's responsibility. I waited outside. If he was absent, I tried to escort them through with my eyes closed.

"Oh, Mom, you gotta see this."

"No, I don't gotta."

Garter snakes are a North American species. There aren't any in Africa. In fact, I never heard of any harmless snakes in Africa. Where we lived in Zaire, they were all deadly, ranging from the little lethal viper to the enormous python who could hug its victim to death. Venomous varieties in between included cobras and mambas.

For me living with the constant possibility of snakes being present was more than a challenge or a cross to bear. It was an exercise in subduing terror—stark fear. I never completely won that battle, but I did somehow reduce my fear to manageable proportions. I managed this mainly, I think, for the sake of my family and other persons who might depend on me not to fall apart in an emergency.

Living in Mont N'Gafula—out in the low-rent district, as I sometimes called it—we were too far from medical help in Kinshasa, should someone get bitten by a snake. The venom works quickly; first-aid needed to be swift and sure. We kept in our refrigerator an antivenin kit that I prayed I'd never to have to use. Doctor and nurse friends talked me through the procedure of using the kit. I'm not a nurse. I'd never given anyone an injection, but I figured I could if it meant the difference between life and death. I would have liked the luxury of a little practice, perhaps shooting a syringe of water into a grapefruit. However, not only did we not have grapefruit, we didn't have extra syringes with which to rehearse.

Even Mama Yemo Hospital in Kinshasa was short of these, though I understood they eased their predicament slightly by finding a way to sterilize and reuse so-called disposable syringes and needles. What was meant to be a one-shot deal could thus be stretched a time or two. I admired the ingenuity and inventiveness of some of the Mama Yemo staff. And I joined in the effort to help the hospital by saving glass jars for use there. Some of these would be used as specimen jars while others would be incorporated into homemade medical apparatus. My thrifty nature applauded the lack of waste. At the same time, I was appalled by the hospital's need.

Fortunately for my composure, we seldom actually saw a snake in Mont N'Gafula. However, we learned to recognize the pattern their bodies left as they wriggled across the dirt yard near the house. We kept a wary eye out for these tracks and traced them to reassure ourselves that a snake hadn't entered our home. If the tracks indicated that horrendous possibility, a ginger but thorough search of the dwelling ensued. Our concrete-walled, L-shaped, one-story house was usually open in Zaire's warm climate. Even closed it was sort of open, as there were no screens and not all the doors and windows shut tightly. Iron bars at the windows and on the glass doors provided security against human intruders. Creepy, crawly, and slithery invaders could find access.

Those purposeful searches for snakes in the house never produced anything except temporary peace of mind. Actual snake incidents always came unexpectedly. I was glad of Victor's and Joseph's vigilance. Each of them, in separate incidents, dispatched a snake on the veranda just as the creature was about to slither into the house. I was glad, too, for our little tiger-colored domestic cat, which was adept at snake killing—though not adept enough, as it turned out. My husband found our cat dead beside the car one morning. We surmised that it lost a battle with a viper. Cat, its name as well as its genus, would be sorely missed. He combined an independent spirit with a lovable personality, and a talent around the house for dispatching unwanted animal life. With one swipe of a paw, Cat would zing a roach or a beetle off the veranda. In at least one instance I think Cat saved a life.

Our lone bathroom was at the end of a long hall, off which were the children's bedrooms. Jim's and my bedroom was probably intended to be a den or study, as it was off the living room. In any case, we had a long trek to the bathroom. Very early one morning, I was sleepily trudging enroute there when I saw something on the hall floor. *Karen's lost her hair band again.*

I started to reach down to pick it up but decided to answer nature's call first. Returning from the bathroom, I was wider awake and saw that the "hair band" was a recently dead snake, a viper. I'm convinced Cat killed it. I'm also certain the snake would have gone into one of the children's rooms had Cat not stopped it short.

Some people like snakes. Okay, to each his own, but somehow it always surprises me to find that someone I know actually owns snakes—on purpose. Returning home one dark midnight in Mont N'Gafula, where of course there were no street lights, I volunteered to get out of our car and open the gate. As I did so, a disembodied voice in the dark greeted me a moment before a flashlight snapped on.

"Oh, John, you did give me a start!" It was our Scotsman neighbor from down the road a bit. "Everything all right? Are you just out for a late night stroll?"

"Well, no. I've lost me pet python, and I don't know where to find it."

Shades of Little Bo-Peep. Was he teasing me? I wondered. No. Further explanation was forthcoming, and he really did have a pet python, except now he didn't have it and that bothered him. It bothered me too.

"So, ta-ta. Give us a shout if you find me pet python, won't you?"

"John, I can guarantee it. Except if I find your pet python, that shout is going to be a scream."

It had been an interesting conversation. Until then I'd never thought of a snake as a guard dog, but that's the function this python served. Like me, most Zaireans avoided snakes when possible. John made sure all his local workers either saw the snake or were aware of its presence in the house, and the fact that it sometimes roamed the rooms at will. No jungle drums of the past were needed to spread the word. Grapevine gossip worked just as well because nothing nor no one went unnoticed in Mont N'Gafula. The few Europeans remaining there (we were the only Americans) kept large dogs to guard against robbery. John and his family kept two or three dogs in addition to snakes and other animals.

When we moved in, several people advised us that a large guard dog or two was necessary for our protection. I vetoed the idea. Maybe my gut instincts were naive, but I felt our best protection lay in developing a mutual liking and trust with the local Zaireans. Besides, I wasn't too fond of big dogs. I tended to feel intimidated when a dog was big enough to put its paws on my shoulders and look down at me. And I most certainly was not going to entertain the idea of our having a python protector, even though Victor and Joseph confirmed the validity of John's story.

Despite my dislike of snakes, I found facts about them interesting. Victor told me spitting cobras were thought to aim their venom at the white of a person's eyes. To avoid being blinded, village people put something white at chest level if they had to walk through an area known to contain these cobras. Should any of them receive a stream of venom to the eyes, the person might hope for a companion to immediately provide a stream of urine. This was believed, in such cases, to be a somewhat effective eyewash. My own eyes blinked rapidly at just the thought of that solution.

I learned snakes not only travel on the ground but also from tree to tree. Some trees of the wooded area next to us shaded our property, with branches extending over one end of our house. The occasional "thunk" on our roof worried me—particularly after neighbors told us of finding a dried snakeskin under the eaves of their house. From the skin's markings and length, they surmised it might have been shed by a python but, because of timing, probably not John's pet.

One day I heard shouts about a serpent from the wooded property's caretaker, which was actually the Swiss Recreation Club and used mostly on weekends. Victor joined me briefly at the window to point out the snake, and I told him I hoped the snake would be caught and killed. He went out to speak to the caretaker and soon a number of men arrived to hunt the snake. Their eventual success cost me a case of my husband's beer. I had not realized that my wish would be their command. Therefore, I was surprised to have the dead snake triumphantly presented to me along with a demand for money. This I refused, which upset the leader of the group. I asked him to wait and went to the kitchen to ask Victor's help. He explained, and convinced me, that I should give the men something for their efforts, but I was adamant it wasn't going to be money.

I probably missed the chance to become the pseudo-St. Patrick of Mont N'Gafula. Had I paid money for a dead snake, Mont N'Gafula might have become as snake-free as Ireland, where, legend has it, St. Patrick drove them out. Except that in Mont N'Gafula there would have been a mountain of snake bodies piled up in our yard. Neither our budget nor my nerves would have stood the strain. The case of beer, minus one bottle saved for my husband, was a negotiated settlement of my perceived debt. None of the men were totally happy about receiving just one bottle of beer for their efforts, including my husband on his return from work that evening.

As time went on, I learned to recognize the distressed twittering of wild birds that told of a snake in their domain. But no more large-scale snake hunts ensued. However, I was shocked one day to overhear young Jim and his friend, Johannes, planning their next viper hunt. Obviously not everyone in our family shared my aversion for snakes. Johannes came by his interest naturally from his stepfather, John, the python hunter. The thought of these teenage boys hunting vipers terrified me, but, realistically, I knew there was no way I could enforce an order against it. I settled for giving them a lecture on how lethal and quick the viper could be, and the boys patiently put up with it. Privately I prayed for their safety—to good purpose perhaps, as the boys survived their snake encounters. A couple of years after we left Zaire, our family was saddened to learn that Johannes and his sister Ella, Karen's friend, did not survive an encounter with a lethal drunken driver.

Even Kinshasa International Airport had its share of snakes. One evening, my husband walked through its dark and deserted outside passageway. There was just enough light to discern the black mamba he disturbed. I was disturbed when he told me about it. Fortunately, the snake chose flight not fight, and so did my husband.

Jim told me too of the delayed DC-4. At first light, a mechanic went to climb up to the plane's nosegear strut only to find it already occupied by a green mamba. The mechanic needed to step up on that strut in order to reach up and plug in the battery cart. This would provide electrical power to the airplane. But the snake was there before him, having coiled itself firmly for a snooze in the night. The sleeping snake was automatically assigned to the category of sleeping dogs (and sleeping lions?): the mechanic and everyone else let it lie. Periodically someone would check to see if the snake was gone. Finally, the well-rested serpent disappeared, and the flight took off hours late. I wondered to what category the airline charged the delay.

My husband's best, or worst, snake experience occurred at home in Mont N'Gafula, where he arrived early from work one day. No one was home that mid-afternoon except Joseph, who was ironing on the veranda. Sam remained unusually quiet in his cage. Jim proceeded to relax in our living room in his favorite chair, his latest copy of *Flight International* in hand. Peace and quiet reigned, disturbed only by the rustling of pages as Jim read his magazine. But wait—there was a rustle, and he hadn't turned a page. He glanced up to see a cobra crawl out from under the sofa just a few feet away. The afternoon remained deathly quiet, but peace had fled, and I suspect Jim would have liked to, too. He eased himself out of and behind the chair. The movement caught the cobra's attention. Jim then had no doubt of the type of snake he faced as the serpent paused, raised its head, and flared its classic hood. Jim no longer enjoyed the quiet and shattered it with a shout.

"Joseph! Quickly! There is a serpent here."

"Oui, *Patron*." Joseph entered with a machete in hand, took one look, gulped, turned on his heel and fled.

This was too much for Jim, whose French also fled. He yelled in English, "Joseph, come back here!" It was part command, part plea.

Joseph didn't understand English, but he hadn't deserted. Instead, he'd rushed out to exchange the short machete for something longer. He returned carrying a long-handled shovel.

The commotion caused the snake to retreat under the sofa. Jim outlined to Joseph the plan of attack. If they were lucky, they would be attacking the snake and not vice versa. Jim worried that the snake would escape into our bedroom-cum-storage room, whose door was next to the sofa. With the unavoidable clutter in that room, the snake would have plenty of places to hide. Jim forced himself to walk carefully to the bedroom door and close it, keeping one eye out for the snake all the while. Fortunately, that door was among the few in the house that fitted flush with the floor. Once the door was closed, the cobra could not slither under it.

That task accomplished, Jim again joined Joseph. The two of them bent to take hold of the living room rug. On the count of *un, deux, trois,* they yanked the rug from under the sofa. And riding the rug was the cobra, quite literally spitting-mad. Because Jim was wearing glasses, he felt his eyes were better protected from the cobra's venom than were Joseph's. Consequently, Jim's plan called for him to distract the snake while Joseph dispatched it. The plan worked.

I arrived home later with the children to be greeted by an excited, voluble Victor rushing out to the veranda. Once I heard "snake in the house," I was too tense to sort out French verb tenses. I wasn't sure whether we were talking past or present. I also wasn't walking into the house until I found out. My French comprehension needed some help, and I glanced around for clues. Joseph was quietly, methodically ironing. I knew he liked to iron clothes, but that grin on his face was out of all proportion to normal job satisfaction. Jim strolled out just then with an unnatural nonchalance and a grin that matched Joseph's. Obviously Victor's snake was past tense.

We found the living room only slightly the worse for wear after combat. The children dashed outside to view the corpse before Joseph flung it far into the overgrown field behind us. I chose to be a practicing coward and stayed put. I had no desire to see that snake, dead or alive.

I couldn't help but wonder, though, whether that was the only snake. Since arriving in Kinshasa, I'd always heard that cobras come in pairs, or at least one should assume they do. Newcomers were invariably told the story, perhaps apocryphal, of the trick some children decided to play on their mother. A cobra had been killed inside their house. Then the children, so the story went, took the dead cobra and placed it in their mother's bed. That evening, they encouraged their mother to go to bed early. The children then waited in excited anticipation for the scream, which never came. When they tiptoed into the silence, they found their mother dead—a victim of the live cobra coiled around its dead mate.

I'd made sure that my children, particularly my practical-joker sons, heard that story more than once. It sprang easily to mind as I surveyed our living room and listened to my husband's latest-and-greatest snake story. There was no way I was going to bed that night unless every nook and cranny of our house was searched and shown to be snake-free.

It was.

# Food

iving off the local economy in Kinshasa was far more of a challenge
than it had been in Nairobi. My coping skills were tested, but I was
determined to successfully contend with whatever problems came
my way. I hoped that my children would take their cue from my positive
attitude and do likewise. Most of all, I was determined not to *be* the problem.
Overseas I'd heard enough of, "Such a shame about so-and-so. His wife just
couldn't handle life here, so they had to leave." Sometimes that was true.
But it still seemed the era when, rightly or wrongly, wives got blamed for a
lot of things.

I once overheard two American men talking. "Why did so-and-so leave
his contract early?"

"I don't know. His wife probably couldn't cope."

"Oh, do you know her?"

"No."

Right. Or maybe wrong.

Most of the wives I knew overseas shared my wanting-to-cope attitude.
I was regaling some of them in Kinshasa with my account of a particularly
horrendous week of problems overcome in Mont N'Gafula when, attracted
by the laughter, a young American Embassy wife wandered over to listen.
She soon startled me with, "How can you live like that? I don't mean to be
rude, but I just wouldn't put up with that kind of life!"

"Well, aren't you lucky you don't have to."

I felt that the official Americans in developing countries were sometimes a little out of touch with the real world. They often lived in big, beautiful houses that were well equipped, even if with standard-issue furnishings. Official Americans were usually able to employ more or less competent, local staff to help run and maintain their homes abroad. Somewhere they had at least a mini-department of bureaucracy to soothe and smooth problems. Someplace too there would be a private commissary in which to shop for familiar food. While the commissary might not be stocked with the hundred-plus breakfast-cereal choices of their favorite supermarket back home, a more than adequate supply of whatever was needed could usually be counted on.

As unofficial Americans overseas, not representing our government in any way, we lived off the local economy. We weren't entitled, nor did we hope, to shop at the commissary or share in its bounty. I was conscientious about this. If it looked to me as if a natural friendship was developing between me and someone who had commissary privileges, I tried to minimize embarrassment by bringing the subject up first. I knew it was against the rules for them to share commissary goods, and I made it clear that only friendship, not goodies, was my goal. They would never have to worry that I'd ask for, or expect, anything from their private supermarket. In this one respect, I sometimes felt a little sorry for official Americans overseas, in that they could not always be sure they were liked for themselves rather than their access to things American.

I remember one woman—not an American—who had lived in many developing countries. I overheard her confide that her first priority in each place was to cultivate someone connected with the American Embassy commissary. On hearing this, I smiled inwardly, and a bit ruefully, as she had seemed to be promoting a friendship with me. Was she in for a surprise! Sure enough, her initial enthusiasm on meeting me and my American accent vanished when she learned I had no commissary connection.

Some other embassies and companies also had access to private stock. I learned this when a British woman in Zaire not-so-gently informed me that, though we were friends, she wouldn't be able to buy anything for me. At first I didn't understand what she was talking about. Buy me what? I didn't want her to buy me anything. She mentioned sugar, but I hadn't asked nor even hinted, at least not knowingly. Obviously she thought I had.

"Hey, the only game I'm playing here is bridge." But I don't think she was totally convinced, and though we continued to play cards, our friendship was never quite the same.

Many of my memories of Africa have to do with food, particularly when we lived in Zaire, where there was an increasing shortage of food during our years there. Food was such a large part of my family job—finding food, budgeting for and buying it, disinfecting it, or—in a number of cases— salvaging what I could of the food when the bugs got to it before I did. And of course preparing and cooking it. In this I had Victor's help. He told me he'd once been a premier chef in a French restaurant.

Victor was a good cook and felt his talents were wasted on housecleaning duties. When he asked permission to train Joseph, our yard man, for those tasks, I readily agreed. As time went on, Victor did most of the cooking, and I did all the baking and specialty things, such as making mayonnaise and peanut butter. As Victor put it, "Restaurant? C'est moi. *Patisserie?* C'est Madame."

I also made the salads. I think my family considered my potato or macaroni salads my personal specialties. Or perhaps these were home-country comfort foods for which Victor just couldn't have the right touch.

It was in our African travels that I learned to disregard the phrase, "as American as apple pie." Apples were a treat there, and on hearing my hostess announce that the dessert would be apple pie, my taste buds all but swooned in anticipation. Far from home, they salivated in expectation as my brain conjured up a delicious image of American apple pie. My brain and its image went tilt at what was set before me. The concoction resembled a piece of apple pie only to the extent that it was a triangular wedge. I ate it and I suspect it was quite good, but my taste buds and mental-image-center insisted on conversing. They wanted to shout "cheat" at every bite. A single crumb-crust filled with flavored applesauce and topped with ordinary cream still does not meet my American definition of apple pie.

Victor and I shared food ideas. Via Victor, I think I introduced plantain chips to Kinshasa. I'd learned to make them in Puerto Rico and considered them a great substitute for potato chips. Unlike me, Victor was good at deep frying things and he liked to do it. Certainly it was a pleasure for me to turn this chore over to him.

He promptly improved on my tedious method of thinly slicing the plantains with a sharp knife. The potato peeler, which Okech had tried to talk me out of when I left Kenya, made short work of these green banana-look-alikes. Victor wielded that potato peeler more efficiently than Okech, though not with the same enthusiasm.

I would have liked to have left the gadget with Okech, but that simple potato peeler was an essential part of my kitchen, and I had no way of replacing it. Receiving something like that in the mail from abroad was unlikely. There were just too many opportunities for things to go missing in Africa's mail service. And should something actually arrive in the mail, import duties could make it costly and inconvenient to pick up. Early on, I gave up the idea of asking anyone back home to send us anything.

When I thought of utilizing Victor's expertise with deep frying, doughnuts came to mind. Doughnut *holes* came to mind when I experimented with a recipe and couldn't get it to work. Each cake doughnut insisted on oozing into a single blob. Forget it. I told Victor to scoop up a blob to begin with and plop it into the hot oil. It was less work, certainly less frustration, and the taste was the same. Everyone within sampling distance declared them a success. When a local Zairean asked what they were, Victor proudly proclaimed them to be *beignets Americain*.

Later, when it came time for us to leave Zaire, Victor asked for some of my recipes. He was going to be an entrepreneur, beginning with plantain chips and *beignets Americain*. I realized he had already done his market research. Not for nothing had he encouraged my generosity. Feed the hungry indeed. And if they like it, sell it to them? Why not if they can afford those few *makuta*. I wished Victor and his family well in their pursuit of a good living. I hoped my recipes might help.

Life in Africa was a do-it-yourself course in back-to-basics. Except for toilet paper and the occasional box of rough tissues, which would never be mistaken for Kleenex, we used practically no household paper-products in Africa. We used cloth napkins daily out of necessity, not elegance. Actually, we used and reused them daily for maybe a week. By that time they were distinctly lacking in elegance. I bought wooden, carved-animal napkin rings for our family. Each of us had a distinctive holder, so we'd not get our napkins mixed up. After each meal, we'd refold our napkin and place it in the appropriate napkin ring. In order to avoid squabbles, I designated which ring was for whom. I tried for some appropriateness in this. For instance, the skinny lion seemed made for skinny Michael, and the children agreed that their father should have the stern-visaged, mad-looking African-mask napkin ring. Jim accepted it in good humor. Left for me was the carved fish which, if there was to be descriptive character commentary, I preferred to think of as graceful rather than cold.

When we washed our hands, we dried them on cloth towels. We cleaned up spills with rags, not paper towels. The bacon was drained on a newspaper if we had one, or it dripped grease on us if we hadn't. "Brown-bagging it" had meaning only for commissary kids. Our children took their lunches to school in plastic food-storage boxes. When these, in Zaire, contained my prized plantain chips, chocolate cookies, or peanut brittle, my kids sometimes exercised their bartering skills. They traded with the commissary kids for Cracker Jacks or American candy bars.

Back-to-basics really came into play regarding food in Zaire. I learned to practice the art-of-the-possible, as in—There are twelve people coming to dinner, what can I possibly feed them? What food was on hand? What food could I afford to buy? What food could I even find to buy?

With adequate answers to these questions, I looked forward to my dinner party for twelve. Our Mont N'Gafula vegetable man was a help. He walked the area once a week carrying a wooden box atop his head. He always seemed glad to set it down at our place and have a mug of tea with Victor and Joseph. That box seemed bigger and heavier to me than its meager contents warranted. I wondered if it might be the only container he had available. But I didn't have any lightweight substitute to offer, so I didn't tamper with the status quo.

I appreciated this extra source of produce even through the weeks of very limited choice. That was when our dinner vegetable became part of a predictable counterpoint. It was green beans one night and a spinach-like vegetable the next. This vegetable routine didn't quite extend ad infinitum, but my children remember it as ad nauseum.

For my dinner party, I was lucky to get enough lettuce and other ingredients for a fresh green salad. I knew some of the people on the guest list did not eat fresh salad at every home to which they were invited, but I knew they trusted me and my kitchen. At my house, they wouldn't worry too much about ingesting any meandering microbes.

Came the day and it was time to disinfect the salad greens only to find there was no bleach, my disinfecting agent of choice because it was usually available. However, Victor had opted for a whiter-than-white wash last laundry day. He had even used my small, precious, reserve bottle of bleach. His profuse apologies didn't really help as I thought of and rejected killer-cleansing alternatives. I had to think of something to rescue the salad because there simply wouldn't be enough food without it. The guests were due in two hours. It was Sunday. The stores were closed even if we had time to get there and back. Victor told me there was no bleach to be had in the village. He would know because he owned the village store, a micro-mini operation consisting of a shelf in his hut. My neighbors were gone, so I couldn't borrow anything. With bleach unavailable, I racked my brains for a substitute.

Liquor was out too, though we had sufficient. Heaven knows I'd been creative before in grabbing the gin bottle. I didn't really know how to mix a good martini, but in a pinch I'd used gin to disinfect things from cuts to cabbage. And though I didn't use it to drown my sorrows, I did use gin once to drown and preserve a large termite for one of my children's science classes in Kinshasa. According to a neighbor who had a fondness for what he called juniper berry juice, that use was a great waste.

But this time, I felt I couldn't use liquor as a disinfectant because a couple of the guests were teetotalers for religious reasons. They were tolerant of others imbibing, but I felt that risking a whiff of booze on their bites of salad was beyond good taste in more ways than one.

Then I thought of a solution. It was purported to kill germs. Mouthwash. Why not? I couldn't think of any reason why not, except embarrassment perhaps if my guests found out. Well, I certainly wasn't going to tell them. I read the ingredients on the bottle of mouthwash and it seemed lethal enough. It certainly smelled powerful. Despite rinsing the salad greens with boiled, filtered water after disinfecting them, a faint odor remained. I hoped no one but me would notice.

The guests ate heartily of everything, including the salad. Coffee and drinks were served in the living room amidst complimentary comments about dinner.

"Marilyn, that salad was a real treat. It had a delightfully piquant flavor. Are you willing to share the recipe for the salad dressing?"

*Not on your life*, I thought, knowing my homemade salad dressing hadn't provided the piquancy. I struggled to swallow my coffee and sense of humor at the same time. It might make a good story, but later—much later.

"I suspect from that gleam in Marilyn's eye that there is a secret ingredient, *n'est-ce pas?*"

"Oiu. Oh, yes. Mais oui." But no way was I ready to share that the secret ingredient was mouthwash!

# One Christmas

Not every dinner in Zaire turned out successfully. There was a Christmas dinner there that still churns in memory. It probably churned in some stomachs for a while too.

Unlike Thanksgiving, with its turkey or something resembling it, our family pursued no truly traditional menu at Christmas. If not exactly a moveable feast, we considered it a flexible one. Well, somewhat flexible. My husband and children would expect something a little familiar and pleasing to the family palate. For that matter, so would I. This precluded a number of food items in Zaire, including the national dish of *poulet moambe*. Only our two Jims liked this spiced chicken and palm nut creation served over rice. In retrospect, and with more experience of various national dishes, it seems pretty mild.

Another time, another country, and midnight found me clutching my stomach and groaning, "God deliver me from the national dish!" He did . . . all night long.

In Zaire, I conferred with Victor about Christmas dinner. I wanted to invite friends, possibly including a family of seven. I wanted to share our holiday dinner, but was hesitant to issue the invitation for fear I wouldn't find enough food. Things were getting increasingly scarce.

"*Pas de probleme*, Madame." No problem. As the years and our international moves went on I grew wary, and sometimes weary, of "no problem, no problem." In whatever language, the phrase became a warning signal for me. It wasn't definite, but chances were the phrase indicated there might well be a problem.

Victor assured me that a few kilometers farther out in the country was a European farmer who would be raising chickens for the holiday. Victor knew someone who worked there, so he could send word that we would like to buy ten or twelve of them. We were only feeding a dozen or so people. I thought maybe I was mixing up my French numbers again. Like in the beginning when I explained our coffeepot to Victor in my meager French and told him how much coffee to use. Instead of eight spoonfuls he used eighteen, thinking that was what I said. And maybe it was. Regardless, "Madame's *café dix-huit*" became an in-house joke. Out-of-house too, I suspect, as Victor and Joseph would share that one with friends.

"Oui, Madame. *Dix ou douze* (ten or twelve). They are small chickens, and I will roast them to perfection."

We carried on the conversation in French because Victor spoke no English. Okay. Ten or twelve. I revised my mental image and liked the looks of ten or twelve little chickens. Sort of like squab or little game hens, right?

A few days before Christmas was the time to go pick up our little chickens. Victor had assured me that I needn't worry about there being enough space for them in our refrigerator. In fact, he'd laughed at the idea and said something in Lingala to Joseph, who also chuckled. At the farm with Victor I found out why. We were buying chickens on the hoof. In fact they still had to be corralled. No large flock was neatly penned, but rather I glimpsed a few scraggly chickens scattered and scratching in the dirt. Victor spoke to the farmer in fast French and then told me I was looking at Christmas dinner. These eight chickens were it, all the farmer had left, and he had other customers. I could tell he wasn't too happy at having to sell them to me. I figured that was all right because I wasn't too happy at having to buy them. But the guests were invited and food was scarce. My face must have reflected my disappointment as I gave Victor the money to pay.

"Ça va, Madame. It's okay. Pas de probleme. There are enough chickens."

"Oiu, Victor. Merci." He was right. Eight of these chickens would be enough. But despite his reassurance, I couldn't quite shake the feeling that things weren't okay and there was, or would be, a problem.

A piece of twine was produced and as each chicken was rounded up and caught amidst much flapping and flopping, Victor tied its legs into a long string. As he lifted the lot into the back of the car, I wondered if this gave new meaning to stringy chicken. My sense of humor was grasping at straws, or string, or maybe hanging by a thread.

Back home again, with the chickens having been surprisingly quiet in the car, Victor and Joseph agreed between them that, in answer to my question, there was no need to build a cage. I thought that this was when we could have made good use of our chimp's first cage, the small chicken-coop one. My instincts had been right, and it was in good use as a rabbit hutch next door at our neighbors'. Being only three days before Christmas, Victor and Joseph decreed that Sam would have to share his cage with the chickens until death did them part a short time hence. Our chimp looked apprehensive and bah-humbug as his uninvited Christmas guests explored his space.

Our children weren't pleased either when they arrived home from school to find Sam looking so unhappy. My main concern was that these kids not be traumatized by the killing of Christmas dinner. After all, these children were transplanted from the American suburbs. Chicken for dinner there was purchased raw, wrapped in plastic and lying prone, not upright in feathers and running for life. As for myself, I could remember my mother raising chickens when I was a child. Chicken dinner then began on the hoof too. Running around like a chicken with its head cut off was a phrase that held real meaning for me. With that in mind, I decided I should prepare the children before Victor and Joseph prepared the chickens.

In my still-limited French, I tried to sound out Victor and Joseph on when and how the chickens would be killed. *When* was the day before Christmas. *How* eluded my French comprehension, and sign language didn't help. I couldn't understand their waving hands. They understood my dramatic portrayal of chopping the chicken's head off and thought the idea barbaric. In all the barefoot dignity they could muster, Victor and Joseph stood tall and informed me they weren't savages.

With a startled but sincere apology, I somehow smoothed over that contretemps. At least I needn't worry about headless chickens running about. I told the children not to make friends with the chickens, and no, I didn't know how they would be killed. And no, they definitely were not to question the servants about the method! Just wait and see—or not see, if they preferred.

Two days later Michael came into the house to ask, "Mom, do you know that Joseph is pinning chickens to the clothesline?"

"He's what?" Was my English comprehension in trouble too? I thought he'd said....

"This I've got to see," exclaimed young Jim as he rushed out. We all followed.

*I can't get away from the idea of stringy chicken*, I thought inanely as I watched Joseph. He was quite literally stringing them up. In his slow and methodical manner, he caught each chicken, twirled a short piece of string around its legs, dexterously tied a knot, and then clothespinned the string to the clothesline. Upside-down, the chickens docilely awaited their fate, except for one or two that curled a head up to try to stare Joseph down. I watched only a moment longer as he wielded a thin sharp knife with deft efficiency. I could see that nothing was going to go to waste. Victor was there with a basin to catch the blood. It would go into soup or something for his family. Precious little is wasted in poor Africa.

Christmas morning brought the sounds of our children examining their stockings that Santa had filled. I set out a plate of banana cake. Zaire's food shortage was causing me to rethink what constituted a nutritious breakfast. We opened our presents, then drove to St. Luke's for its Mass in English. Michael would be one of Father John's altar servers, and Karen would be one of the guitar accompanists. I would help lead the singing at church. I had trouble picking up the starting note as I listened to a guitar. I hoped I wouldn't lead the congregation astray.

While we were at church, Victor and Joseph would arrive at our home in Mont N'Gafula, along with Noel, a temporary helper aptly named for the season. Victor had assured me that I could leave the preparation of Christmas dinner mainly to him. I had questioned the need for both Joseph and Noel to work on Christmas Day, but Victor, with that happy twinkle in his eye, told me they were needed. When I persisted that maybe only one of them was needed I was told, in effect, to butt out. Victor of course did this very politely, with talk of Christmas being a time of gifts and not a time to ask a lot of questions. I acquiesced, thinking that perhaps overtime pay in addition to the Christmas bonus was the custom rather than giving the day off to as many employees as possible.

At St. Luke's. From left: Michael, Karen, Jim, Marilyn, Jim Jr.

On the way home from church, I worried a little that Victor and Joseph might not be there. I needn't have. They and Noel lined up in our driveway to cheer our arrival and call out Christmas greetings as we slowly drove through their surprise gift. Our gate was decorated with flowers and palms, and likewise-decorated arches spanned the driveway at intervals.

"Triumphal arches?" my husband asked me.

Despite all due respect and appreciation, I thought they looked more like squatty, flower-covered wickets in some giant's game of croquet. But I didn't dare say this out loud for fear one of the children would quote me.

We drove through the decorated croquet hoops. The arches, flowers, and cheering made us feel a tad like visiting royalty. Close enough. We were being honored, all of us, but probably in particular, my husband. Our staff was impressed that Jim went on state visits with President Mobutu. And so he did, sort of. When President Mobutu commandeered a DC-10 from Air Zaire, Jim was, in a manner of speaking, commandeered too to go along as navigator-cum-flight-operations coordinator. This manner of welcoming home, our Christmas present, was usually reserved for chiefs and VIPs. It was special.

As I helped in the kitchen, I felt that the rest of the day was destined to be an anticlimax. I was right. Of course it was great to have friends with us to share our Christmas dinner. The thanks we offered beforehand was heartfelt, for our families, friends, and the food.

Once we began eating, however, anything heartfelt about the food soon seemed likely to be heartburn. We chewed, and we chewed, and we chewed. At this point I would have gladly settled for my ubiquitous stringy chicken, but those little birds were as tough as the proverbial shoe leather. After a few bites, I gave up and voiced, along with apologies, what everyone was thinking. The chickens were tasty but tough to the point of terrible, and practically inedible.

The guests left a short time later—probably to go home and have a snack. One said when leaving, "Marilyn, I can't thank you for that chicken, but in all honesty, I can say the gravy was delicious."

I appreciate honesty and a sense of humor, so I genuinely smiled. And it was nice to know I hadn't completely lost my culinary touch. Still, to be thanked for the gravy that Christmas was small comfort.

Those croquet hoops were great, though—a very comforting memory.

# Continuing Adventures With Food

◩ ◪ ◩

Food and food shortages continued to play a major role in my life in Zaire. Sometimes it was food for thought, as when Victor—facetiously, I hoped—said he could cook cat and I would think it was chicken. Should he ever do so, I told him, he could think about another job. He assured me he was joking. Hah.

Joseph had cooking talents I was unaware of until I discovered that he'd cooked bats in my favorite frying pan. On my stove. In my kitchen. My God! I cut short his earnest explanation that they were fruit bats, quite clean and tasty, the fruit they ate giving their meat a good flavor. If my mind could take it all in, my stomach couldn't. That ceased to be my favorite frying pan. Unfortunately it was my only good-sized frying pan, so it continued in use, well scrubbed.

Rumors that Kinshasa bakeries would soon close because of lack of flour caused fresh fervor in reciting the Lord's Prayer. "Give us this day our daily bread" took on real meaning and a new intensity.

Soon after the bakeries closed, word reached me that friends had a hundred- pound sack of flour for me. I must go and get it. It was waiting for me at a house in Mimosa Compound, west of Kinshasa. This large group of prefabricated houses, fenced-in and guarded, was sometimes laughingly referred to by the international community as the Golden Ghetto. It wasn't really luxurious, but they seemed to have everything there— including a modern, American, suburban atmosphere and neat, green lawns sprinkled with water pumped from the nearby Congo River. Or the Zaire River, as President Mobutu decreed it should be.

The residents of the compound were doctors and medical personnel, with their families, on special contract with Mama Yemo Hospital. They were an international group with a number of Americans among them. One of these was my resourceful benefactor, though I suspect she acquired the flour through an international connection.

That very morning Victor had told me of a news bulletin he'd heard on the local radio. (I always encouraged him to pass along any worthwhile news as my French wasn't up to broadcast speed.) President Mobutu had just decreed there would be no hoarding, particularly of flour—no exceptions. Anyone, Victor went on, caught with a hundred-pound sack or more would be automatically jailed. It was the new law. Victor didn't know of our windfall, or that my morning errand was to collect that flour. *Great, I'm about to become a lawbreaker*—and I found that a scary thought. Not that I was going to actually hoard all that flour, but I had to get it home before I could share it.

I realized this might depend as much on my unknown, untried, untested acting ability as on my driving. A sixty-mile roundtrip constituted the driving part. The part where I acted as if everything was natural and normal would be needed at police or military barricades. Along my planned route, there were several of these checkpoints to pass through at night. But in the daytime, if I were lucky, there might be only one.

*Please, God, let me be lucky. Let them search my car on the way in and not on the way back. And, please, God, let me be a hell of an actress, or they will search the car both ways.*

I felt my best chance was to leave immediately for Mimosa. Maybe the word would not yet have been passed to the barricades for extra vigilance against hoarders. Possession of a hundred-pound sack of flour, if discovered, would condemn me on the spot. I was taking a chance, but the flour was needed. So was my husband's job. I hoped I wasn't about to get us kicked out of the country.

As I drove to get the flour, I couldn't help but worry about the barricades that might be up. They were manned by the military, who were sometimes nice men, and sometimes a ragtag lot who might be drinking or suffering from a hangover on the morning watch. One never knew what the mood of the moment would be, or whether their guns were loaded. Rumor had it that they often weren't, that soldiers sold the bullets or that their superiors hadn't armed them in the first place. More than one person asked, "After all, in their place, would you want to arm that lot?"

But there were also enough sounds of gunshots plus stories making the rounds that indicated these soldiers had real firepower, at least some of the time. I knew I didn't have the kind of nerve a neighbor had who, annoyed one day for being stopped at a barricade near our homes, reached out from her Land Rover and gently pushed the soldier's gun aside saying, "Don't point that silly thing at me. You know who I am. I'm just going to get feed for my animals."

I didn't have her commanding presence, her command of French, or her internment experience in a Japanese prison camp in World War II.

Nor would I be able to bribe my way through. *Baksheesh*, bribery—it was common in Zaire. My husband and I had talked at length about this when we first arrived. *When in Rome...*, and, *To get along, go along*. Well, yes, up to a point, but I thought bribery over the line. It was against my principles. Besides, I told Jim, I'd never be able to do it well, nor maybe would he. And our lack of French might get us in trouble if we offered a bribe to the rare honest person. Or the whole thing might get us easily set up for problems with the authorities if someone took a dislike to us.

"Money talks in any language," Jim claimed.

"Yes, but we don't have enough to even whisper. Honesty is the best policy."

We argued it out and agreed that we would never offer nor pay any bribe for any reason. So far as I know, we didn't—though each of us found ourselves in situations where it might have smoothed the way.

My typical manner at the checkpoints was one of friendly respect tempered with a touch of caution. Usually, but not always, this was returned in kind. It was so that morning at the only checkpoint I encountered enroute to Mimosa. My car was searched, including the trunk, but I had nothing to hide, so it was easy to stay relaxed, more or less.

The same men were on duty when I returned. I stopped my car, left the motor running, and rolled down my window. Only one man approached and they all kept their rifles slung. So far it looked good, but I was nervous.

No, not nervous but plain scared and trying not to show it. I've heard of hearts racing pitty-pat. Mine felt like it was going *thumpety-klunk*.

"Madame, you are back so soon."

"Oui, monsieur. My friend was not at home." This was true. Her gardener had loaded the flour into the trunk of my car.

The soldier leaned forward for a cursory look into the car. Then he stepped back, saluted me with his hand and a smile, and waved me through the barricade.

"Merci." And I silently sent up a thanks-be to God. *Thank you, thank you, thank you.* I mentally chanted that mantra as I drove safely home.

The flour was stashed on the veranda in a metal barrel I'd gotten for that purpose from a missionary friend. I hastened to share a good bit of the flour, both to be helpful and to get our portion down to what might be nearer the legal allotment.

One hundred was suddenly a magic number in our fight against the food shortage. Victor's number-one wife arrived one day with a hundred-pound sack of peanuts on her back. I didn't know whether to be shocked or impressed at her carrying that weight. Certainly I was grateful and glad to pay. I could count on Victor not to overcharge me. I knew better than to bring up the subject while his wife was there, but later I asked Victor if he ever carried those heavy loads. No, he assured me. He wasn't even sure he could without hurting himself, but his wife was trained to it. And so she seemed to be, with her spare and angular frame that was obviously used to hard work.

Victor's wife was certainly no plump young matron of leisure. Sometimes in Africa, a married woman's extra pounds and pretty plumpness were considered a sign of her husband's love and esteem. Her added *avoirdupois* testified to the world how well cared for she was. Those pounds proclaimed that she didn't have to work too hard. Her well-clothed weight reflected favorably upon her husband, who was thought successful because he could provide the good food and clothes, plus pay other people to do the work.

Victor appreciated his wife working hard. He was trying to get ahead in his world, and she was helping. This was his number-one wife, his first one. It was awhile before he confided to me that his big, happy family included a second wife, younger of course than the first and probably a tad plumper and prettier. Having two wives added to Victor's prestige. At least Joseph, who

186

couldn't afford any wife, seemed impressed. Or maybe Victor believed the definition I once saw that said, "Polygamy is having more than one spouse, and monotony is having only one."

It would be awhile before we could use the peanuts that Victor's wife brought to us. They were just harvested, still wet, and needed to be spread on the veranda to dry. Eventually I'd make a lot of peanut butter and a little bit of peanut brittle. We'd enjoy snacking on some of the peanuts too. First, though, they must be dried, shelled, roasted in the oven, and then most of their papery hulls removed. I was glad to have the household staff to help with some of these steps. My children also pitched in.

I was glad too that my American electric blender worked all right on a transformer. In Kenya I hadn't needed it and even wondered why I'd bothered to bring it. I could buy mayonnaise and peanut butter in the Nairobi stores. In Zaire, I considered that blender essential.

Peanut butter sandwiches weren't part of the Zairean diet, but some of the local recipes called for peanut paste, so even in the villages peanut butter was made. There the women used a mortar and pestle. I counted my blender among my blessings.

If things came in threes, our third hundred arrived on Joseph's shoulders. He brought a huge stalk of bananas. There were probably well over a hundred. I could give the children free rein on these. With so many bananas on hand they could help themselves whenever they wished. Of course our chimpanzee considered himself one of the kids and thought this rule applied to him too. Sam still had to be watched when he was out of his cage.

Though our food supply was in better shape, shortages continued to be a way of life. I had to ration toilet paper for a while. We came close to that cowboy phrase of the old West, three squares a day, applying to more than meals.

When it came to the basics, we always muddled through somehow. There would be a fortuitous find, a helpful friend. Enhanced, even creative coping skills came into play, and I wasn't the only one good at this. In fact, I was always learning.

One of my neighbors came to borrow an egg. With apologies, I explained I had only one and was about to use it. She could see I had the blender ready and the ingredients for making mayonnaise laid out. When she ascertained that, yes, it was going to be mayonnaise, her face lit up.

"But how fortunate," she exclaimed. Then she pointed out that I could make mayonnaise using just the yolk of the egg. And she could use the white of the egg for her meringue. With adaptable precision, that valuable egg was shared.

The incident made me think of a coffee-shop conversation I'd overheard in the United States. There, in the land of plenty, a woman in the next booth was sharing with a friend her memories of a brief assignment in a small European town. "My dear, it was so primitive the eggs sometimes had feathers on them!"

Whoopee. Maybe she expected Easter-egg stripes? At least she had eggs.

I also thought of our personable young egg-man the year before in Kenya. He delivered eggs door-to-door on a bicycle, not the best mode of transport for fragile cargo. Still, he was trying to better his life until rain-slicked roads caused too many skids and scrambled his profits. His thinking too, perhaps. He committed suicide. Despite haggling being the locally accepted way, I regretted the times I bargained down the price for his eggs.

# Coping

🮥 🮦 🮥

Having servants in Zaire didn't mean a life a leisure for me, but there was an increased aspect of gracious living. The good china was used almost every day for evening dinner, which Victor usually cooked and served. A small bell sat beside my place at table. Its gentle jangle brought Victor from the kitchen to clear away and serve dessert.

At first, Victor thought he should serve us each dish individually, and he adamantly insisted on this method if we had a guest whom he considered extra important—an ambassador, for instance. We preferred family-style service, with the main course on the table so we could help ourselves. Actually, except for the "important" times, I think Victor came to appreciate family-style service of dinner. It meant he could stay in the kitchen and get a head start on the washing up, or simply rest as we ate.

Victor sometimes snacked a bit during this time, but his usual main meal was rice plus whatever he cooked at noon for himself and Joseph. Sometimes Victor added a small can of mackerel to their rice. I'd originally bought these cans of fish to supplement our cat's diet. When Victor and Joseph asked permission to use them, I agreed. I wasn't about to feed the cat better than the servants. In fact when I paused and he thought I was pondering their appeal, Victor rushed, with a smile, to use this very argument

At my request, Victor worked a split shift, having off each afternoon and a day-and-a-half on the weekends. He spent much of his time off working too. He and his family tilled a plot where they grew manioc and peanuts.

I appreciated Victor's willingness to work through our dinnertime. I

189

also appreciated having after-dinner coffee with my husband without the worry of after-dinner dishes. It was nice to have someone else washing and drying them—particularly someone else who didn't try to tell me it wasn't his or her turn, as my children did.

My food lessons continued. I learned to shake the packets of macaroni before opening and dumping the contents into the boiling water. I later heard of Shake-n-Bake. This was my own method of shake-n-boil. If insects were hiding in the macaroni holes, I preferred to discover the bugs before their bath. As with a lot of lessons, this one came from experience. Trying to get those tiny corpses out of their hot tub was tedious.

At the time, I didn't always share food stories with my family for fear of putting them off eating. None of our children were overweight when they were growing up—quite the opposite, if anything. Michael in particular was very thin. My husband was the only one of us who gained extra weight in Zaire. Perhaps this could be attributed to the local beer, Primus. Jim thought it excellent and it was cheap. For instance, at the airport restaurant where he lunched, liters of bottled beer were less than half the price of the safe, imported liters of drinking water. My husband tried to convince me that I should applaud his frugality.

Bottled Coca-Cola and Fanta Orange were the drinks of choice for our children. They were fascinated to observe Victor and Joseph, when offered the occasional bottle of soda, remove the bottle caps with their teeth. Personally I was horrified but grateful that the men joined me in warning the children not to try the same trick. Knowing my children, I bet at least a couple of them tried it anyway.

Sometimes sodas were in better supply at our house than our boiled and filtered drinking water. The soda was purchased by the case, usually several at a time and most often at the back of Sedec. This was a variety store and supermarket near the American Embassy in Kinshasa. Going to shop at Sedec gave us a reassuring look at our American flag flying nearby at the embassy. We seemed to need that occasionally.

It had taken awhile to get our soda shopping up to speed. One had to turn in a case of empty bottles in order to purchase a case of full bottles, and it had to be in-kind. But if one were newly arrived in country, how could one have empty bottles?

"I do not know, Madame. That is not my problem. No bottles, no soda."

I felt like someone applying for a first job. No experience? Then no job.

Kind new friends provided us a case of empty bottles. A short time later I felt as if I hit the jackpot in being able to buy three cases of empty bottles from a departing American Embassy couple I met by chance. I took a chance and bought a card table from them too, sight unseen. The bottles were fine. The card table was rickety and overpriced.

We bought our car, a Jeep Wagoneer, from another departing American Embassy person. This used vehicle looked good on our short test-drive. Turned out it wasn't, but it became our problem. As if we didn't have enough. The seller was gone, and we had been too trusting of our fellow countryman. We'd let his friendly American manner disarm our buyer-beware instincts.

We all learned to cope with the occasional unpleasant food incident in Zaire, sometimes by adjusting our standards or expectations. When newly arrived, I complained to the supercilious maitre d' at a Kinshasa restaurant about the bread we'd been served.

"But, Madame, I really don't understand what is your problem or what it is you want."

"Bread without worms would be nice." This earned me a haughty stare, and the offending bread was taken away but never replaced. It also earned me an uncomfortable look from my embarrassed husband.

By the time a similar situation again occurred (reared its ugly head?), I'd adjusted—or maybe given up on some things. Then I simply muttered, "Oh, great, extra protein," and didn't bother the waiter or his arrogant boss. I didn't eat the bread either.

Sometimes I managed to cram a lot of things into a day. Like the day I decided I had just enough time before picking the children up from school to make cinnamon rolls for their afterschool snack. That would be a nice surprise for them. I didn't have time for the rising that yeast dough would require, but I could stir up some biscuit dough—from scratch of course.

I mixed and patted out the dough and spread a bit of canned margarine on it. Next went cinnamon and sugar. Then I felt fortunate to have a small cellophane packet of raisins recently purchased. I quickly opened this, sprinkled the raisins on the dough, and turned to throw away the empty packet. Out of the corner of my eye I caught movement, turned back to my culinary creation, and stared in disbelief. The raisins were rebelling and marching lock-step off the dough. Damn their little bug feet! I'd been in too much of a hurry and forgotten to shake the package.

My telling of this story caused laughter, but I think I missed the real inspiration of the moment—a fact I realized years later when I saw the California Raisins dancing on American television. I wonder what experience might have prompted their creator's idea.

Our kitchen stove was our only stove, because in Zaire we were close enough to the equator that extra heat was considered unnecessary, though we occasionally envied those who had a fireplace. The stove was what, as an American, I considered normal-sized, as was the kitchen itself—unlike another house in Kinshasa we'd looked at that had a tiny kitchen and a tremendously large living room. That kitchen would be crammed with the addition of a stove and refrigerator, whereas the living room would never fill up, at least not on our budget. One look at its length and I told Jim I wouldn't know whether to furnish it as a living room or a bowling alley.

The house in Mont N'Gafula was large enough and cheaper to rent, a factor for us. Best of all, it had been available immediately, and we all felt it would beat living at the Memling Hotel.

I liked having a larger stove and oven again. The only problem with the oven was that its door hinge lacked screws on one side to hold it properly in place. But it closed mostly all right, and with a little practice, I developed a dance-step maneuver that used my foot to facilitate the door's closing. Cookie baking became a quick routine again, grabbing one cookie sheet out of the oven and shoving another in, using a pot holder for only the pan coming out. One day my system glitched, or my brain did, and I found I'd reversed the process. My unprotected hand held, though not for long, the cookie sheet hot out of the oven. That hand also held instant blisters, to which I applied ice water and prayer. Both were effective, but that hand was tender a long time. What a stupid and painful mistake.

With the developing food shortage in Zaire, I took to hiding the cookies sometimes because my kids went through them so fast, particularly the chocolate ones that were their favorites. They soon caught on to the fact that the Nido cans might hold more than powdered milk. Those cans were good for storage. They were also good as drums when covered with animal skins and decorated by local skilled craftsmen.

When all my hiding places had been discovered, I resorted to locking the kitchen at night, both the outside door to keep out prowlers and the inside one to keep out my cookie monsters. I found out much later that our older son simply took this as an added challenge. At the time, I'd suspected Joseph had developed a taste for my chocolate cookies, but I didn't say anything to him. I'd already had an indication from Joseph that he thought me a tad stingy.

Flies were a terrible problem at times and we didn't have screens. In the kitchen, especially in hot weather when we needed the doors open, it was a real chore to keep flies from contaminating the food. At times they dive-bombed me and fought for the food. And as baker or cook, I often had both hands busy. Sometimes I recruited one of our kids to stand in the kitchen and wave off the flies until I could get the food safely into the oven, or wherever. After it was cooked, I used a couple of nylon-mesh food-umbrellas to cover the food and foil the flies.

On one particularly trying day, as Victor and I both were busily preparing food and fighting flies, Victor asked in exasperation, "Madame, why do you suppose the good God made flies?"

"I don't know," I said through clenched teeth, "but when I see the good God, it is the first question I am going to ask the good God." I too was exasperated, my patience with flies at an end. Victor thought my reply humorous, and I heard him laughingly repeat the conversation a number of times.

He also told of Joseph's reaction. Joseph thought me blasphemously presumptuous to think of questioning God. But what really got to him was my apparent stinginess. He uncharacteristically burst out with, "But Madame, the flies...the flies eat only a little, Madame!" Between us, Victor and I tried to set Joseph straight on stingy versus sanitary.

The kids weren't the only ones who liked cookies. Our chimpanzee did too. And, like the children, Sam wasn't above snitching some when my back was turned. Just how brazen he could be was shown on a cookie-baking day when the children were home.

"Keep that animal out of the kitchen," I ordered to all within earshot. Sam was running through the kitchen in a game of chase.

193

"Ah, Mom, we're just having fun."

"Have it someplace else." Perhaps the cross note in my voice caused Sam to scamper for the safety of young Jim's arms. From there, by the door, Sam reached out a submissive arm to me and pursed his pliable lips to give a grunt of apology. Or at least we all took it so.

"See, Mom, he's sorry."

And certainly Sam seemed so. He held out both arms to me in supplication.

"You see, Mom, he feels bad. He wants to come in to give you a hug. Sam hasn't really seen you this morning."

"Sure he has—every time he ran through the kitchen." But I relented. "Okay. One hug, two cookies, and out you all go."

I stepped back from the table, took my apron off and set it aside. Before going back to baking I'd have to go wash up again. Oh, well, love is worth a little extra effort.

Sam snuggled into my arms, his face beside mine, his chin (what he had of one) resting on my shoulder. It was a super hug—until I realized Sam's ulterior motive. I hadn't stepped far enough from the table. He had a long reach, and his hands and feet were full of cookies.

"Way to go, Sam," said Jimmy.

"Sam, you have to share," said Michael.

"All of you, get out of here," said I. The boys grabbed their two allotted cocoa snaps and chased after the chimp to share in his cookie caper.

There were days in Zaire, as perhaps anywhere, when life seemed difficult. I remember once reading a to-know-yourself article that suggested that in order to know one's strength, one should think of which tribute might appropriately go on one's tombstone. In Zaire, I decided my epitaph might read "She coped." Oh, did I cope—and there was plenty to cope with. But thinking back, maybe I had a good teacher. I grew up financially poor, but my mother was good at employing the Great Depression motto: "Use it up, wear it out, make it do, or do without."

Some good things can come out of poverty. Our family's tradition of a birthday pillow-present was born the year in which there was little money but still the need to make our children's birthdays special. Waking up to a small—and in our case, inexpensive—birthday-surprise on the pillow was an added treat and a good idea, one they now carry on in their own families. That particular year, all presents we gave were on the cheap side, budget-priced to our limited means. Our children's birthday excitement was big, though, and partly maintained throughout the day by my periodic permission to open another of several inexpensive presents. Of course, I baked each one's favorite birthday cake—and hoped that being money-poor was overcome with the richness of caring. Still, I always liked the thinking of the person who said, "I've been rich, and I've been poor. Rich is better."

I kept hoping the bakeries in Kinshasa would reopen. Sure, I had flour now but I'd never worked with yeast. Cakes, cookies, and quick breads all took baking powder and seemed simple to make. Over the years I'd developed a modicum of expertise in that type of baking. I could even bake a good pie from scratch. But the thought of baking real bread intimidated me. I was sneaking up on it though. When the store had yeast one day, I bought some. And when a friend offered me loaf pans, I took them—gratefully, albeit a tad reluctantly, realizing that my last excuse was gone.

Still, I hoped the bakeries would be back in business soon. We missed that good bread, though I didn't miss the mob scene that often went with it. Everyone knew the bread would be ready for sale about mid-morning and that the quantity might be limited. Bakeries' supply seldom matched demand. Consequently, people milled around waiting, and all rushed forward at the first glimpse of bread.

The Zaireans didn't, at least at that time, line up and take turns. Probably because the Belgians didn't line up and take turns. My irrepressible young Nigerian friend noticed this and said, "I'm glad the British taught us to queue!"

I later shared this comment with a British gentleman, adding that I too thought the civilized custom of queuing was a good contribution to society.

"Yes," he replied. "I think we British did begin that custom of queuing." A short pause and he added, "Of course we probably also introduced the practice of bribing one's way to the head of the line."

Queue or line, there rarely was one in Kinshasa. At the bakery, when the loaves of bread were ready for sale, a mini-mob scene ensued—sometimes not so mini. People of varying degrees of cleanliness surged forward and tightly packed the room. Each person lifted an arm and waved money to pay. The aroma of the freshly-baked bread was great, but it usually was pungently overpowered for me. Whichever way I turned, my nose always seemed at armpit level.

The bakeries were closed a month or more before I worked up the courage to try baking bread. By this time we were craving that simple taste, and I figured anything short of disaster I could produce in that line would be appreciated. It took me almost all day, beginning with the sifting of the flour through a clean nylon stocking in order to get the bugs out. Keeping some bay leaves in the flour was supposed to keep weevils at bay, but those hardy little creatures seemed to take them as an added taste treat.

Those first loaves of bread looked a little flat and lopsided, but their aroma was right. It was pure, freshly baked bread smell, unadulterated by armpit odor. It was all a nice surprise for my family when they arrived home at day's end.

"Could we just have lots of bread and butter instead of dinner tonight?" asked Karen. The full mouths and nodding heads around her indicated it was a popular thought.

"Why not," I said and gave Victor the night off, along with some bread.

My bread baking got better, practice making, if not perfect, eminently acceptable. Even the shape and color of the loaves looked right. The time the task took became less. Though still a chore, there was lots of satisfaction. Once or twice, I even found the slam-banging and punching of that bread dough remarkably therapeutic.

Sam approved the results of my efforts. Our chimpanzee liked bread as much as any family member. Perhaps he thought he wasn't getting his share. Certainly he tried to get more than that one day. He was in his cage. Or so I thought until I returned to the kitchen to check on the loaves of bread set to cool. I was just in time to see Sam heading out the door with a whole loaf of bread under his arm as if he was carrying a football. He saw me and took off down the length of the veranda, dodging chairs and obstacles like a broken-field runner. I took off after him, acquiring unexpected help when Chocko, our parrot, swooped down on Sam from the veranda railing. With Chocko's pecking interference, I caught up with Sam and we tussled for possession of the bread. With the thought that half a loaf was better than none, I settled for my cleaner half when the bread broke. I took it back to the kitchen and then went outside again to settle with Sam, first closing the doors so he couldn't try another end run.

I didn't think Sam should profit from his thievery, at least not by an entire half loaf. I needn't have concerned myself. It was all taken care of. Chocko was placidly pecking his way through a chunky trail of bread on the veranda. I looked around for Sam and saw that Joseph had appeared. The two of them were near Sam's cage, and as in his cookie caper, Sam was expected to share. Joseph held out a hand to Sam, who, already chastened and cowed by Chocko, offered up the offending bread. At least I would have found that bread offensive after the tussle and trip through the driveway dirt. Not so Joseph, who simply divided it into inside and outside parts, and gave Sam back the dirty crust. Munching his share, Joseph put Sam back in his cage and proceeded to mend where the chimp had broken out.

# Health

░ ▨ ░

W hen we moved to Africa, I felt keenly the responsibility of keeping my family healthy—making sure they had the required immunizations, balanced meals, good health habits, et cetera. This was important anyplace, but the harsher health realities of Africa seemed to elevate important to imperative.

I was glad we'd already progressed through all the childhood diseases. In Karen's case regarding measles, she'd had the new immunization vaccine a year or so before. Evidently it didn't work, because in Kenya she came down with one of the worst-ever cases of it. That was an unpleasant surprise. A pleasanter one was the fact that, in Nairobi, the doctor made house calls.

In Nairobi it was recommended that our two younger children receive immunization against tuberculosis. The shot was recommended because we expected to be in Africa for quite some time. Tuberculosis is common in the third world and sometimes threatens to make a worrisome comeback in the rest of the world. So Karen and Michael each received a BCG shot, the Bacille Calmette-Guerin vaccine. This resulted in a somewhat ugly depression on a forearm of each child for a while. Longer lasting, I was told, is that they will forever test false positive to a TB test.

After Africa and back again in the United States, this false positive caused slight problems. In the United States the BCG shot is not common, but the test for tuberculosis is. We sometimes had to fight being boxed in by American bureaucracy.

"All the children must be tested for tuberculosis. It's the rule."

Sometimes an explanation worked. Sometimes it didn't.

"All children who test positive for tuberculosis must be treated. It's the rule."

And so on up the bureaucratic ladder. It was time consuming.

In Africa we tried as best we could to guard against major health problems. When necessary, we took prophylactic pills for malaria, and every six months we received immunization shots against cholera. The effectiveness of these shots was debatable. However, we were grateful for getting our shots at the airport or through the airline clinic. There the needles were sterile. We didn't feel the need to bribe someone to use a clean needle, a common practice some places in Africa even before the advent of AIDS.

Antibiotics were highly prized in Africa, not only for their miracle-like effectiveness but for the price they could bring. Sometimes poorer patients took a prescribed drug just until they felt better, and then they sold what remained. Unfortunately, the condition for which the antibiotic was originally prescribed often remained too. It was temporarily suppressed by a partial dose of antibiotic, only to burst forth later with even more virulence.

For people with money, it was easy to self-prescribe medicine, even antibiotics. This practice might not have been wise, but drugs were available and their sale was either unregulated or much less so than in the United States. Over-the-counter drugs sometimes applied to everything in the pharmacy.

In Zaire we didn't have a doctor who made house calls, except for the occasional one or two we knew socially. I generally considered it bad form to bother them about business. My husband was on direct contract to Air Zaire, so we were eligible for treatment at the Air Zaire Clinic. Many people at the clinic did not speak English, or were uncomfortable doing so. This mandated my attempt to have our symptoms figured out in French.

One time when I was ill and my husband was preparing for a trip, he urged me to see a doctor the next day. I knew I would have to drive the children to school, but the clinic was in a totally different direction. The thought of the extra driving, and then of forming French phrases to explain how I felt seemed too much. I found myself saying, "I'm too sick to see a doctor!"

There was a more casual attitude toward cleanliness and sanitation in Africa than I was used to in the United States. This casual attitude was often dictated by circumstances and necessity. Lack of access to clean water, or to any kind of water at times, affected people's health, as did lack of knowledge and health education. As witness: "But Madame, the flies eat only a little."

And the mosquitoes drink so very little, but their impact is huge via the spread of yellow fever, dengue fever, and malaria. We were immunized against yellow fever before leaving the United States. It was nice to have an immunization shot that we didn't have to worry about again for ten years. Researchers are working on some kind of immunization to guard against malaria. Success in that would be great because the malaria bugs are developing their own immunity to the various pills used in treatment or prophylactically.

When we lived in Zaire it was generally assumed that anyone who lived there for long would get malaria in some form. One could only hope it would be a mild occurrence. In our family it was Michael, our younger son, who suffered the bad case of malaria. Fortunately, treatment eventually worked, but it was a worrisome time. Always slender, Michael became so very thin. He could win a game of hide-and-seek by stepping behind a tree trunk—a sapling at that.

I tried to gear myself and my family to the health environment in Africa without getting paranoid about it. British friends in Nairobi told me that, in their experience, Americans living abroad could be too germ conscious. In their stringent efforts to avoid all germs, perhaps some Americans got zapped extra hard by disease when something virulent slipped through their defenses. This seemed a reasonable statement to me. Of course in Nairobi one could usually drink the water without fear of disease, and the mile-high elevation probably helped kill off some bugs. The potability of tap water elsewhere in Kenya was suspect.

In Kinshasa it was a little different. Almost all foreigners boiled their drinking water, yet dysentery or related diseases were not uncommon, even in Kinshasa's international community. I stressed to both our household help and my family the importance of washing one's hands, particularly after bathroom use. At least I tried to.

"Wash your hands."

"Sure, Mom. We know. Cleanliness is next to godliness. Right?" Our children were sometimes egged on by a grin from their father. So was I.

"I'm only asking you to wash your hands, not perform a choral rendition of 'Nearer My God to Thee.'" Cleanliness might be next to godliness, but it also seemed next to impossible at times.

I tried too, with varying degrees of success, to get across the importance of disinfecting a cut or scrape when it happened. A break in the skin was a doorway for infection. If I was available, I didn't mind taking care of these things for my kids, but they were quite old enough and capable enough to do for themselves, if they only would. Occasionally, having warned them in advance that I didn't wish to be interrupted in a task except in case of emergency, I greeted their interrupting me anyway with an exasperated, "You'd better be broken or bleeding!"

One Friday evening when my husband and I were hurrying to get ready for a party at one of the embassies, young Jim asked me to look at his leg. He said he'd hurt it a week or so before.

"Jimmy, I really don't have time now. I'll look at it in the morning." I figured if it had already gone without my attention for a week, it could go another twelve hours.

My husband was almost ready to leave, and I was not. I raced to trade my robe for a long dress, and when I passed through the living room again, young Jim spoke up.

"Mom, I wish you'd look at my leg."

"No. I'll look at it in the morning. You are not broken or bleeding, and I'm running late." Running was the operative word all right. Despite my long skirt, I sprinted down the hall to the bathroom to put on my make-up and do my hair. Then it was back through the living room enroute to find my earrings. Almost ready.

"Mom, I really think you ought to look at my leg."

I kept moving as I exploded with, "James, I am *not* looking at your leg now unless you have an infection so bad that there are red streaks running up and down!"

"Like I said, Mom, I really think you ought to look at my leg."

His answer stopped me midstride. Red streaks? An infection that bad? Sure enough. And no, he hadn't disinfected or cleaned the small cut when it occurred. Now the small cut was festering and a big infection had set in. I did what I could with thorough cleaning and disinfecting and a little bathroom surgery. Young Jim wasn't yet running a fever, and no medical help was available that night. I'd done all that could be done for the time being. Nothing would be served by my husband and I staying home, though I briefly contemplated it. No, there was no point in forgoing our evening out. We could still get to the cocktail party within a reasonably diplomatic timeframe. The party was at one of the African embassies, and the ambassador's wife was a friend of mine. We would only be gone about three hours. I felt that young Jim was going to be very sick, but not in that length of time.

I was right. Jim Jr. woke up the next morning with a high fever and a lump in his groin. I pointed out cause and effect and the advisability of listening to his mother. "Wash your hands and disinfect cuts." He was too sick to argue. I took him to the doctor, who concurred with my diagnosis and good advice and, more importantly, prescribed the antibiotic and treatment to cure him.

The often stoic acceptance of pain by the Zaireans was something mentioned and marvelled at by foreign doctors we knew. It was marvelled at by me too. I knew one Zairean woman who had major breast surgery with only the slightest local anesthetic.

I tried to emulate her fortitude when I was in the dentist's chair, and he worked without Novocain. The dentist explained that he had only a little Novocain on hand, and he really needed it for a patient coming in that afternoon. That patient was scheduled for far more complicated and painful dental work than my relatively simple filling.

Varying versions of that story were used on my children too, usually in lieu of Novocain. I can still remember staying with them when the dentist let me, so they could clutch my hand. Their pain clutched my heart. I told them to be brave, that it would be over soon. So it was, but I think their fear of dentists lingers on. And in their mind's blur of memory, some of them are apt to allocate more sadism than altruism to that particular dentist.

Our son Jim participated in a poorly planned piano-moving experience for the American school in Kinshasa. No one thought to tie the piano down after several boys manhandled it to the bed of a pickup truck. The teenagers stayed aboard for the ride, but not for long. When the pickup truck made a sudden stop, boys and piano hit the ground. It was a classic mass-in-motion physics lesson for the schoolboys and Zairean driver. No one was seriously hurt, though the piano suffered a bit. The boys were lucky to suffer only glancing blows from that loose piano.

I was lucky the man with the message about the accident spotted me in time to wave me down. I was driving to Kinshasa; he was driving to Mont N'Gafula to tell us about young Jim. He'd been taken to Mama Yemo Hospital along with the other boys, injuries undetermined. At Mama Yemo, I was told they didn't know whether young Jim was there or not. They weren't being unkind, they simply didn't know. However, staff pointed me in the direction of two large wards where my son might be and suggested I search for him. With some trepidation, I did so. That was a terrible trek. My heart seemed to swell with fear. I was fearful I would find my son in that hospital and fearful I would not. He was not there. As I sat in my car wondering what to do, where next to check, I saw young Jim approaching.

"Am I glad to see you!" we exclaimed in a unison greeting. He too had been pondering what to do next when he suddenly spied my car. Jimmy was anxious to tell me about the accident, but I wanted first to hear if he'd seen a doctor.

"Yes," Jimmy said and named a doctor we knew at the hospital. The doctor had checked him over and released him with a diagnosis of mild concussion and bruises.

# Incidents

Some weekday mornings I dropped the children at school and went on to whatever function the morning held. If it was too early to arrive someplace and I had no shopping errands to fill the time, I sat in my car at the school and studied my French, read a book, or wrote letters.

One morning I arrived at a Women's Club meeting where the social hour was in progress prior to the scheduled speaker's address. Ladies were standing around chatting or circulating among small, informal groups. Most of them balanced coffee cups and cookies. A friend spotted me and made her way toward me, allowing herself to be only briefly detained enroute. I got the feeling she had been waiting for me, but I was unprepared for the urgency and tone of her smiling greeting.

"Marilyn, keep smiling no matter what I say and pretend we're talking about something innocuous."

"Aren't we?"

We weren't. She said it was very unusual for her husband to do so, but he'd told her to tell me of a disturbing report he'd heard the day before. Jim and I had guessed some while back that her husband worked for the United States Central Intelligence Agency. These kinds of guesses we kept to ourselves, but I would confirm our guess to Jim the next time I saw him. Though when that might be was anyone's guess. Jim was with President Mobutu and entourage aboard an Air Zaire DC-10. It was turning into a sort of presidential fly-about to various countries willing to accept a state

205

visit. The trip had already lasted far longer than anyone expected. And therein, according to my friend, lay part of the problem.

After all, the Cold War was on, and world powers vied for friends in Africa, particularly heads of state. Some of these became adept at playing one world power off against another in order to increase the largesse of the befriending country. Zaire's President Mobutu was a friend of the United States, but this hadn't prevented him from visiting communist China.

"Marilyn, do you have any information that President Mobutu is not returning to Zaire?"

"Good heavens, no!"

"You don't have any information or anything hinting at it?"

"Certainly not!" My denial was vehement, and I forgot to smile.

My friend reminded me of that before she said, "Your son Jim Jr. is evidently telling people that President Mobutu is not coming back. Marilyn, this is serious."

"I understand that, but something doesn't compute. My son simply wouldn't do that. He's done some stupid things, but he wouldn't do that." I felt certain of this, but to prove it was another matter.

We paused as other friends joined us and then, when we could, drifted away naturally to continue our smiling conversation. My smile muscles felt as if they were starting to tremble. In fact, all of me felt that way.

"This needs to be cleared up quickly," my friend said.

"I agree," I replied, "but I need more information. Where is this coming from? Who says my son is saying this?"

My friend hesitated briefly and then told me. She named the man who bounced into her husband's office the day before. I'd met the man a few times and thought him somewhat a braggart. The man's story was that the day before, he'd gone on a picnic outing to the Congo River with a family who had with them my older son, Jim Jr., a friend of their son. The boys went clambering off over the rocks and exploring the river bank. The adults set out the food, and over food and drink their conversation turned to President Mobutu's extended trip. They speculated about when he would return to Zaire. The hot and sweaty teenagers returned just then. With silence and all eyes upon them, my son allegedly blurted into the void, "Mobutu's not coming back!"

The man pounced on this statement and tried to get additional information. Whereupon my son, in distressed confusion according to the man, tried to insist that he didn't really know. To the man's way of thinking, it was a clear case of *methinks he doth protest too much*.

"I know that Marilyn had a letter from Jim," someone at the picnic offered.

This somehow clinched it all for the man. He got it into his head that we'd had a letter from my husband, that the letter contained news that President Mobutu would not return to Zaire, thus creating a political power upheaval, and that my son accidentally let this information slip. The man thought he possessed an information coup the CIA would love. And he thought he knew whom to take it to, my friend's husband.

At the Women's Club meeting, we were instructed just then to take our seats. I chose one away from my informative friend. Away, in fact, from anyone I knew well because I needed time to calm my mind and ponder what I'd just heard. I needed time to think clearly. I tuned out the talk and tried to organize my thoughts.

In my heart, I knew this stupid story of my son and talk of President Mobutu was false, but I needed more than my motherly instincts to prove it. I ran the story through my mind again. I knew the picnic family, and it was true our sons were friends—they might well have been together. But what was that about my getting a letter from Jim? He *never* sent us letters when on these trips. This was purposeful. He didn't want to feed anyone's thinking that we might have private information about President Mobutu. If the trip lasted a couple of weeks or more, Jim might send us a picture postcard, innocuous, no hidden messages. I'd received one last week. So the letter part of the story was false.

Now when was this picnic supposed to have happened? Just a couple of days before. On Sunday. Yes. Okay. Sunday meant we went to church. What had we done after church? Occasionally there were invitations for one or more of the kids to go with someone, to join friends someplace. But no, this past Sunday we were all together. Except Roxanne was away at college in Spain, and big Jim was away on President Mobutu's trip. But the rest of our family was together that Sunday, including young Jim. We'd gone to church, enjoyed fellowship and refreshments in the church garden after the service, and then I'd driven us all home, where we spent a quiet Sunday afternoon—all of us, including Jim Jr. A feeling of relief flooded me. The whole stupid story was false. It hadn't happened. It couldn't have happened.

My relief was short-lived. After the meeting, I quickly explained to my friend that my son was with me and his father had sent a mere postcard, never a letter.

"But Marilyn, something happened along the lines of the story to cause this man to go to my husband."

"Maybe so, but he's totally mixed-up. My son wasn't even there."

"I believe you," said my friend, "and so will my husband. But he's going to need to know more about that picnic and what really happened. Can you help? Unobtrusively of course, so as not to make a big deal of it."

My friend reminded me that we'd see each other again the following day. We were both invited to a bridge party at one of the African embassies. If I found any further information on the false story, I could tell her then and she could relay it to her husband.

*Oh, great, life is just full of surprises. Now I'm supposed to work for the CIA?* But I agreed to find out what I could. After all, it involved my husband and son. Except that it didn't, blast it. They weren't at all involved. And what was that old saw about how you can't prove a negative? Okay. So I'd try to prove the story positively false.

It proved easier than expected. I managed a conversation with the mother of the picnic-family. The one who allegedly had my son with them. I got the name of the boy mistaken for my son and what that boy had actually said. Which was simply, "Maybe he's not coming back!"

Sounded like, "Mobutu's not coming back!" At least it did to the eager ear of the man who wanted an information coup, and who mistakenly thought he was looking at and listening to my older son. The whole thing was ridiculous.

In chatty groups of expatriates sharing experiences, I've heard it said more than once that it takes a special kind of person to live overseas, particularly overseas in developing countries. At which point someone in the group is sure to add, "Yeah, it helps to be crazy."

Certainly crazy things happened. A pilot told us of going to Kinshasa's airport one morning when it was still dark and chilly. Arriving there, he walked over to greet some local men huddled around a small fire. The pilot was surprised to see their fire was fueled with mail from the nearby post office.

I thought it crazy too that I couldn't count on picking up our mail when my husband was gone, particularly if he forgot to give me the key. I checked our postal box at Kinshasa's airport post office only once a week when Jim was gone. I figured by then there should be something there from someone. I was still unaware that mail sometimes fueled a fire.

On my husband's first extended trip out of country, he forgot to leave me our postal-box key. Not considering it a real problem, I identified myself and inquired of the postal clerk whether there was mail for our box. He checked and held up a sheaf of envelopes. The top one I recognized as being from my mother. Maybe I didn't recognize a bid for baksheesh, a gratuity, a tip. A bribe? I didn't get my mail. What I got was a little humiliation. I was told I needed my husband's written permission to pick up the mail. Words failed me. I didn't know how to say in French, "You've got to be kidding."

The postal clerk seemed to enjoy my discomfiture. What really bothered me was that my husband also enjoyed the story later when I told him. Jim readily gave me written permission and seemed to enjoy that too, though he swore through his chuckling that I misunderstood.

That wasn't the first time I had to have my husband's written permission to do something, such as leave Zaire without him—just like any wife in Zaire who had no special exit visa. This held true when I went to Kenya for Roxanne's graduation and to bring her back to Zaire. The whole policy gave real meaning to the expression, "It's a man's world."

When my husband needed to make a business trip to Europe, a jaunt unconnected to President Mobutu, Jim invited me along. It was too good an opportunity to pass up. I hummed a few bars of a song about Paris as I looked forward to my first time there. And of course if my husband accompanied me out of country, there would be no problem in my leaving Zaire. Well, maybe a few. For starters, what to do with the kids, and who would look after the house?

What-to-do-with-the-kids was solved in a very ecumenical way. The American School of Kinshasa was founded by Protestant missionaries in the days when Kinshasa was still Leopoldville. Along with the school, the missionaries established hostels where the children of missionaries stationed in the country's interior could live and be looked after during the school year. The managers of three of these hostels kindly agreed to room and board a child for us during the duration of our trip to Europe.

Joseph, our gardener and part-time house person, would look after our house—and unbeknownst to me, cook up his mess of bats in my favorite frying pan.

My husband dropped me and our luggage near the Custom's baggage check and went to park the car. I expected to wait there for Jim but it wasn't that simple. Two officials rushed toward me and said, in French of course, that because I was Portuguese, all my luggage must be especially gone through. I gathered that, for some reason, it was not a good day to be Portuguese. It had something to do with Portuguese traders in Zaire. I dug in my purse for my American passport while I tried to explain I was American, not Portuguese. No, not Portuguese-American. I wondered if my dark hair and brown eyes mislead them. By the time I dragged out my passport, the officials had already decided between them that I most likely wasn't Portuguese after all—mainly, I gathered, because if I were, I'd speak better French. Almost everyone has a better reputation for languages than we Americans.

My husband arrived just then. We got our luggage squared away and next went to Currency and Passport Control, where Jim took my passport and presented it along with his. The man there was pleasant as he spread open our passports and picked up the official stamp. As I waited behind Jim, my view of the official was somewhat blocked, but I heard the antiquated implement clang down twice to stamp our exits. The man closed and handed our two passports to Jim, who in turn handed me mine. Our trip to Europe was about to begin—and it was a good one.

I was still basking in its glow when we returned to Kinshasa. I looked forward to picking up our children and resuming life in Zaire.

Jim got ahead of me disembarking the plane, and in the surge of people toward Immigration, I couldn't catch up. He looked around, caught my attention, and indicated he would continue through. I nodded. I knew he wanted a word with some of the Air Zaire people. We'd meet up at some point after I passed through Immigration. Jim got through there quickly with his American passport and Air Zaire identification.

My turn came and the immigration man looked at my passport and then at me, back and forth with suspicion. "Is there a problem?" I asked.

I understood few words of his rapid-fire reply. I explained that I didn't speak French well and asked him to speak slowly so that I might understand. He questioned me in slower French. Why did I want to enter Zaire? I lived there. No, not alone. I lived with my husband and children. Yes, American. All American. Where was my husband? I looked around and saw that Jim had disappeared. I tried to explain that my husband and I arrived together on this flight, but he'd gone ahead of me to talk to some Air Zaire people. He worked for Air Zaire, and yes, we'd left the country together the week before.

A supervisor arrived at the immigration man's side, spoke to him briefly, and examined my passport. Then the supervisor turned to me.

"What is it you want, Madame?" he asked.

"I wish to enter Zaire," I replied.

"But no, Madame. You cannot come into the country when you have not left it!" He waved my passport at me and continued. "There is no exit stamp. You are already here." He declined to let me through the barrier.

I shook my head. I knew I'd understood the French, but the logic escaped me in any language. Yet, I tried again.

"If I have not left Zaire," I said, "then why am I here? On this side of the desk?"

"I do not know, Madame. You are causing a problem."

The arrival of my husband and some Air Zaire staff was a welcome relief. With their help, the problem was eventually sorted out. Somehow that clanging exit stamp hadn't imprinted on my passport. Certainly it had sounded official, but it taught me not to assume. Ass? U? Me? It was true.

# Thivery

One of the rewards of living in Mont N'Gafula was that there was less crime than in Kinshasa. Reasonable precautions preserved the illusion of pastoral peace. Bars on windows and doors kept out intruders and served to remind us not to get too complacent. Outdoor lighting around the house attracted bugs but discouraged prowlers. Choosing wisely when hiring employees helped, as did treating them fairly and justly.

Choosing common sense over impulse to charity saved one from the con artists, some of whom even found their way to Mont N'Gafula. We newly arrived expatriates were considered fair game wherever we were. We were all considered rich—and so we were, in comparison to the wrenching poverty so prevalent in Africa. But one can't save the world singlehandedly, and it is too physically taxing and emotionally draining to weigh the merits of each individual request for money in places such as Africa. I made it a point not to give even coins when asked, except to one or two beggars to whom I consistently gave because I chose to do so and not because I felt threatened or forced. We contributed money at church and to organized charities of good repute. It would be a constant hassle if we gave money to individuals in Zaire and similar places because, somehow, word goes out that one is a soft touch. Fortunately, word of one's consistent "no" goes forth too, which eventually results in fewer requests for largesse.

But con men are creative, and one in Zaire took as a challenge my reputation for consistent firmness in matters monetary. Or maybe he discovered that my firmness was somewhat a façade, difficult for me to maintain at times. Possibly my heart needed to harden a little. Its heartstrings could still be too easily tugged.

In actual fact, this particular con man used a different approach. Victor informed me there was a man out at the gate who said he had a message from my husband. I suggested to Victor that he invite the man onto the premises, and I would speak to him on the veranda.

"No, Madame. It is better that you go to the gate."

That should have clued me in right then, but it didn't. I asked Victor to accompany me to the gate in case I needed an interpreter of French into simple French. The message, supposedly from my husband, was that this man had greatly helped my husband when he had car trouble earlier in the day on his way to work. When asked, he assured me my husband was fine. The man further explained that Jim had wished to reward him for his great assistance and help. However, according to this man, my husband did not have the proper notes in his wallet to do so; he had only larger zaire denominations. My husband told him though, after learning he was going to be near our neighborhood that morning, to see me, that I would reimburse him for the help he had given. Plausible? Perhaps. Without a telephone, I had no way of checking with Jim until next I saw him. I turned and quietly asked Victor his opinion of the man's veracity.

"I do not know, Madame."

I suggested to the man that he return that evening to see my husband. The man pointed out this was not possible as he had no car; he lived far away and was in the Kinshasa area only to take his sick daughter to the doctor. It was for this reason, and to buy medicine, that he really needed the money now. In fact, the man said, he was in our neighborhood hoping to find one of his relatives from whom he could borrow money, but his relative had moved. To be paid for helping my husband was a godsend.

"Madame, my little girl is so very sick. The need for money is so very big. And, Madame, your husband promised me you would give me fifteen zaire."

At the legal exchange rate then, that was the equivalent to about thirty dollars. I doubted my husband would be that generous, but then I didn't know exactly what had happened. I still didn't know *if* anything had happened on my husband's way to work that morning. Was the man at the gate, now near tears and obviously distressed, a liar, a cheat, and a good actor? Or was it all for real, including the sick daughter? We'd lived in Zaire almost two years by then. If a scam, I'd not heard of this particular approach to relieving one of money. However, to assuage my lingering doubt and to make up for my possible gullibility, I refused the man's request for fifteen zaire and gave him only seven.

Even this amount was too much for Victor and Joseph. They wouldn't speak against the man, but after he left, they politely let me know they thought I hadn't used my best judgment. They also let me hear their muttering to the effect that, if Madame was going to throw money around, maybe she should toss it in their direction—they who worked so hard.

I felt I had goofed, and my husband confirmed it that evening. He'd driven to and from work without incident and hadn't sent—nor would he—anyone to collect money from me.

Thievery in Kinshasa was practically an art form. In addition to the artistically constructed potato basket with no middle, there were the seemingly tamper-proof packs of cigarettes that contained eighteen rather than the normal number of twenty cigarettes. But who would bother counting? A person buys a sealed pack of cigarettes and doesn't think about it not containing twenty. If the pack finishes faster than usual, the smoker assumes his or her habit increased, not that the number of cigarettes decreased. The rascally roadside tobacconists increased their profits with a delicate touch that worked the pack and its seals carefully open. These were resealed with a quick touch of heat. The one or two cigarettes extracted were sold separately to those persons who had the nicotine habit but not the means to indulge it by the pack. The pack itself was sold at normal price to people of means.

In Kinshasa there were pickpockets who could remove wallets and watches with Fagan-like fingers. Women watched their purses, knowing they weren't the only ones looking out for them. I clutched my shoulder-strap bag tighter when jostled, and eyed with suspicion the man with the newspaper draped oddly over his hand and forearm. Sure enough, I glimpsed the scissors the man held at the ready. When I got home and examined the strap of my purse, I found it cut half through.

Another favorite trick for purse snatchers was to motion to a lone, woman driver that something was wrong on the opposite side of her car.

When she stopped, got out, and went around to investigate the possible flat tire or whatever, it was hoped her purse would be left on the seat. Thus it could easily be snatched by a nearby accomplice.

This trick was tried on me a number of times. It didn't work because I automatically kept my purse with me, but several times I was gullible enough to get out of the car as asked. This by the smiling and charming young urchins working their scams at the open-air market. Perhaps they tired of their unprofitable game in my case. They weren't so charming the day they surrounded my Renault and started rocking it with me inside. That time none of us were smiling. And no one helped. Though maybe I didn't stick around long enough for aid. The situation seemed dangerous, and I felt it might escalate quickly. More than assistance, I wanted out of there.

Later when I was home and wasn't shaking, I told Victor of the incident. How I was scared for my own safety but also for someone being injured when I gunned the engine, backed up, and got out of there—though my rearview mirror pretty well assured me the teenage boys weren't hurt. Victor told me not to waste my sympathy. He also told me that I shouldn't go to the market by myself anymore. Victor said if there was a need to go there, he should accompany me. I agreed and that plan worked well.

Having growing children with growing feet meant I became known at the Bata shoe store on Boulevard Trente Juin in Kinshasa. Shoe sizes were in the European mode rather than American. And transactions naturally took place in French. Of course, French wasn't natural for me, but the salesclerks there were very patient and understanding. My understanding and a clerk's patience were put to the test one day. Also his courage.

"Look at the shoes, Madame…"

What did he think I was doing? I *was* looking at the shoes. But what else was the clerk saying? Whatever it was, it didn't seem to have anything to do with shoes. I finally figured it out, much to the man's relief. The gist of it was that I was target of the day—or hour—for the thieves milling around outside the shop, looking through its large plateglass windows. Apparently a plan was afoot to relieve me of packages and purse as I left the shop.

The clerk warned me of this at some risk to himself. He was breaking the unwritten rule that one didn't rat on one's own. He was Zairean—so were the thieves—I was not. If the thieves thought he had warned me, the clerk would be beaten. He begged me to be aware but to please act normally.

I thanked him, seemingly for the shoe information, and he drifted off to other tasks as far away from me as he could get. My body meandered around the store while my mind raced. I looked at shoes and conversed with Karen about them. I was glad she was my only child with me that day, but I was no longer in the mood to buy her new shoes. Then I decided it would look most normal if I did and went on with the task at hand. All the while, by some form of osmosis and the occasional "normal" glance out the window, I tried to soak up information about the potential robbery scene.

By the time we bought the shoes and were ready to leave the shop, I felt I knew which man in the group outside was the leader. Most of his men, five or so, stayed around him. Two or three others were stationed a short distance away, but they wandered back and forth. Amongst them, they had both directions from the doorway covered.

I tried to unobtrusively time to the optimum our departure out the door, with Karen beside me all unaware. She was annoyed when I insisted I carry her shoes. We exited and turned toward the larger group of men who thought things, and we, were going their way. After three steps, I stopped short as if I'd just remembered something. Karen stopped too and looked at me, as did the would-be thieves.

"The American Embassy," I told Karen, loud enough for the men to hear. "I just remembered I need to go to the American Embassy."

I stressed the American Embassy part for the men's benefit, hoping they would comprehend those words even if they didn't speak English. It might give them pause. But I didn't pause. I smilingly grabbed Karen's hand as I turned and said, "Let's hurry."

Karen was used to my fast walking pace. She trotted beside me as I hurried us off in the opposite direction from the group of thieves-in-waiting. As I'd hoped, we swept past their cohorts coming toward us. Inwardly I enjoyed the looks of surprise on their faces.

We continued on toward the American Embassy. I risked a look back before I gave Karen her shoes to carry. I told her to hold them tight because a thief might want to grab them. It would be a long time before I shared the whole scary scenario with my daughter.

We entered the embassy, and I thought of something to ask the receptionist. I knew the thieves weren't following us. However, I felt one might have been detailed to follow us those few blocks, just to see if we actually went to the American Embassy. It couldn't hurt to go there, and doing so might take away, if we were watched, any idea that the clerk had warned me. Thanks to that warning, we'd gotten away in a rather adroit manner. Where in the world had I picked up that kind of planning in order to avoid trouble? It seemed to come pretty naturally. Thank God the strategy worked.

Only my instincts warned me of a rip-off another day, but by then it was too late. Young Jim, Michael, and Karen were all with me in Kinshasa for shopping. We bought shoes that day too, for all of us, plus a couple of other things. We also bought a few groceries, and my sons were carrying these in two open, cut-down cardboard boxes from the store. It had been a good outing, and we were headed back to our car when I suddenly remembered we needed coffee.

Biblical writers may have considered bread to be the staff of life, but it is coffee that jumpstarts my being each morning. Nescafé was the brand of choice in Kinshasa. Usually it was the only coffee choice, and one felt lucky if those cans were on the shelves. We were near the corner store that was most likely, in all of Kinshasa, to have coffee in stock. I knew too that we couldn't all crowd in there with our stuff.

It seemed a good idea to leave teenage Jimmy and Michael to guard our purchases on the one corner, while Karen and I crossed the street to get the coffee. The boys were glad to set the boxes down, and we piled all our packages in them. Tired, my sons leaned against the large pillar at the front and center of concrete steps that curved to either side. These led to that building's large, corner entryway. I then took a minute to speak to the one-legged beggar nearby and to give him a few coins. He was always sitting near that corner, and from the time we first arrived in Kinshasa, I appreciated his friendly greetings and upbeat manner.

The store had Nescafé and not many customers, so I was able to accomplish my coffee errand quickly. I remembered to save my receipt to give to the guard at the door on our way out, so there was no hassle there. But the instant we were out that door, I sensed something was wrong. The sense of unease was so strong that I put out a hand to hold Karen back from running ahead. I paused before descending the steps outside the store. Surveying the street scene, I could find no cause for my alarm. My sons were where they should be. Everything and everyone seemed normal—yet somehow, not quite. Still, I couldn't figure out what, if anything, was different.

I mentally shook myself and decided that if the whole world seemed out of whack except me, then—just maybe—I should reconsider *me*. It was past lunchtime and I hadn't eaten breakfast. Hunger hallucinations? I put my paranoia aside, but about halfway across the street the sense of something wrong came on strongly again. *What is going on?* I wondered. Then I realized what was bothering me—people passing seemed unusually glum, and no one was making eye contact with me. Quite the contrary. Even the most casual glance was evaded. I looked to my beggar-man friend. His demeanor was slumped and sad as he studiously avoided my gaze. What was I missing? Then I had it—or didn't have it. There was something missing all right.

"Where are the packages?" I asked my sons. They were each standing guard duty, tall and foursquare astride their boxes. They looked down in dismay and then up and around in disbelief.

This brief tableau brought a wide grin to the face of a young man nearby who walked over, gave me a slight, gloating bow, and said, "Bonjour, madame."

"Don't 'bonjour' me, you thief!" I was furious, knowing there was nothing I could do about being ripped off.

"Mom," said Jimmy, "he didn't take anything. He was just talking to us."

"About school and stuff," chimed in Michael.

"Oh, I just bet he was!" I snapped. My sons genuinely didn't know how the packages had disappeared. They'd even shoved the boxes up against the steps by the pillar. Then they'd straddled the boxes.

"But you forgot to watch your backs. And to look at your boxes," I pointed out. Then I quickly explained that this fellow held their attention while an accomplice grabbed what he could. Given my sons' unawareness and how much was missing, I wondered how many trips were made or how many accomplices there were. As if to prove my point, another young Zairean man came around the corner, grinned at me and made as if to take something from one of our boxes. I stamped my foot in futile anger, and together the two young men left empty-handed and laughing. We all knew there was nothing I could do. Going to the police was useless. They would consider the matter too trivial to bother with and would think—if not outright tell us—that we should have been more on guard.

The beggar man glanced at the thieves' retreating backs and then risked a look at me. "Truly, I am sorry, madame," he said in soft French and then turned away.

*And so you should be. You could have warned my sons.* I regretted these thoughts immediately and was glad I hadn't voiced them. Such reasoning was unfair. Anyone warning my sons risked retaliation, a beating at best, and I didn't even want to think about the at-worst possibilities.

"Pick up what's left," I said to my children. "We're going home." Home meant Mont N'Gafula.

"But what about our stuff that's gone?" asked Karen.

"You've got the operative word, and that's 'gone.' There's nothing we can do about it," I replied.

"Can't we buy more shoes?" persisted Karen.

"No. The shops have already closed for Saturday afternoon. And even if Bata were open, I don't have enough money to buy everything again."

"But it's not fair!" wailed Karen.

"So who ever said life has to be fair? It isn't always," I told her. But I understood her feelings. I could have done a little wailing myself right then, but I was the mom—and in charge, in control…sort of.

"Are you mad at us, Mom?" asked Michael.

"A little," I acknowledged.

"We were kind of stupid I guess, weren't we?" said Jimmy.

"A little," I agreed. "Or maybe even a lot, blast it!" It was very quiet in the car going home.

Because of the rampant thievery around Kinshasa, one learned to be on guard, but so many people were good too. Sometimes when one least expected it.

"Where are your books and things?" I asked Jimmy another day. We were in the car on the way home from TASOK, The American School of Kinshasa. Mike and Karen had their stuff, but I'd just realized young Jim was lounging carefree and empty-handed there in the back seat. He wore shorts, which meant he'd changed clothes after school. He should have been carrying those clothes, plus books, and the plastic box for his lunch.

Jimmy looked around in surprise and said, "I don't know. I thought I brought everything to the car."

We'd only gone two or three miles from the school, so I turned the car around and headed back. Soon we noticed people waving at us. This was not terribly unusual and we returned their greeting. Then we became aware that people were not so much waving *at* us as trying to wave us down to stop.

"Hey, that guy's got my jeans!" exclaimed young Jim.

The man was trying to return them, not run off with them. We stopped. Up and down the road people waved young Jim's things at us. He was right in thinking he'd brought his belongings to the car, at least to the car's top. That's where he'd set his things and forgotten them while he waited for the car door to be unlocked. He was lucky that time. Everything was smilingly returned to him.

Sometimes the only thing stolen was my composure. Occasionally that seemed the target. Indeed, I believe my composure one morning was the sole target of a segment of the Zairean army. They'd established a new base, which I passed every time I went to or from Kinshasa. There were usually soldiers standing around the base entrance. I formed the habit of giving them a friendly smile and wave. This was often returned in kind. As some of the soldiers came to recognize my car, they even initiated the greeting.

I thought this was the case one morning as I returned to Mont N'Gafula after chauffeuring my children to school. A sergeant, with upraised arm, stood among a handful of soldiers in camouflage gear. They were complete with attached tree branches and twigs. It was only a moment before I found out how good the camouflage was. As I swept past, the sergeant with the upraised arm smiled at me, but instead of waving, he brought his arm down in a swift gesture—whereupon his troops leapt out of the line of trees just along the road, scaring me at least half to death. My car swerved left and right a couple of times before I got it back under control. I looked in the rearview mirror to see the sergeant doubled over in laughter, and his grinning troops staring after me. Their joke worked. I put my arm out the window and gave them a wave as I continued on. In unison, they all waved back.

It was good to have a decent car. The older Jeep Wagoneer that we'd bought from the departing American Embassy man cost us in patience and repairs. Victor, fully aware of its disabilities, bought it from us for a nominal sum. Having a relative who was a mechanic made him see that vehicle in light of its potential as a taxi bus or cargo transport.

I think that machine needed a resident mechanic, of which our family boasted none. Friends tided us over with the loan of a car until we bought one Renault and saved up for a second one for me. My Renault was a flesh-toned, pinkish-peach color—not a color I'd opt for if I had a choice. It was distinctive, and coming or going, people certainly knew it was me.

This was the car the soldiers recognized when they jumped from the trees and scared me. It was no joke another day. I always hoped to pass the army camp without getting stopped, but I wasn't always lucky. Often the men were marched out and across the road while all traffic stopped. Sometimes the marching men were slowed to a shuffle or stopped, and traffic, usually sparse, waved through. Sometimes mine was the only car, and I'd be motioned to hurry up and go through as the sea of soldiers parted.

One morning as I drove the children to school, it looked as if the whole army camp was marching out. I judged I'd probably make it through but was ordered to stop. Of course I did so, though I was surprised at the order. The soldiers were also stopped, and it seemed to me that I should be allowed to continue, but the delay went on—and for no good reason that I could see. I inched my car forward a foot or two in hopes that the officer in charge would notice and tell me to proceed. He noticed all right. I didn't understand what he said, but I had the impression it equated to I'd better not try that again. I'd never seen this officer before—and I would have remembered. He was one of the tallest men I'd ever seen. He towered over the troops. His was a formidable, commanding presence. And we were all his to command. Nobody moved—not soldiers, not me and—I hoped— not my children.

This officer spoke to three men seeming of lesser rank standing near him. I wondered if the trio was getting a dressing down. It seemed so. In the midst of this, the tall officer turned briefly toward me, and I thought he motioned me forward, to continue on. I did so and hit the brakes when the officer, going for his sidearm, whirled in my direction. I met his gaze and it was not a pretty sight. His face contorted in rage as he stalked toward me. He reholstered his gun before he reached me, but his hand hovered and twitched in its vicinity. I had the distinct impression he would like to use the weapon.

My children obeyed my hurried command to say not one word. Even in

English I found it difficult to speak with my heart in my mouth, but from somewhere I also found the French. Speaking to the officer, my French was almost voluble as I apologized, verbally kowtowed, and groveled our way out of there.

"Mom, did you see him go for his gun?" asked young Jim when we were a mile or so away.

"Yes," I answered shortly. Part of my brain thought it a silly question since it was the gun that got me to grovel. But my kids were safe and they still had a mother. My heartbeat returned to normal as I continued my chauffeuring duties, but for a while there it felt like it was outracing the car.

I was not sorry, soon after that incident, to have my chauffeuring chores eased for a while by a road washout. It added to my husband's workday, though. Jim was forced to drive the long way around to work, through Kinshasa instead of by the back road that, near Limite, got him onto the airport highway. With the longer route necessary anyway, it made sense—to me at least—for Jim to take a few extra minutes to detour by the school to deliver our children.

# Party Time

Ｚ Ｎ Ｚ

With varying degrees of success, we entertained friends in Mont N'Gafula, but over time I felt we fell far behind repaying the kindnesses and invitations extended to us. Not that we operated on a quid pro quo basis—that was not possible, expected, or desired. Still, I wanted to do something to show my appreciation, to dispense hospitality on a larger-than-usual scale so as to invite more of the people we knew. I pondered the idea of hosting a large cocktail party, perhaps for a hundred guests or more.

I ran the idea by my husband. Jim had questions but no real objections if I wanted to do it and thought I could. He pointed out that we didn't have the resources of many of our friends, and he wondered about food. I knew that even a cocktail party needed food, an assortment of nibblies substantial enough to constitute a light meal. In fact, some guests even skipped dinner in favor of grazing at these events, particularly if they felt obliged to attend more than one party in an evening. I assured Jim that if I decided to go ahead with my cocktail-party idea, there would be more than just a mountain of plantain chips to munch. I was good at estimating food amounts needed, and creative enough to put together palatable possibilities from the local economy and the few imports Zaire allowed. No, I reassured my husband, there would be nothing too weird with any canapé combinations.

Victor greeted the cocktail-party idea with enthusiasm, but he too wondered about food. We agreed we'd need to serve at least two hot hors d'oeuvres and several cold canapés—these in addition to bowls of plantain chips and peanuts. I shared some thoughts on food possibilities, and again Victor was enthusiastic. I knew his enthusiasm augured well for the success of the project.

We discussed some logistics. Victor knew someone who could be our bartender for the evening, and I pointed out how the furniture could be rearranged and a bar set up. Victor vetoed my idea of augmenting our drinking-glass supply with plastic ones. He knew the owner of a bar who would loan or rent us some glasses if Victor asked. I understood this might be a favor and not an option available to everyone. Even if it were, I wouldn't have known about it except through Victor. He definitely made life easier for me, and I thought back to when I first hired him.

It was the custom in Zaire to provide uniforms for household employees when they were hired. So, soon after we met, Victor and I went to a Kinshasa shop where uniforms were sold. He told me he needed two pairs of white uniform shorts, two pairs of long white trousers, and two or three white slipover tops. These looked similar in style to the top of a doctor's scrub suit. This much clothing seemed a tad excessive to me, so we negotiated the size of his working wardrobe. I pointed out that he could wear only one outfit at a time. Victor pointed out that he needed to be wearing one outfit while he washed the other. That seemed reasonable, but if his pair of trousers needed to be laundered then he could wear his pair of shorts. *N'est-ce pas?* And, by his own reasoning, two tops should be enough. He acquiesced in my decision and I thought the clothing complete.

But no. *Mais non.* Victor had saved for last the *piece de resistance.* A jacket, he needed a jacket for serving when we had guests. I wasn't too sure of this, but obviously he was. A jacket was a necessity. It soon became clear that it wasn't just any jacket Victor had in mind. He pointed to the one for the shopkeeper to show me. Victor's whole face was alight as he looked admiringly at that jacket. It was a white martial creation of gold braid and brass buttons, dazzling in its splendor. In its price too. Even if I could bring myself to accept the jacket's gaudy elegance, I would never pay anywhere near what it cost.

By this time Victor had the jacket on and stood in sartorial splendor. I told him he looked very nice before I told him the jacket was too expensive, and I wasn't going to buy it. He bowed to the finality of my words. With the shopkeeper's help, we chose a cheaper white jacket, without gold braid and with ordinary white—not brass—buttons. It fit my simpler taste, if not Victor's.

It was those brass buttons he liked most. Before leaving the shop, he lightly touched them again with a resigned air and gave a sigh of regretful longing.

As Victor's time with our family grew, I came close to regretting I hadn't bought him the jacket with brass buttons. There were times when I thought he deserved a whole brass band.

I let the idea of a cocktail party percolate in my brain for a while. With a couple of people who would be on the guest list, I shared my worry that a cocktail party in Mont N'Gafula might be a far-out idea—too far-out. Perhaps people wouldn't come that distance. Maybe I should forget the whole thing and not attempt it? Not to worry, they said. People would come.

The question of what to feed them became easier when I found myself at the right place at the right time, and I bought some of the limited supply of imported canned food that a Kinshasa shop set out for sale. Things were falling into place. The final impetus, if I needed one, was good friends telling us they would soon leave Zaire permanently. I seized the opportunity. We had many friends in common, and after a quick, confirming exchange of glances with my husband, I told the departing couple that we would like to give them a going-away cocktail party. They concurred, and a date and time was agreed upon.

Everything progressed apace. I was grateful for Victor's high opinion of the project, and between us we sorted out the details. I agreed we needed to hire more staff for the party, but I reminded him that Jim Jr., Michael, and Karen would help serve. I don't think this totally met with Victor's approval, but he went along with it. When the kids first got wind of the party project, they immediately wanted to know if they were invited. They knew it was a grownup affair, so didn't seem to mind the conditions I put upon their presence. If they chose to attend, they must dress appropriately for the party—long dress for Karen, suit and tie for the boys. They must also help serve as they circulated among the guests.

A week or so before the party, Joseph began to worry aloud to Victor and to me. "What if it rains?"

"It won't." I had enough to worry about.

But Joseph persisted in clouding the conversation during those days preceding our big party. "It might rain, Madame."

"So if it does, we won't use the veranda."

"It might rain a lot, Madame."

"Joseph, you worry too much. Madame will handle it." This reassurance came from Victor.

"Madame does not control the rain. God does that, and you know there could be enough rain that people might not come to her party."

"God wouldn't do that to me," I snapped presumptuously. I hardly dared to think of all our preparation going for naught.

At least Joseph shut up on the subject, though my ear caught part of a quietly muttered reference about blasphemy.

On party day, I received regrets and word from a segment of my guest list that they would be unable to attend. All African diplomats in Kinshasa—at least the higher-echelon ones—had been invited by President Mobutu to a spur-of-the-moment gathering with him that evening. Their acceptance, no matter how inconvenient, was assured—all but automatic as part of their diplomatic job.

Evening and our guests of honor arrived well ahead of party time. The rains arrived soon after. We moved all party preparations indoors from the veranda. The extra space probably wouldn't be needed anyway.

We chatted with our friends, the couple in whose honor we were giving this party. We'd miss them. We'd had some good times together, but I began to wonder if we'd include this night. I noticed our voices getting louder as we spoke above the sound of the rain. Then the heavens opened up and God sent the deluge. Had I tempted fate, tempted God with my somewhat facetious remarks? Surely not, though I was sure that Joseph thought so. Just then the lights went off. Electric power was out all over Mont N'Gafula.

We scurried for candles, and I voiced thanks that our supply was ample. Then I went to the kitchen to check with the staff. Somehow I knew what I was going to hear, and Joseph didn't disappoint me.

"It is raining, Madame." But then he surprised me by adding, "I'm sorry." And he was, even if he did think it my just punishment.

I made sure that things were squared away in the kitchen. At the moment everything was at a standstill, but we arranged emergency candles and flashlights in case the guests began arriving. There was also a two-burner propane gas stove that could be used for cooking, but we'd have to forgo the hors d'oeuvres intended for the electric oven. As I returned to our guests, all four of them, I wondered if we should just forgo the whole party. We were over an hour into party time, and it was closer to fiasco than fiesta. How embarrassing to give a party and have no one attend. But never underestimate one's friends.

"I see lights," called one of our kids.

"Car lights," chimed another.

"Lots of them," claimed a third as a caravan of cars turned into our driveway. And they kept coming.

It was a great party.

# Moving On

S oon enough it was our turn to leave Zaire. Despite, at times, the inconvenience of life there, we didn't feel ready to go. Perhaps we felt rooted, as we'd invested a lot of ourselves there. Or perhaps it was a case of better-the-devil-you-know, since we didn't know what life held for us elsewhere. We didn't even know where elsewhere was. Jim's contract with Air Zaire had been extended once, and he thought it would be again, but it wasn't. Perhaps he'd worked himself out of a job. A good part of his duties was to train and upgrade local staff in flight dispatch.

Neighbors agreed to take care of Sam and the job of donating him to the Rotterdam Zoo, where they knew the director. That zoo happened to be where the siblings of Elsa, the Kenya lion of *Born Free* fame, lived.

Our family would head back to the United States, but exactly where would depend on job possibilities for Jim. I suspected we'd suffer some reverse cultural shock on our return to the land of plenty. Would all those choices in the supermarket be overwhelming? Or just a pleasant challenge? Would we remember that wall-mounted light switches clicked upwards to turn on? And built-in closets again would be nice.

That thought reminded me to get busy organizing our belongings for sale, including cabinets and wardrobes and most of their contents. Among other things, I'd give the potato peeler to Victor. He'd need it for all those plantain chips he planned to sell. There was even talk that Victor might hire Joseph to work for him.

What would our future hold? Sadness and gladness, pain, sorrow,

231

joy? Surely all of these and, thanks be, always some nuggets of humor. (As it turned out, part of our future would hold a revolution that decorated downtown walls with, "Yankee, go home." And I would smile over the scrawl of one brave, local wag, who wrote underneath: "And take me with you!")

But we left Zaire with a great deal of sadness and a tremendous amount of uncertainty. Would there be another good job for Jim? (Yes, but not until we went through another year of unemployment.) How would our children fare? Would we ever see Sam again? Or Africa? (Yes on both counts—but we did not know it then.) A plague of doubts beset us.

Uncertainty was the immediate, almost overwhelming, problem facing us as we prepared to leave Zaire. I tried not to think that we had come full circle. We seemed to have passed Go, Kenya, and Zaire only to land again on Unemployment.

We were halfway around the world from the United States, where we began. Jim and I decided, after much discussion, to complete our around-the-world odyssey by flying to Paris and London, and then head west to the United States. We liked the idea of our family being able to say that they, literally, had been around the world. Had my husband and I known our future held that in store a few times over, we might have saved our money. However, we didn't know, and under the circumstances, it was a gesture of faith in our future.

In our financial figuring we made sure that extending our travel would not cut into the sum of money we'd need to cover a year's living expenses—should a job not be immediately forthcoming. The budget would be tight, but that was nothing new. Admittedly, the trip extension didn't cost as much as it might because Air Zaire allowed us discounted tickets. Still, it was a tidy expenditure when facing unemployment. That outlay took a little courage as well as money.

For traveling money we went to our bank in Kinshasa for American dollar traveler's checks. Evidently a lot of people were traveling out of Zaire around the same time. We found there had been a run on traveler's checks. The only ones left were of the ten dollar denomination. My husband was more than happy to split that stack fifty-fifty. When it came to signing, we both got writer's cramp.

The ten dollar checks were certainly legal tender, but I wondered if, like cyclamate soda, they were also in the category of America's unwanted leftovers. On that trip, everywhere we went we cashed those cheapskate-looking, ten-dollar traveler's checks. And every clerk and cashier exercised their eyebrows over us and those checks.

On leaving Zaire permanently, currency regulations allowed us to convert a certain portion of our local money to dollars, which we did with the traveler's checks. Any money above the prescribed amount, according to local law, was to be left in Zaire. Jim was paid in zaire, the currency of the country, and we had a problem. It was a pleasant problem in some respects, as I couldn't remember our ever having too much money for anything before. But selling two cars and almost everything else we owned, combined with some savings, put us over the currency control limit for taking all our money out of Zaire.

The black market for currency was an illegal option that my husband suggested we consider. Though we had never participated in it before, we had been approached and were aware of possibilities. These included the possibility of big trouble if we failed or were found out.

There was the story of the man in a fat leg-cast who left Zaire but didn't wait long enough to do his victory dance in the airliner's aisle. The Air Zaire plane was still over Zairean airspace when an incensed government official aboard ordered the pilot to turn back and land. Whereupon, or so the story went, man and money disappeared into custody.

In addition to taking into consideration the repercussions of failure, I needed to work through the ethics of breaking the law. My instinctive law-abiding nature was nervous at the idea. Still, it was our money, we'd earned it, and we needed it to support our family. That worked. I hoped the scheme my husband laid out for me would too. Certainly it seemed reasonable. I particularly liked the part where Jim assured me I could leave it all up to him. He would take care of this awkward money problem.

On the day of our leaving Zaire, we successfully passed through all checkpoints and were in the departure lounge of Kinshasa's airport awaiting our flight. Jim said he'd be back in a few minutes and flashed some Air Zaire identification at the nearby guards. They let him go out through the ramp doors. The guards were used to seeing Jim wander around in the course of his job and were unaware that it had ended. I chatted with our children. They were unaware of their father's errand, or the fact that we were about to smuggle hard currency out of Zaire. Their ignorance protected them, I hoped, and helped to maintain a natural, normal façade in our family scene.

Jim returned with what looked like a packet of mail and said a bit redundantly, "Look, we have mail."

"Oh, good," said I, smiling brightly.

"Here, you have it"—and he thrust the packet at me.

I had to take the package that I knew contained more than mail. My heart started doing its *thumpety-klunk* bit. I would have liked to have clunked Jim over his smiling head right then. He was rewriting the script.

Much later, still annoyed, I reminded Jim that he'd told me I wouldn't have to worry about smuggling out that money because he would take care of it.

"And I did." My husband grinned. "I gave it to you, and you did a great job, just like I knew you would." I didn't know whether to feel complimented or used.

In Paris, we discovered the Eiffel Tower and twilight. Our children marvelled at both, but I think twilight had the edge. After almost four years of living near the equator, they had forgotten dusk and darkness that falls gradually.

In London, Jim didn't feel well and decided to stay at the hotel while I took Jim Jr., Michael, and Karen sightseeing at the Tower of London. Roxanne was in college in California, having preceded us to the United States some months earlier. For the children's sake, I was trying to stay optimistic and cheerful. This despite still not having any firm answers to their questions. "Where will we go to school? Where will we live next?"

There were some job possibilities. All pretty tentative. "Somehow everything will work out all right." I sure hoped I knew what I was talking about.

The Tower of London reeks of history. In the past, people were imprisoned there, beheaded there. Blood flowed there.

It did again the day we were there.

The Crown Jewels are impressive. We had just seen them, and I wanted to move on to the armory in the White Tower. My kids wanted to stop at the souvenir stand. Michael had a penchant for picture postcards.

"No. Let's finish all the sightseeing here first. Then we can stop for souvenirs."

Karen didn't seem to mind this plan but the boys did. Their vehemence surprised me. Surprising too was the fact that it was Michael taking the lead in opposing me. I tended to think of him as the more reasonable of my sons. Here he was on the verge of making a scene, and over something as silly as souvenir shopping. So much was happening in our lives that we had no control over. I'd like to say that I graciously relinquished control of the souvenir shopping, but I didn't. I growled through gritted teeth, "Oh, all right. Have it your way!"

There was nothing gracious about my giving in to avoid a scene. The three of them hurried off, and I contemplated calling out to them that I was going ahead to the White Tower—but I didn't. Instead, I stomped to the nearest bench to sit and smoke a cigarette, something I considered calming.

BOOM!!! Any calm that day at the Tower of London was destroyed. That bang was no firecracker. It was the first bomb the IRA, Irish Republican Army, planted in a crowded tourist area. It was only the second bomb they'd yet exploded in all of London. I knew instantly it was a bomb that had just gone off. Perhaps I knew because I'd just left Africa, and my senses were still heightened to danger. Many people milled around wondering, not believing at first in possible peril.

*Oh, dear God. Where are my children?* I hurried toward the souvenir shop. *Please, God. Let them be all right.*

I saw Jimmy a short distance away. He was helping someone. Somehow I knew that he himself was all right. But Mike? Karen? People were pouring out of buildings. The courtyard was now crowded. Yet strangely there was no panic, except for that threatening to well up inside me.

Then my inner voices kicked in. *Calm down, Marilyn. You've never been one to panic and this is no time to start.* I heeded that inner guidance and took a deep breath—several of them.

"Mom! Mom!" Jimmy had just spotted me. He had a stricken look on his face.

*Oh, God. Please don't let him tell me Mike and Karen have gone ahead to the White Tower.* The injured were coming out of there. The bomb went off there. *Please, God?*

"Jimmy, your brother and sister—where are they?"

"I don't know, Mom. Did you see the blood? There are kids bleeding."

"Yes, I know, but I've got to find Mike and Karen. They didn't go ahead to the armory, did they?"

"I don't think so," answered Jimmy. "Shall I go look for them?"

"No! I want to get us all together, not farther separated. You're sure they didn't tell you to tell me anything?" I could just picture Mike saying, "Tell Mom we've gone ahead and we'll meet you in the White Tower." *Please, God, no!* I silently pleaded.

"No, Mom, they didn't," Jimmy said. Thank heaven for that. I didn't think they would go ahead without a message—but I couldn't be sure.

A Tower guard, a beefeater, grabbed a bullhorn. He was disheveled, minus his hat and picture-postcard perfection. The guard literally pleaded and begged the crowd to clear the area. There was the possibility that another bomb might go off at any time, and the milling people meant that emergency vehicles couldn't get through.

Like a salmon swimming upstream, I edged my way against the crowd. The throng flowed around me as I attempted to move toward the souvenir shop. Another guard tried to turn me around.

"No! I won't leave without my children."

Thank God! Mike and Karen. There they were—just coming out of the souvenir shop. I maneuvered in their direction.

"Where have you two been? I've been looking for you. I was so worried!"

"I had to go back in to pay for the postcards," said Mike. "I ran out with them in my hand. And I made Karen stay with me so she wouldn't get lost in the crowd. I'm sorry it took so long, Mom. Karen wanted to find you."

"A bomb exploded, and you had to go pay for postcards before finding me?" There were priorities and then priorities, but I couldn't fault him. I already had an arm around Karen. I gave Mike a rueful smile and a hug. Then I said with real thankfulness, "If it hadn't been for you, Mike, and your damn postcards, we would have been right where the bomb went off."

Now that my children and I were together, I was ready to leave the area. The ambulances were having trouble getting through to the injured. Dear God, how glad I was that none of us were among them. I sent up a prayer for those not so fortunate. I couldn't help thinking that Mike, God bless his temper tantrum, would get no further argument from me this trip—or ever—when he wanted to buy a souvenir postcard.

As we inched our way out of the Tower, my thoughts went to my husband back at the hotel. What if Jim had the television on? This Tower of London bombing would surely be the main topic. My husband would have no way of knowing we were all right. We should either get back to the hotel or at least telephone him. I didn't want to further spoil the sightseeing day I'd promised our kids, though. That is, if they were still in the mood to continue. We hadn't really had a chance to get in touch with our feelings. Shock had numbed us, but it was beginning to wear off.

I put the choices to the kids. If they wanted to, I was willing to continue sightseeing. Buckingham Palace and the Changing of the Guard perhaps. But we'd have to call their father to tell him we were all right. Or we could simply go back to the hotel if they'd rather do that. It was up to them. What did they want to do?

The boys didn't seem to know what they wanted. It was left to Karen who suddenly burst into tears and wailed, "I want to go *home*. I don't want to do anything else. I just want to go *home*!"

I was caught off guard. Home. Wherever that was. I put my arms around Karen and hugged her. It hit me with such force. Home! The bomb had shaken me, but this was devastating. Every fiber of my being regretted that we didn't have a home to go to. These kids, my kids, needed a home. We had left Africa. We had just narrowly escaped death or injury in England. And we didn't know what awaited us in the United States. Even stateside, there was no real home to go to because we had moved around so much. We seemed adrift on a sea of uncertainty. But I'd heard the pathos and plea in Karen's voice. My heart ached for her. These kids needed a home to go to, yet there seemed nothing I could do about it. I felt so helpless. Jimmy and Mike were strangely silent, but I sensed their solidarity with their sister's sentiments.

"Honey," I said to Karen as gently as I could, "we don't really have a home to go to right now. I'm so sorry." There were tears in my eyes and my voice. Karen pulled back and looked at me in amazement.

"Well, of course, Mom. I know that. I mean, I know we don't have a house-type home to go to right now. But we always have a *home*, wherever we are. When I said, 'I want to go home,' I meant the hotel. That's where the suitcases are, so that's where home is."

My sons made concurring noises. I mentally shook myself. Here I'd been, reading great deprivation and loss into something simple. With immense clarity, our youngest had just stated a significant truth. Home can be, sometimes must be, a state of mind—with maybe a little luggage.

For better, for worse, for us, for a time—my daughter was right. Sometimes...home is where the suitcases are.

To purchase additional copies of *Home Is Where the Suitcases Are*, please visit any of the following locations:

www.Amazon.com
www.barnesandnoble.com
www.bookstore.abbottpress.com

CPSIA information can be obtained at www.ICGtesting.com
Printed in the USA
BVOW072208160112

280667BV00001B/71/P